DATE DUE

DEATH ROW: SPAIN 1936

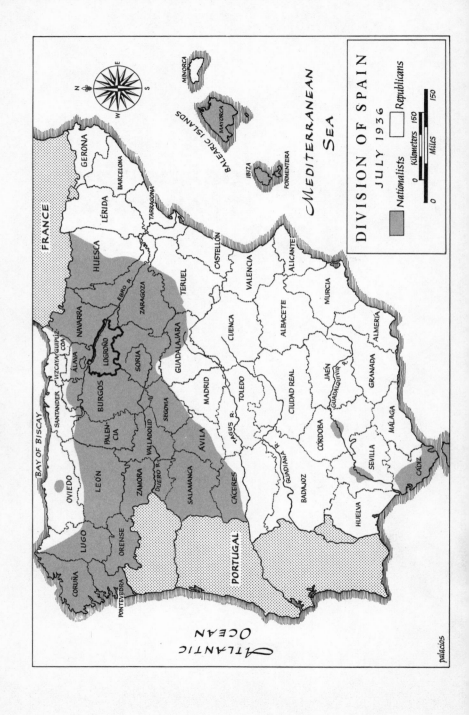

DIVISION OF SPAIN
JULY 1936

Nationalists

Republicans

Kilometers 150

Miles

0   150

MEDITERRANEAN SEA

ATLANTIC OCEAN

BAY OF BISCAY

FRANCE

PORTUGAL

BALEARIC ISLANDS

MINORCA

MAYORCA

IBIZA

FORMENTERA

GERONA
BARCELONA
LÉRIDA
TARRAGONA
HUESCA
NAVARRA
GUIPÚZCOA
VIZCAYA
ÁLAVA
LOGROÑO
ZARAGOZA
CASTELLÓN
TERUEL
SORIA
GUADALAJARA
VALENCIA
ALICANTE
CUENCA
ALBACETE
MURCIA
BURGOS
PALEN-CIA
VALLADOLID
SEGOVIA
ÁVILA
MADRID
TOLEDO
CIUDAD REAL
JAÉN
GRANADA
ALMERÍA
SANTANDER
OVIEDO
LEÓN
ZAMORA
SALAMANCA
CÁCERES
BADAJOZ
CÓRDOBA
SEVILLA
MÁLAGA
CÁDIZ
HUELVA
LUGO
ORENSE
CORUÑA
PONTEVEDRA
GUADALQUIVIR
GUADIANA
EBRO R.
DUERO R.
TAGUS R.

palacios

DEATH ROW: SPAIN 1936

by Patricio P. Escobal

translated from the Spanish
by Tana de Gámez

THE BOBBS-MERRILL COMPANY, INC.

Indianapolis   New York

The Bobbs-Merrill Company, Inc.
A Subsidiary of Howard W. Sams & Co., Inc., Publishers
Indianapolis · Kansas City · New York

Acknowledgments

The author expresses his profound gratitude to the late Federico de Onís and to Professor Navarro Tomas for their encouragement and advice in the writing of this memoir; to Tana de Gámez for her translation; to my son Pedro R. Escobal for his valuable suggestions; and last but not least, to Mr. Rubin Falk, for assistance in the final stages.

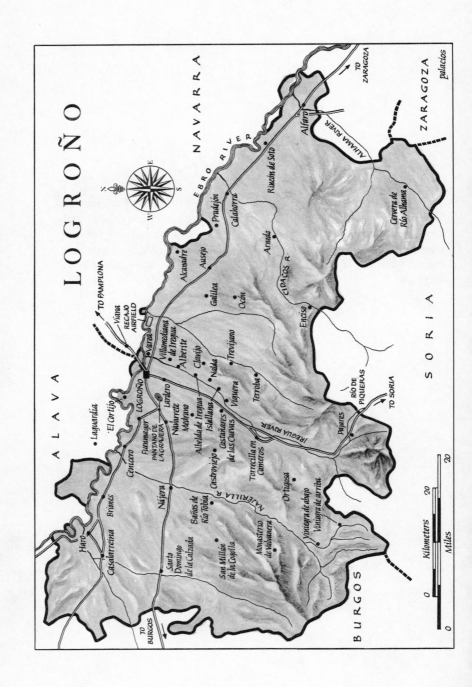

✎ Spain

For one thousand years, from the VI to the XVI century, this was the first nation of Europe: equal to Greece in heroic history, to Italy in art, to France in philosophy. This nation had a Leonidas called Pelayo and its Achilles in El Cid. This nation began with Viriatus and concluded with Riego. Lepanto is in its annals what Salamis was to Greece.

But for Spain, Corneille would not have created tragedy nor Columbus discovered the New World. This is the indomitable land of the Castilian Fueros, as entrenched in the ramparts of its geography as Switzerland, for the Mulhacén is to Mont Blanc as eighteen is to twenty-four.

While Rome assembled in the Forum, Spain was legislating in the woods; twice a month its people met and ruled in the forest, at new moon and again at full moon. This nation had its Cortes of León seventy-seven years before England had its Magna Carta. Its people issued the Ball Game oath at Medina del Campo, under King Sancho.

Since 1133 at the Cortes of Borja, this people gave preference to the Third State, and one city alone, Saragossa, had been sending fifteen deputies to that assembly since 1307. Under Alfonso II this people proclaimed the right and duty to insurrection; in Aragón they instituted the man called Justice to be above the man called King, thus confronting the throne with the formidable *si non*. They denied taxes to Charles V. At its birth, this nation stopped Charlemagne. It defeated Napoleon at its death.

The people of this nation have suffered plagues and ills, having been no less dishonored by the clergy than lions are infested by lice. This nation lacked only two wisdoms: to learn to dispense with the Pope and with the King.

In commerce, navigation, in invention applied to new frontiers, in the discovery of unknown routes, in initiative, in establishing new civilized worlds, this nation has surpassed England with a lot less isolation and a lot more sun. This people have the Alhambra as Athens had the Parthenon, and a Cervantes as we have a Voltaire.

Such was the light spread over the universe by the immense soul of this people that a Torquemada was needed to squelch it.

Clericalism and despotism have conspired to destroy this nation.

Victor Hugo

✑ Preface

As is often the case in human affairs, with the passing of time, indifference and oblivion succeeded the stirring emotions unleashed upon the world by the Spanish Civil War. Thus a brief reminder of the places, circumstances and historical framework accompanying this autobiography will help better to understand the events described in these pages.

The action of this book takes place principally in Logroño, capital of the province of the same name. The city—about fifty thousand inhabitants in 1936—is on the banks of the Ebro river, which, just outside of town, is joined by the torrential Iregua. An orchard famous for its produce extends between the two rivers. As do other tributaries of the Ebro in the region, the Iregua exposes in the summer its sandy bottom and scalloped borders, winding along shallow pools surrounded by poplars. Not far from its banks lie the many small pueblos to which we refer in this book.

Logroño is considered the capital of the region of Rioja, although that region extends to the neighboring provinces, where it takes the names of Rioja Alavesa and Rioja Navarra. Actually, the province of Logroño is part of the region of Old Castile, thus acting as a sort of transitional zone between the barrenness of the Castilian meseta and the lush vegetation of the Basque provinces. Logroño is some ninety miles of rough terrain west from the French border. Soria lies south, its border with the province of Logroño outlined by high forested sierras which are blanketed under snow all through winter. Navarra is to the north, separated by the Ebro. A part of the province west of Logroño is known as High Rioja. The rest is Low Rioja.

High Rioja played an important role in the emergence of Castile, and for some time it engaged in disputes with the old kingdom of Navarre, whose court once was held briefly in the town of Nájera. Several monasteries and places remain as a living testimony to the historical past of the High Rioja: those of San Millán de la Cogulla, Valvanera, Clavijo, and Santo Domingo de la Calzada, the last city named for the engineer saint who built and maintained the road to Santiago de Compostela used by the pilgrims in the Middle Ages. The most important town of the Low Rioja is Calahorra, episcopal site and ancient Roman city whose ruins still stand on the outskirts of town. The province of Logroño abounds in rich farmlands and a great number of agricultural industries. There are also some minor but flourishing industrial plants.

Generally, the *riojano* is a man who enjoys hard work and good humor. He is a good drinker and swears a lot. The political color of the region has always been liberal, with some hardcore Carlists strewn among the pueblos. In 1936 the working class was split between the CNT—Confederación Nacional de Trabajo (National Federation of Workers)—and the Socialist Party, with a marked preference for the CNT in Logroño where there also was a small anarchist sector. At the time, the military garrison consisted of contingents of infantry and artillery and their barracks, plus an air force unit whose field, Recajo, was less than ten miles from the city over the Saragossa highway.

The events described in these memoirs were lived and witnessed during my life as a political prisoner. Of necessity, the feelings, tendencies and expressions of the majority of the characters in this book have a common direction, a natural consequence of sharing a common fate which meant imprisonment to all and death to many.

Few Spanish families came out of the holocaust of the Civil War without having paid blood tribute, often to both sides of the conflict. It seems idle now to argue over the number of assassinations committed by each warring faction. Devastating enough is the fact that the overall number of casualties exceeded one million. But it is a proven fact that the cruelties and murders committed in the zone held by the legal government, the Republic, were perpetrated by the primitive and the resentful, those who had known only a miserable and hopeless life and who gave vent to feelings of revenge and retribution without moral restraint. If not excusable, their blind and savage reaction is at least understandable. On the other hand, similar atrocities committed by the rebel side, the fascists, were commanded and condoned by people classified as law-abiding, educated, religious, the class that had not felt the lash of deprivation and hunger. A cold, premeditated and well-organized perversity was characteristic of their actions.

At the time of the outbreak of the insurrection the situation in Madrid was similar to that of many Spanish cities. A small group of army officers and some two thousand of the new mechanized police force "Assault Guards" stood loyally by the Republic, hence the name Loyalists as opposed to Rebels. The rest of the military and security forces were either in open rebellion or awaiting the propitious moment to join the Rebels. It was the failure of the military commands to obey government orders that put the Republic in the crucial dilemma of having to arm the people or risk perishing. The decision left no margin for hesitation. The conjunction of the rebel forces of the Montaña headquarters with those of the military regions surrounding Madrid was imminent. To delay a few hours meant only one possible consequence: the immediate demise of the Republic. Once the mass of the people were armed, only the foolish or the spiteful could hold the government responsible for the excesses of the rabble.

In 1935 (one year before the outbreak of the Civil War), I was working as an engineer with a private company in Madrid. The victory of the Popular Front in the elections of 1936 gave me an opportunity to return to my former job at Logroño's City Hall, a post from which I had been summarily expelled by the new government that followed the brutally repressed Asturias revolt and the subsequent Socialist defeat of 1934. A full year's service as a municipal engineer in Logroño would be an advantageous addition to my record when applying for a similar post in Madrid. Thus, in returning to my old job in Logroño I planned to serve the five months that would complete the aimed-for year. At first, professional and personal matters kept me traveling to Madrid frequently until I put my affairs in order and made my final trip back to Logroño, unaware that in a few days I was going to be arrested and under threat of death for several years.

Toward the end of the summer of 1935 I had suffered a serious back infection which left an aftermath of pain and discomfort. It was still bothering me when I was jailed, four days after the outbreak of "the glorious Movement," as the fascists called their insurrection.

The provincial jails became jammed with thousands of new prisoners and the falange authorities (the fascists) had to convert several public buildings into what were then called "qualified jails." It was in one of them—a combination of handball court and movie house called La Avenida—that I first was jailed, in July of 1936. Thirty-eight days later I was transferred to another qualified jail, the Industrial School. A second transfer, on November 5th, took me to the provincial prison. Around the middle of February of the following year, a mass transfer of political prisoners brought me back to the Avenida. That second stay at my first jail lasted until the middle of June of 1937, when, in critical condition, I was taken to the provincial hospital. There I remained, in Room Eleven, for over four months, until—by now an advanced case of Pott's disease—I was confined to a house in Pedernales, a small town in the province of Biscay. My illness and slow recovery took nearly three years, during eighteen months of which I did not move from a wheel bed. And confinement did not mean freedom. My case was no different from those of thousands: it had to run its legal course. For any of us, leaving Spain was possible only through acquittal of charges.

Part of the Italian general staff aiding the rebels was assigned to Logroño at the beginning of the fascist offensive on Bilbao, perhaps because being half way between the two northern war theatres— Aragón's to the east and the Basque front to the west—Logroño was the most strategic point from which to direct operations and also coordinate actions with the Navarrese forces of General Mola. The house that was then occupied by the Italian high command belonged to close relatives of my wife, an aunt and uncle who had long been living in Buenos Aires. The family children and their playmates continued to use part of the vast gardens for their games. That in turn brought the family in contact with the Italian officers whose powerful influence—particularly that of General Gustavo Gambara—was to be instrumental in obtaining an acquittal in my case and eventual freedom. I doubt General Gambara will read these pages, but I think it only fair to express my gratitude, both for his help and for the subtlety and discretion with which he extended it. At last, with all difficulties surmounted, I was able to leave Spain in the middle of June of 1940.

I began jotting down the events of my life in prison at the qualified jail of the Industrial School, but fearing the thorough searches we had to undergo with every transfer, I destroyed the notes. Later, during my confinement to bed in Pedernales, a certain peace of mind and long hours of quietude encouraged me to reconstruct those memories while the details were still fresh.

A few days before leaving Spain with my wife and child, with all documents in order and the boat tickets in my pocket, the same fear of being searched and denied exit at the last moment compelled me to leave the notes with a close friend. Sixteen years later, when the material was returned to me, time had left its destructive mark on the penciled notes; some passages were difficult to read, a few impossible. But nothing that was legible has been altered, save for a necessary change of names in certain cases.

❧ Contents

Part I

The Avenida Prison

In the XVIII Canto of the Inferno, Dante describes the hideous spectacle of the Ninth Circle, where those who have sown civil and religious strife in the human family are punished. The sinners present horribly mutilated limbs which, no sooner mended, are again broken by a devil in charge of inflicting this ferocious torture.

THE UPRISING
AND MY ARREST

Madrid, mid-July of 1936. I am in a small café on Alcalá Street, across from the park of El Retiro, well past the hour of evening. I sit at a small table, waiting for my brother-in-law's car to take me back to Logroño. The warm Madrilenian night is full of strange rumors. The Spanish army in Africa has rebelled and the spread of the insurrection to the peninsula is expected momentarily. Confident, unaware of the impending foreign intervention, the government of the Republic awaits developments.

My companions arrive close to eleven o'clock and we leave Madrid by the road to France. Twice we are stopped by Civil Guard patrols between Buitrago and Aranda del Duero. After a hasty and late dinner in Burgos we reach the outskirts of Logroño at dawn. We are stopped again by a team of Civil Guards, at the road gang

3

station by the roadside. After a telephone call to the secretary of the provincial governor, we are allowed to proceed and enter Logroño.

It's nearly seven in the morning of July 19, 1936 when at last I go to bed. I sink into deep sleep until almost three in the afternoon. Two hours later I am out, walking the streets. The town seems shaken. There are rumors of an uprising in the nearby army barracks. Assault Guards pass by, carbines on their shoulders. Groups of workers and labor leaders are meeting on corners. There is a state of general unrest. By eight o'clock the crowd on the Portales promenade is so thick it looks like the eve of San Mateo, the town's great yearly festival. Troops of the infantry and artillery garrisons walk along with the civilians. The local republican leaders believe a military uprising is doubtful, reasoning that if the army officers were planning a rebellion the troops would be confined to barracks, not walking freely and mingling with civilians. With more accurate information and a little daring, it would have been possible to surround the barracks with the help of the Assault Forces, the city police, the Civil Guard and members of the leftist organizations, and thus prevent the soldiers from returning to headquarters. But nothing is done. The night passes while a series of secret messages are dispatched between garrisons. Just before sunrise, the accord between the infantry and artillery garrisons is complete. Not so at first with the air force commanders: White, chief of the Recajo airfield, resists until the last moment, finally acceding to pressure from a group of air force officers and yielding to the ultimatum sent from the other garrisons.

The next day by seven in the morning the troops and their commanders take to the streets and swiftly capture communications, transport facilities and public buildings, imprisoning legal authorities as they work. There is no armed resistance. The forces of Security, Assault, police, and Civil Guard, under pressure from their respective commanders, fall instantly into the ranks of the fascist rebellion. Despite the absence of armed struggle, several are assassinated that day, among them a young fellow I know, Arejuela, an employee of the municipal sanitation services.

Many react against these murders, finding them barbarous. For the rest of the day the insurrectionists establish firm contact with the Requetés of Navarra—as these reactionary militias with red berets were called following the name given to the recruits of the Carlist wars of the 19th century in Spain—and begin to jail civilians by the hundreds, requisitioning all manner of vehicles, looting the homes of prominent leftists, among them the house of Jesús del Río, a provincial representative who fortunately is away in Madrid. The twenty falangists being held at the provincial jail are promptly released, together with several common prisoners, the most ruthless, who had agreed to collaborate in the insurrection.

The negligible forces of Falange—hereto less than two hundred throughout the province—begin to spread their propaganda, rioting as they march through the public squares, wearing their blue shirts and chanting their bizarre anthems.

Next morning all municipal employees are called to gather at City Hall. In the great official salon of the building several hundreds of us are addressed by Captain Conde, an artillery chief, who stands surrounded by several officers.

"The rebellion called The Movement has no other aim than to overthrow the Madrid government," he tells us. "It is a Republican uprising that seeks only order, well-being, and the glory of Spain. No one who does his duty has anything to fear. The cooperation of all public servants will be necessary for a few days, perhaps only a few hours, until the new government takes command of law and order to save Spain from anarchy, chaos, and communism."

We disperse at the end of the briefing, with only a small group of municipal employees taking the harangue seriously, although many believe that the captain spoke in good faith. The murders have been only a sad but inevitable adjunct of any uprising, they say. Surely, they will be the last ones.

Out in the streets the troops are marching to the strains of the hymn of Riego, the Republican anthem. Thus they continue to march for several weeks, until playing or singing the gay strains of the brisk, historic liberal anthem becomes a subversive act serious enough to be punished by death. (However, weeks after the start of the uprising the fascist revolution is still attempting to camouflage itself under the guise of a "republican" Movement, as Captain Conde said to us at City Hall, and as repeated days later in the speech of fascist general Yagüe to the Sixteenth Company of legionnaires at the capture of Badajoz:

"Legionnaires, you deserve to triumph because as you face those who know only hate you know how to love, how to sing and laugh. Madrid is far away, legionnaires, but we shall arrive there because those who fell fighting for Spain will rise from their graves to guide our steps in the fray. Legionnaires of Company Sixteen: how few of you remain, and how proud I am of you! Hail with me: Long live Spain! Long live the Republic! Long live the Army!")

That very night after Captain Conde talked to us at City Hall, the number of murders—including those reported in the neighboring towns—rises above one hundred. Next morning terror reigns rampant in the city and province of Logroño. Noble feelings and generosity go underground to give way to a moral breakdown verging on villainy. The local newspapers print maps of Spain with superimposed arrows that point to the advance of the insurrection. The shafts of the arrows start at the provinces held by the rebels, the points piercing deeply into surrounding territory to give the impression of a blanket seizure of the nation. Actually, less than one fifth of national territory is under fascist control. Sensational news accompanies the maps: The troops from Africa have already crossed the Strait of Gibraltar! The Republican government is in crisis! Fighting in the streets of Madrid and Barcelona will last only a few hours before the rebels take over Spain's two largest cities! . . .

From only several dozen members scattered through the province, the political party of Falange grows into hundreds in a few days and into the thousands in a week, its inflation attended by a corresponding rise in assassinations. They begin to arrest anyone who tries to keep out of sight, reason enough to refrain from staying home. I walk through town and watch the exuberant joy of some citizens. On the bridges across the Ebro I see contingents of Requetés from Navarra (Carlist volunteers), reactionaries who had been trained and made ready for instant mobilization. These Navarrese—many without weapons—are quickly equipped at the artillery barracks in Logroño and integrated into columns marching to the war fronts. I am not aware that my innocent attitude as an observer is being taken for a gesture of defiance. "Such a confirmed republican should not display his daring by walking the streets as if nothing were happening. Instead, he should be hiding his shame at home. . . ." Meanwhile, well-known citizens of the town are among those assassinated by the execution patrols. The governor and his aides . . . Chief Erce of the Urban Guard . . . Bernal, president of the Leftist Republican Party . . . Ulecia, head of the Night Watchmen's Corps . . . lawyer Rupérez . . . Dr. Vallejo, a physician. Young ladies who tremble at the squeak of a mouse or faint at the sight of blood are sending hundreds of innocent people to jail and death through their thoughtless denunciations. Kindness and compassion become such crimes that anyone moved to exercise them is immediately suspect and risks his life. Only the priests can express themselves freely without jeopardizing their personal security. But with some exceptions, the angels of peace, messengers of the Divine Word, are too busy kindling the flames of fratricidal fires from their very pulpits and with all their strength.

The morning of the third day after the outbreak of the rebellion I again walk over to the bridges on the Ebro. There I find a relative of mine, Captain Jalón, already in uniform and sporting the large red beret of the Carlist reactionaries, looking quite satisfied with the events. The forces of fanaticism, ignorance, and cruelty in the province are falling like a plague over the city, bringing sorrow and desolation to many families, including mine.

In the afternoon I go to the Hijelmo, a small bar on the street of June Eleventh, not far from where I live. A Carlist Requeté has just shot and killed a tenant of the building on the doorstep and a group at the bar is talking about it. A dangerous socialist who was trying to escape, they say. As I leave the place in a few minutes, I hear the comment of a city employee standing at the door: "They killed him like a rabbit and they have the nerve to say he was trying to escape. Escape where? The doors were covered by the rest of the armed patrol!"

Another friend of mine is murdered, Modrego, a freight agent who worked at the railroad station, a young fellow who had very dark hair and an open, friendly manner. He loved to swim in the Ebro where I frequently found him in the summer, rowing his small boat. . . .

I spend the morning of the fourth day at a family country place outside town with my wife and newborn son. When we return to the city to lunch with my in-laws, we find two security guards and a secret police agent awaiting me in a car in front of the house. Courteously, the agent shows me his orders to take me to the Civil Government offices. He must notice the terror reflected in my wife's face, for he assures us it will be a matter of some simple statements which will take no more than a half hour to set down. He adds his regret for the delay this means for the family meal. . . .

A few minutes later I am escorted out of the car and into the Civil Government building. There I am kept for two hours in a large room crowded with dozens who also await an uncertain fate. A policeman I've seen around town works laboriously over a mound of papers on a desk. From time to time he stops and runs his eyes over the lines filling the room. At last I am taken into another office where there is only one man sitting at a desk: the Chief of Police. He questions me about my activities of the past few days. I explain I had just returned from Madrid four days before and therefore know little of what was going on in Logroño in my absence. I hardly had a chance to rest from the trip when the uprising started. As for the past couple of days, my life has been the same as ever; the only thing I know of the developments is what any passerby can see while walking the streets.

With a meaningful grin the Police Chief assures me he has exact information as to the reason for my trip to Madrid: to help organize the resistance against the Movement!

I explain the purpose of my journey: strictly professional, as can be proved easily by glancing at the correspondence on my desk at City Hall. I don't deny being a republican, but the Commissioner knows very well that I am an unimportant member of the Leftist Republican Party. Is it logical to suppose that someone without rank in a political organization is going to be entrusted with a mission of the sort he has just mentioned? Changing to a confidential tone, the Chief names the most serious accusation weighing against me: that I am responsible for keeping hidden several caches of arms and explosives. If I reveal the location and other pertinent details nothing unpleasant will happen to me. That alone will be proof of my willingness to cooperate with the glorious national Movement. Otherwise. . . .

It isn't difficult to see that the fictional charges have no other purpose than to give a semblance of legality to my arrest.

"Sr. Comisario," I tell him, "I say and repeat that I have never been a leader of local politics in the province. As a municipal official I have dealt with the Civil Government enough for you, who should be well informed, to know the purpose of my trips to Madrid. As for those weapons and explosives, I doubt they actually exist, but if they did I assure you it would be none of my business. At the point of that pistol on your belt I couldn't tell you anything different. And if I did it would be a lie."

At a sign from the Police Chief the team of guards witnessing my interrogation from the door steps closer. The Police Chief orders me to follow them and gives them his instructions: "The usual."

"To the coop?" asks, smiling, one of the guards.

A slight nod from the Chief of Police both answers him and ends the questioning. Now, handcuffed and flanked by the two guards I cross the small square of the Institute on the way to the Avenida prison. My white trousers and my escort call attention. The handcuffs press annoyingly on my wrists. I look up and walk lost in dark thoughts. As we turn the corner I catch a glimpse of the lower windows of the Círculo Logroñés, a social club of the town. There are faces peering behind, some expressing curiosity, others a gleeful satisfaction. A few, anxious to take in every detail of my misfortune, press their noses against the thick panes. Seen from the street through the disfiguring glass, they look like monsters. They are the people who at the slightest social stir always use the same expression: "What we need in this country is a man who wields a big stick and flogs hard."

Those unconditional admirers of the Big Stick policy were called *flagellomanes* by Poli, Policarpo Rivas, a friendly jailmate I was soon to meet.

AT THE AVENIDA JAIL

At a cubbyhole by the jail door a sergeant briskly enters my name, political affiliation, and other registration details. Once the entrance requirements are complied with, they free me of the handcuffs and push me into the Avenida's indoor court. In other times, the building was a great jai-alai palace. Later it was divided, part of it to be used as a movie house and part as a handball court—which requires a shorter distance between player and wall than *cesta* and racket games. It is the latter section that has been converted into a qualified jail known among the prisoners simply as the Avenida, where I find myself surrounded by friends and acquaintances, all anxious for news from the outside. I do my best to satisfy them, and when I tell the details of my arrest I find out that this is "the coop," as the guard called it. I am told so by a former prison official, now one of my fellow inmates.

A cloud of dust and the conglomeration of humanity—some 900 inmates—packed in that small space make it difficult to recognize it as the court I know well from the days when I went to see the handball matches. Now quilts and pallets are rolled and piled up everywhere and all manner of blankets and clothing hang from hooks and nails on the wall. The effect recalls the Madrid Rastro, the fleamarket. The tension caused by the war news keeps everyone in a state of frenzy which precludes a full realization of the immediate horrors that surround us.

After obstinate efforts to pile all bundles against the walls, a narrow passage has finally been achieved. It offers our legs a welcome chance to stretch out, and we call it "the treadmill."

In one of my maneuvers in that bedlam I land near the former prison official, Don José, the one who has informed me of the "official" name given to this jail. He is truly a fine person, this graying gentleman. I met him in 1934 during the socialist revolution of October, when I was the prisoner and he the jailer. Now, beside him, I meet a distant relative of his, a skinny young cabinetmaker. He tells us how one of his co-workers at his shop was machine-gunned and two others sent to jail. He passes on the information he has received from a friendly soldier with whom he managed to exchange some conversation when they changed the guard. Cataluña and the Basque provinces, save for a small sector of Alava, are firmly under government control. In the center of the peninsula the war fronts are in Somosierra to the north of Madrid, and in Sigüenza to the east. The failure of fascist General Mola—military governor of Pamplona and supreme chief of the Navarrese forces—to push on across the Sierra to Madrid has enabled the government to wipe out the attack of the Fifth Column inside the capital, thus preventing it from making contact with the rebel forces. All of this has shattered the morale in the fascist rearguard. With touching faith, the little cabinetmaker believes that in a few days the republican troops will be coming down the mountain pass of Piqueras on the way to Logroño. His relative Don José tells him, smiling wistfully, "They'd better hurry if they want to find us alive."

Among my first contacts at the Avenida jail are Ruiz, a towering man who hereto has been a postal official; young Policarpo Rivas; Salvado, a state veterinarian; Pepe Mato, a close friend and a colleague of mine at City Hall where he is chief of the municipal laboratory. With his great mane of white hair and imposing height, Mato has the look of a patriarch. He is kind and cultured and well liked in our city. He tells me how he has tried to improve sanitary conditions in this sorry human heap of the Avenida by talking to Captain Contreras, a medic from the artillery regiment placed temporarily in charge of supervising sanitary conditions in this qualified jail. The interview was cordial, but fruitless. "I tell you, this is not a jail. This is a pigsty," Mato says now. "Here one can really apply the famous sign mentioned in the Divine Comedy: 'Abandon all hope, you who enter here. . . .'"

I am summoned to the reception office and given a pallet, a blanket, and some cigarettes. The rest of the afternoon I spend talking with Policarpo, whom we all call Poli, a man of middling years, sparse blondish hair, and a fair complexion. He too believes the fascists will have a scant chance for victory if they fail to take Madrid and Barcelona, and for a long time we speculate about it.

At dusk a non-commissioned officer appears at the door and shouts with all his might: "Line up for chow!"

In comes a platoon from the nearby artillery barracks, carrying three immense kettles. When the lids are removed to reveal a cold sickening mass of chickpeas and potatoes, the same words of disappointment echo through the waiting lines: "Cold again." I soon learn the meaning of those words. Despite its abominable flavor and quality, the stew is edible so long as it reaches us while still warm. But not even the hungriest among us can swallow more than a couple of spoonfuls when it is cold.

Time for taps, and as the command resounds through the compound, we grab our pallets and blankets and spread them on the spaces they assign us on the floor. Following the corporals' instructions we leave a narrow passage between each two rows. The powerful lights that once were used to light up the night matches are now left on all night. It is impossible to escape their glare, even with eyes tightly shut. They seem to burn right through the eyelids. But more ominous discomforts prevent us from falling asleep.

Around ten o'clock a dead silence descends over the court and its nine hundred inmates. It is the calm that precedes the hour when the execution list was read nightly at every prison, and called "La Saca." Some thirty minutes pass and we hear the purr of an approaching motor followed by the screech of brakes. Evidently, a vehicle is stopping at the jail door. In a moment, a platoon of "blue shirts" (falangists) bursts into the court from the rear door and stands in double file. The non-commissioned officer who acts as warden reads slowly from a list of names until he has called seventeen prisoners with "provisional freedom permits" signed by Benlló, the Civil Governor. The official signature seems to guarantee that the "saca" will not be a mass murder, although it is some kind of an improvement on the old "fugitive law." (In old days of social strife in Barcelona when General Martínez Anido was governor and Colonel Arlegui chief of police, labor leaders were transferred at night from one prison to another, to be assassinated under pretext of having attempted to escape. The maneuver was known as "compliance with the fugitive law.") But now at the Avenida we are not as certain of the fate of the condemned as we are going to be soon. Most of them, hoping to be able to defend themselves in what is supposed to be a night trial, leave confidently. The good-bys are brief. As we hear the truck starting down the road a certain relief is felt by all. The melancholy night reaches us only through the black holes of the transoms above. Our eyes remain glued to those rectangles until with the approaching dawn their blackness diminishes. Only then is sleep possible, for at night the dreaded Twenty Eight—as the sinister truck is known in the compound—can always return for a new load. With the light of dawn we get a few hours of reprieve.

I feel as if I had been left in a dark cave from where seventeen long shadows have disappeared like fading ghosts. In a moment I must go to the latrine. What I see there could turn the strongest stomach, for two small washbasins and two toilet bowls are all the sanitary installations on the ground floor. There are better facilities in the balcony, what has been the spectators' first tier of boxes, but those are off-limits to the prisoners. Back on my pallet I cover my face with a towel in an effort to evade the glaring beam and try to concentrate on getting some sleep.

At six o'clock a piercing bugle call sends us to our feet. Reveille. The moment quilts and pallets are rolled and piled up against the walls, the cleaning chore begins. There is an inch-thick coat of dirt formed by the floss and fuzz of the smelly quilts, by papers, spittle, cigarette butts. The summary mopping only manages to stir the fetid mass and leave it ready to trap the dirt of the new day, my first in jail. A sergeant approaches me and proposes to make me corporal, explaining that, being educated and well liked, I better than others could help organize the confusion. I decline, offering instead to cooperate with whomever he designates as corporal in my section. Morning passes slowly between frequent arrivals of new prisoners, departures of those being transferred to other jails, and a suffocating heat which precludes much activity. The sweltering sun falls vertically on the tin roof, turning the enclosed court into an immense dark oven.

The men take to grouping according to their towns. One of the delegations nearest to me is from Nalda, a pueblo of the lowlands of the Iregua, at the edge of the hilly region that surrounds most of the province. My mother was born in Nalda, and I find out her brother Matías has been arrested in another group. Some of them tell me that he and the Mayor of Nalda were separated from the others when the truckload of prisoners arrived in Logroño, to be jailed instead in the small Falange barracks. (As I learn, later, that version is incorrect. It was in the sacristy of the Marian Fathers' convent where my uncle Matías spent his last hours.)

Among the group of Naldeans there is a giant of a fellow called Juanón, Big John, well over six feet, with a face like an apple tanned by the sun. He plays the shepherd's drum in the town festivals, and because of his expansive chatter and gestures he seems to be leader of his group. Smiling, he assures me that by now there are only women and children left in Nalda. The men—those who could—

have fled and are hiding in the hills. In a matter of a few days all will return to normal, he assures me. But I am worried about uncle Matías, who besides being a local judge, always was a political leader of the town's liberal party. . . . Trying to get more information about him I manage to speak alone with Eustaquio, the senior member of the Nalda group. I learn no more from him, but in his clever, direct words I find a marked contrast to Juanón's optimism.

"There are only a half dozen rightist nobodies in our town," he tells me, "but they are a bloodthirsty lot. The churchmice are no bigger in number but twice as bloodthirsty, women and all. They encourage the men with their prayers of 'Holy Virgin of Villanueva, give us strength to shoot them all.' "

The monstrous blasphemy rings in my ears for some time.

There are six women being held in the first tier of boxes, among them a Normal School teacher, Felisa Vidorreta. She is known in town as an able teacher who also tutored at home. We were arrested the same afternoon and met briefly in the halls of the Civil Government building. Now I remember her quick gesture and whispered words as we crossed one another: "They can't, they cannot win."

In a few days the good teacher is shot. Two of her former pupils are among the execution platoon.

I receive two visits in the afternoon almost consecutively: my wife, and a falangist group with which I have had cordial relations but whom now I cannot possibly consider friends. They offer to help me as best they can. The fascist arrows embroidered on their blue shirts seem to stab my eyes. I thank them for their intentions but I tell them I don't need their help, adding that I have no idea of the reason for my being in jail, together with so many others who are known for their honesty and integrity. Surely, their very gesture in coming to offer help proves that they themselves believe my arrest is an injustice. . . . Their visit is short; half embarrassed, they leave, mumbling their offers of help.

In an attempt to improve sanitary conditions, some of the notable inmates have several talks with the bugle sergeant who is actually the prison chief. Pepe Mato, the most articulate, points out the dangers of an epidemic and its consequences, not only for us but for the population of Logroño. Pepe's earnest conversations with the sergeant result in the beginning of some organization in this infernal chaos. We are granted permission to sweep again in the afternoon, and from somewhere are brought cans of disinfectant to be mixed with the mop water. The swarm of flies diminishes, but the toilets remain in the same filthy condition.

Chow and the recurring hardships of night are no different from those of last night, except that the "saca" is moderate; there are only six names on the execution list.

HOODLUMS IN UNIFORM

This morning I get to talk with Adolfo Moreda, magistrate of Barcelona's Supreme Court, a short, bald man of forty six with a youthful countenance and an infinite reserve of stories. I have been told that in the socialist uprising of 1934 Don Adolfo refused to surrender Barcelona's Palace of Justice to the army troops. Only recently the government of Don Manuel Azaña has named him president of the Supreme Court. To celebrate his promotion, the nearby town of Alverite, his birthplace, invited him to the yearly festival, where they were going to name him Favorite Son. The magistrate spends his summers in Ordesa, a poetic corner of the Pyrenees, but this time he cut short his vacation and proceeded to Alverite to receive the honorary title. After spending a few days in his town visiting friends and relatives and attending parties and dinners given in his honor, he came to Logroño hoping to rest from the festivities before returning to Barcelona and his work. And it was here, at the Gran Hotel, that the start of the insurrection caught him. Next morning, July 19th, he was denounced by a well-known marquis of the province. The arrest was carried out so swiftly, that Don Adolfo arrived in prison still wearing his country hat, carrying only a few essentials gathered in haste. Now he tells me how he was received at the then almost empty jail together with nine other new prisoners. For fifteen minutes they were kept at rifle point against a wall, arms raised and in dead silence.

The scene ended when some important falangist burst into the court-yard and, after insulting the terrorized prisoners, commanded the platoon to continue making other arrests.

At noon a considerable number of prisoners are transferred to the fort of San Cristóbal in Pamplona, relieving the crowded conditions in our compound. But this small comfort doesn't last long; before nightfall new arrests take up the space left by the departed.

During one of our many discussions about the war, a bricklayer called Amós raises an arm with fist closed, socialist style. A stool pigeon tells the sergeant, who comes running and forces Amós to give the fascist salute. "Like this," the sergeant tells him, giving the heil Hitler copied by Spanish fascists. "The closed fist is out of fashion. Nowdays you have to stretch your arm and open your hand. And be thankful that this time I give you only a lesson in gestures."

I take part in an interesting conversation about the "sacas" with Magistrate Moreda, Don José the former prison official, a protestant pastor called Angel, and several young labor leaders. We arrive at the conclusion that our suspicions are correct: The nightly lists of prisoners with "permits of provisional freedom" signed by the governor are actually death sentences. Adolfo Moreda is the only one who thinks differently. With his congenital optimism and believing as he does firmly that the fascist revolt is close to failure, he cannot conceive its leaders willing to implicate themselves so obviously. There is a certain logic to his reason. Later it becomes general knowledge that in the most difficult moments at the beginning of the fascist Movement, some of its prominent leaders considered the possibility of suicide, so greatly had they involved themselves with their crimes.

Don José tells us of his confidential talks with a colleague who has been sent here as an expert to help organize this qualified jail. The man told him of so many bodies found in the common grave at the local cemetery—among them some of the prisoners that were "taken" out of our prison last night—that Moreda's arguments lose all strength. A cloud of pessimism descends on all in our talkative group.

At last, one of the Nalda group tells me the true fate of my uncle Matías. He was taken just before dawn from the sacristy of the

Marian Brothers' convent and pushed into a truck with fourteen others. The entire group was executed in the pond of La Granjera, a few kilometers from here. The memory of my mother's brother, that handsome giant with his vivid green eyes and rosy cheeks, machine-gunned ruthlessly, desolates and enrages me. Years were to pass before I could learn all the details of my uncle's tragic end. He was arrested with the others in the dead of night. His hunting dog followed the truck all the way to Logroño, waiting and hovering around at all stops. Several times he tried to get into the Marian Brother's grounds, only to be kicked out at rifle butt by the soldiers of the guard. Limping and whining he spent the warm July night facing the holy enclosure, until at dawn the transport truck took the fifteen Nalda prisoners to La Granjera, one of the execution grounds just outside the city. An influential relative of ours was able to obtain a special permit to claim my uncle's body and bury it in my mother's mausoleum. When my relatives arrived at the execution grounds, the others were already buried in the common grave, but Matías' corpse was laid face up to the sun, his body pierced by bullet wounds. Stretched out close to him, whining softly, was his hunting dog.

Here they come from the artillery barracks, carrying the great kettles. This time the stew is almost hot, so we proceed to devour it. After dinner we walk "the treadmill" until taps and time to lie down. We remain waiting in this dungeon, each inmate deep in his own ominous conjectures, awaiting the "saca." It calls for sixteen victims, all of them from surrounding small towns. The last one on the list, his muscles paralyzed by terror, is pushed out of the court as his bowels give out through his trouser legs, leaving a stinking trail behind. The moment is too tragic to provoke a single snicker in the compound, but the awaiting execution patrols make up for our silence with strident peals of laughter.

Several days pass with the same routine of takes and transfers, while some organization of this sorry human heap is achieved. The greatest improvement has been the assigning of a service corps to the job of cleaning the latrines. A picturesque peasant of the town of Nájera, Macario—slight, swarthy, with very dark straight hair— is put in charge. Two prisoners are named by the sergeant as his assistants. More than a few of the survivors of the Avenida prison may well owe their lives to this small sanitation team headed by Macario.

During the early hours of morning the queues outside the toilets are so long and move so slowly that some of the men cannot hold themselves till their turn comes to reach the bowls. To avoid the revolting spectacle some of us learn to beat the rush by starting early for the latrines. A young light sleeper next to me becomes my personal alarm clock. We lose some sleep, but we even manage to wash before pandemonium starts.

I see Macario and his helpers sunk to their knees in human feces, working without rest until the latrines are spotless. When I ask my friends about this strangely selfless soul, I am told he has been accused by a shepherd of his town whose resentment had to do with a question of women rather than of politics. Since his charges are light and his accuser a humble, unimportant man, perhaps Macario could negotiate his freedom, but his services at the Avenida are so crucially needed that it would be futile for the poor fellow to try it. During the months he is detained at the Avenida he receives extra food rations, gift cigarettes and other privileges from the prison authorities in an effort to keep him from complaining.

They have closed all accesses, barring even the little sunlight that seeps through the high windows of the second and third balconies. Only a few timid threads of light steal at an angle between wall and ball court. By noon they grow to a brilliant strand projected against the wall. Every morning twenty of us take turns to follow the sun spots. Like sunflowers we face the welcome light for a half hour, after which the enclosure returns to its dusty shaft of gloom.

Suddenly an order is given to stop all incoming gift parcels. The restriction lasts for a week and draws different interpretations from the inmates, from the possibility that the Republican forces have taken Saragossa, to the rumor that a monarchist conspiracy has spread to the rebel zone with the help of many young officers. Whatever the reason, the results are dismal, for from then on the stew never fails to arrive late and cold. But hunger is not the worst we suffer from this mass isolation. Of the three vital essentials now denied to us—food, clean clothing, and tobacco—it is the lack of the last one that we resent the most.

I have made a valuable purchase, a pair of dark glasses to protect my eyes from the irritating glare of the powerful spotlights they keep on all night. Bought them from a soldier, a soccer fan who remembering my performances with the Real Madrid team, let me have them at a fair price.

One of the women held in the first tier of boxes has suffered the same fate as teacher Felisa Vidorreta. The others were transferred to the provincial jail. Now the guards have taken over the balcony and use it as a rest and recreation area.

The "sacas" continue relentlessly, with no less than twelve victims nightly, except Sundays. Evidently, being a sacred day to what calls itself a holy crusade, it calls for temporary compliance with the Lord's Fifth Commandment.

A new development: spies in the prison! They appear suddenly among us, four young fellows who look as pale and meek as novice priests. They say they've been brought in with a new group of arrests, but in truth they have been sent by the police authorities to mingle with the prisoners. The lack of skill of the apprentice informers is so obvious that in a few hours they raise our suspicions. As I am talking with Angel, the protestant pastor, one of them approaches. I give Angel a sign, we break up and walk away. Rambling, we wind up at another end of the court with Ruiz the postal employee, Ramos, and Poli. They are talking about the same thing. Ramos, a grade-school teacher, young, fat, and short, is laughing.

"The human brain is a magnificent instrument, but few know how to use it. Look over there," he tells us, pointing to one of the spy teams who a few yards from us are trying in vain to strike up conversations with the men. Their mere approach has an instant effect: At the sight of them the groups break up and disperse like small chemical bodies disintegrating at a drop of acid. Others, with more or less subtlety, walk away slowly without looking back. In a few days a new team of spies joins the amateurs, but they are unable to improve the poor technical quality of the corps. When one of them has a row with a prisoner, the sergeant lets the cat out of the bag. "You guys are no good for the job," he tells them in his witty Andalusian accent.

The stool pigeons are assigned to the service of inspection and control of visitors, where they perform their duty unabashedly. Indifferent to side remarks, to indignant looks and gestures, they stick their heads between mother and son, husband and wife, brothers, and friends, until it becomes impossible for a man to exchange a word with his visitors without being heard by the zealous bunch. In a few days they disappear from our midst, probably transferred to other jails to carry on their "secret" mission.

One night I witness an unforgettable scene while I lie on my pallet on the cement court. Magistrate Moreda is on my right. It is around eleven thirty, past the hour of the "saca," when we hear a clatter of sabers, boots, and spurs, together with much laughter. It's coming from the stairs that lead to the first tier of boxes. In a moment a group of artillery officers and two civilians appear leaning on the balcony railing, their eyes searching intently among us. It is not easy to find someone in this labyrinth of quilts and blankets. Even with the help of the Andalusian sergeant they have difficulty in spotting the prisoner they seem to be straining for. At last, amidst cries of satisfaction and nodding to one another, they shout: "There! There he is!" They are pointing in my direction and for a wild moment I think I am their prey. My fears subside instantly. Moreda has his face covered by a towel, trying to protect himself from the glare of the powerful lights, as I used to do. Now, with my cherished dark glasses, I can see the scene in all its details.

"Enjoying a good bed, president of the Barcelona Court?" cries one of the officers. "There he is, with his salary of hundreds of thousands of pesetas, while these hungry nobodies admire him, as they do other sons of bitches called *chiefs*. The kind who wear collar and tie are the worst!"

"He doesn't move," cries another one. "He's making believe he's asleep. The fake!"

"Maybe we should go down there and kick him awake!"

"Who would believe it of his excellency the magistrate! There he is, shitting in his pants from terror!"

"There'll be no peace in Spain until we exterminate his kind."

"Hey, you! You are not fooling us. We know you can hear us! One of these days we're going to give you a train ticket to Barcelona. We don't want bad riojanos and traitor Spaniards in this province!"

"That's exactly what he would like, a train ticket. Better leave him here as an example to these idiots."

For some minutes they keep up their insults and provocations led by Captain Conde and another artillery officer. Only Captain Contreras, the medic, and the civilians in the group, don't say a word. My face contracts with rage and indignation. How can serious, adult, commissioned officers conduct themselves like common ruffians in front of a vast, defenseless audience? At last, tired of pouring insults and convinced of the futility of their provocations in the light of Moreda's immobility, they leave the balcony with the same clatter of boots, spurs, and sabers that preluded their arrival.

Hundreds of voices raise an angry hum in this field of pallets, until the sergeant shouts, "Forget it! Everyone back to sleep!"

In a moment Moreda turns to me. "If I had moved," he whispers, "I probably would be on my way to the cemetery now. They came for me but didn't dare take me because they are unsure of their victory. We've often said that, you and I. But I can tell you now: I never dreamed they could sink this low. Hoodlums in uniform."

An approaching corporal sent by the sergeant halts our confidences with his stare. Moreda and I withdraw to our thoughts and fall asleep eventually.

In the morning we hear rumors that the isolation tactics will end in a few hours. We again can have visitors, food, cigarettes . . . ! Those from far-off towns who seldom receive packages or visits will share at least our food and tobacco. Yes, let them lift the ban!

THE PROTESTANT PASTOR

One of the inmates who most attracts my attention is Angel, the protestant pastor. He looks to be in his forties and has a dark face with a straggly beard and very dark eyes, all of it crowded above a small frame. His closest friend here is Marcelino Bello, the anarchist. Both are vegetarians, both have the same mild, gentle manners. There seems to be a strong kinship between them. In spite of the many bizarre things one sees in this jail, this friendship between minister and anarchist draws general curiosity. Angel serves in the town of Pradejón. His home and small chapel have been ransacked and set afire by the rabble of the town, encouraged in such charitable undertaking by the local authorities. He owns a few parcels of land which he himself has tilled and tended. With the sale of that produce and by tutoring children on the side, he has lived an ascetic life verging on penury. He salvaged only his Bible from the catastrophe that destroyed his small possessions. He always carries it with him and consults it often to enrich his conversation with dozens of quotations. This afternoon we are walking the treadmill when Angel's inseparable friend, Bello the anarchist, is called to the visitors' room. During Bello's absence I hear an interesting exchange between the pastor and Poli, the lawyer.

"You never leave that book behind, do you?" Poli remarks, pointing to the Bible.

"Why should I? This book is full of fundamental truths which can comfort me in the worst moments."

"How I envy you for being able to find such easy solace. I wish it were that simple for me. I've read the Bible, but I doubt it could comfort me."

"Then, I believe you haven't read it as well as you should. I myself didn't understand it until I read it for the third time, and then it changed my life. Now I know the meaning of tranquility."

"If that's what the book gives you, a sedative could do as well."

"Not exactly. The gospel gives you a lot more than tranquility. Patience, resignation, the strength to love your fellow men as they are, whatever they may be. . . ."

"That's really something! You mean that even when you're suffering humiliations and abuses, locked up in a pigpen, you can still love your jailer and your torturer? Don't you think that beyond a certain point of endurance men are justified if they turn into beasts? I could accept the theoretical generosity of pardoning the offenses we ourselves receive. But . . . what about those inflicted upon our loved ones? If your wife, brothers, and children had suffered what many families of those here have gone through, the mere mention of the word love would be an insult to your ears."

"I don't pretend to be above pain. I suffer as you or anyone. But there is a difference between us: I struggle to eradicate hate, while you kindle it."

"At times I too feel evangelic, although in a different way. Perhaps because I have an impulsive temperament, man's inhumanity to man can breed in me tremendous feelings of revenge. They don't last long, I assure you. But this is different, my friend. This gets worse every moment! I can overlook a push, a scratch, perhaps even a wound. But if they persist in hitting me on the same place, the day comes when the wound turns into a cancer. No, dear pastor. I respect saintliness but I don't hope to attain it."

"I too am not a saint, although I'd like to be one. Now I want to prepare myself, to wash my heart of all stain for the approaching journey. To die forgiven, without hate."

"Then, you don't admit the possibility that we may be saved momentarily?"

The pastor smiles wistfully. "Perhaps, but not for me. Whatever the result of this struggle, I think this violence will last for years. In the matter of feelings we have regressed rather than progressed. Even the jungle beasts kill only for food. Whereas here. . . ."

Emilio, a lanky medical student who often joins us in our talks, has been listening quietly, but now breaks his silence to take up Poli's side.

"If those who are now in command were in our place, they'd suffer our same fate at the hands of these fiends in charge of executing us. Big criminals always buy little ones to do their dirty work for them. And after all is said and done, despite the guise of patriotism and religion, this civil war is actually a class struggle. The rich backed by the ambitious military, by religious fanatics, and the stupid fascists, all trying to regain power by the only means possible after their defeat in the February elections. Actually, the source of it all is the unjust distribution of wealth."

"Evil and ambition are not the consequences of capitalism, even if capitalism could contribute to increase them," replies the pastor. "I for one detest communism or any form of dictatorship."

"But why do you believe it so impossible to achieve through politics what you find so attainable through religion?"

"It is only natural that I place greater value on religion than on politics. Jesus Christ captured the world by preaching nonviolence. And in our day, Gandhi with his hunger strikes is a greater menace to the British than the most courageous fighter. Assuming that Man could achieve his best goals through communism, the road of cruelty and violence that leads to those goals is enough to forego them. Violence doesn't change Man inwardly; religion does it. Any system that pretends to achieve the best in Man without first changing his spirit, is utopian. I mean, change man's spirit in order to change society, using no other weapon than religion."

"Well, look around! See what your weapon has accomplished in more than a thousand years?"

"This is not religion. This is superstition, ignorance, evil. Doubly hideous in this case because they are masked in holy vestments."

"Wake up, my friend. Man has no drive other than what he requires to fulfill his needs. Once those needs are satisfied, there is no weapon that can move him."

Orders to resume communications with the outside finally are implemented and again we receive packages, visitors, and through them, news. The execution's lists are reduced considerably, too. All of which creates in us a general state of optimism, not so much for the privileges we regain as for our belief that it signifies defeats on the fascist fronts. Organization of our daily life reaches the discipline and order of military barracks, said to be the only poetry in such enclosures. Along with the corporals, another team of prisoners is assigned as liaison and assistants to the guards. They are given extra privileges in exchange, but few of them take advantage of their position to bully us, and not one is guilty of being an informer.

For several days we receive strange evening visitors. Much as they would come to see a circus, several young ladies accompanied by a few officers stand at the first tier of boxes to watch us. Judging from the gay expressions on their faces, they seem to enjoy looking at the sea of human misery extending beneath them. Although their comments do not reach us we note they invariably end in general laughter.

Another one of my jailmates at the Avenida is Andrés Salvado, the state veterinarian, man of few words with a pleasant dark face and slender build. This afternoon I ask him about the Cabezón brothers, with whom I've struck up a cordial friendship during my stay in Logroño. Amancio Cabezón, head of the family, is branch president of a British chemical concern which does a considerable business in agricultural provinces like Navarra, Valencia, and Rioja. He is well known and liked in Logroño for his wisdom, kindness, and dependability. He has been town councilman several times, and up to the outbreak of the fascist uprising was deputy mayor of Logroño.

A few years ago Amancio built himself a country home in Albelda, near the lowlands of the Iregua. He continued to add land purchases until the property became quite a farm. The land is tilled by tenant farmers of the surrounding pueblos. Because of his kind nature and the excellent terms he offers in his work contracts, Amancio is on the best of terms with his farmers. Now Salvado tells me that soon after the start of the fascist uprising, a falangist patrol commanded by "friends" of the Cabezón family burst into Amancio's farm with orders from the Falange committee to capture him dead or alive. As Salvado talks I cannot help remember the times some of those very men and I have stopped at Amancio's house after picnics and excursions to the nearby sierras, only to be invited to stay for a snack, a dance, some entertainment . . . and all that went with the generous hospitality of that friendly house.

And now, those very same men. . . .

The loyal and courageous farmers tipped off Amancio and helped him go into hiding, Salvado tells me, so the search was fruitless. But all the time it was taking place, a well-known falangist of town kept his pistol pointed at Amancio's wife. Frightened as she was, the poor woman couldn't control her indignation. "For heavens' sake, Jacinto," she exclaimed. "Put that ugly thing away! We know each other."

"Exactly," replied the "chivalrous" falangist. "That's why I keep my gun on you, because I *know* you."

In a couple of days, Salvado adds, the three Cabezón brothers gathered at Amancio's hiding place and from there managed to reach the French border through the province of Navarra . . . disguised as priests! Theirs is one of the rare escapes from our province, one as celebrated by Amancio's friends as lamented by the falangists to whom he was a coveted prey.

In an effort to enlarge our walking space—the treadmill, in prison argot—we pile up most of our quilts and pallets in the center of the court, thus leaving a kind of eliptical track surrounding the mound. Soon we discover another advantage to the Himalaya of our bedding: It obstructs the guard's view at certain angles, leaving us some coveted "dead spaces," as we call them. Undetected, relishing our new "freedom," we hold political discussions and exchange impressions regarding the war. The promenade and the "meetings" cease instantly the moment we hear the word "Chow!" shouted by a guard from the door as the kettles are brought in. We are still not being fed at regular hours, and "dinner" continues to reach us cold almost every time. The silent faces of the men express joy or dismay, according to the temperature of the stew which gradually becomes worse and less, until we reach the point of near starvation. Not infrequently we see ravenous youths fighting the rats for a slice of stale bread.

One of the prisoner-aids is Fermín of Nájera, a mature man of strong build and a good disposition. He gets along well with everyone, jailers and prisoners, and under orders of the Andalusian sergeant he's been put in charge of reading the nightly list of the "sacas." Tonight, as he reads the ninth and last name, Martín, a young fellow I haven't had a chance to meet, springs to his feet like lightning from his pallet and sprints in a mad race in the opposite direction to the door. As he reaches the end of the narrow corridor between two rows of pallets, he hurls himself with all his strength, head first, against the radiator. He is dead instantly. Breath is suspended in every throat in the compound. The sergeant calls hysterically for the medical assistant. When death is officially established they wrap the body in a blanket and take it away. In a few minutes we hear the truck starting down the road with its eight condemned and one corpse, on the way to the execution grounds and the cemetery.

The blood and bits of brain on the radiator and surrounding floor are covered with sawdust, to be swept away in the morning. The men come around to examine the suicide site and weapon. There are commentaries about the "nocturnal" fight, a reference to night sessions at the bullring when even after a sprinkling of sawdust the mounds of strewn entrails of the disemboweled horses seem all the more macabre for the lights and shadows created by the powerful lights beamed on the arena.

"He was dead, all right. Dead, I tell you," I hear someone say in the morning as I myself approach the radiator. Later I learn the reason for that categorical affirmation. It seems one of the prisoners swears that as they took away the suicide he saw the body move under the blanket folds.

The Andalusian sergeant, who never shows cruel instincts and does no more and no less than comply with his orders, is promoted to petty officer a few days after the suicide of our young jailmate. The comment among the cynical is that the promotion has been earned "in the field of battle."

Because of the constant movement of prisoners caused by takes and transfers, it is difficult to remember all faces at the Avenida, and except for friends and comrades I see them only as old faded photographs. But I will never forget the face of slight young Martín who preferred death by concussion to the bullets of the execution platoon.

THE BOMBING AND END OF BELLO THE ANARCHIST

It is mid-afternoon, and over the drone of the human beehive we suddenly hear rifle shots. Silence descends on the compound instantly. Now, besides the increasing barrage of the shots we also hear a hum of approaching motors in a crescendo that soon drowns all other sound.

"Planes!"

"Sounds like Republican trimotors from Madrid!"

Panic spreads in the prison. Only the Andalusian sergeant—now promoted to petty officer—displays some alertness by brandishing his pistol through an open window on the first floor and emptying it, apparently at the blue sky. Next to me Don José's relative, the little cabinetmaker, is about to faint from terror, limbs trembling, teeth chattering. . . . In great confusion most of the men run to take cover under the balcony of loges. A few seconds later the "bombs" fall on the north section of town. Panic increases in the compound.

Magistrate Moreda climbs up on a chair and raises his voice.

"Quiet! Keep your heads! It's nothing, there is only one danger. Can't you see? The guards up there, ready to shoot us!"

It is true. The guards are pointing their rifles at us, obeying the commands of the officers urging them to re-establish order. Impressed by Moreda's serenity and sensible words, the men remain fixed in their places, pushing and struggling no more.

A prison official rushes toward Moreda, and straining to be heard in every corner of the court, shouts: "No one can give orders here! I am the one in command!" The fulminating glare above his immense beak of a nose is met by Moreda's serene glance.

"I don't mean to interfere with your duty. I am only trying to help stop this panic before it ends up in useless bloodshed," the magistrate says quietly.

The eagle-like prison official shakes angrily, further enraged by Moreda's words. "You shut up like the others!" he thunders. "You are nobody here! Nobody! You hear?"

Slowly, Moreda turns his head and remains silent, the picture of dignity.

The prison returns to normal while fantastic news reaches us. The outskirts near the river are smoldering in shambles; the spires of the church of Santiago have collapsed, razed by a bomb; one of the pilots was captured and lynched; there are hundreds of wounded; two bombs landed on the soccer field of the Sport Club. . . . Spurred by the feverish imagination of frustrated, isolated men illusory rumors run wild but soon burst like bubbles when we hear the truth. The bombing has been done only with Madrid newspapers thrown from a Republican plane. The state attorney and other notable falangists of the town quickly drove in their cars and picked up the rain of news from Madrid. Only a few of the newspapers have reached the hands of some pedestrians who were caught out on the street during the "bombing."

The powerful lights are switched on. Now Moreda is walking the treadmill with a slender chap, an office clerk in better days. I know him slightly, he owns the only map in this jail where we can follow reported war operations.

"Intolerance is a form of fear," Moreda is musing as I join them. "Knowing we are in command of events and have reason on our side makes us tolerant, even kind, almost subconsciously."

"Exactly," replies the young fellow. "It's that tolerance which always dooms us. Remember that old political story? 'You liberals always lose because according to your ethics you cannot kill us reactionaries. Where, we reactionaries cut your heads off quite simply and lose no sleep over it.' "

"Perhaps, at first appraisal. But notice how the reactionaries always lose at the end. They may have their temporary periods of victory, but soon they're swept back to their lair. And when they reappear they seem to have lost some of the spunk they had before. You can see that plainly in history."

"Yes, your honor, but history also tells us that the reactionaries abuse the freedom we liberals grant them after they lose, the freedom they never grant us when they're on top. Isn't there a way to stop them from using the means we ourselves give them to defeat us?"

"The leftists always lack energy when they get in power. I said *energy,* notice, not *cruelty.* That is something I detest."

"Words, only words. . . . Cruelty, energy, justice. . . . They are all conditional! Who can tell their limits? What is called energy here may well be cruelty over there. What we consider justice here may be called an outrage elsewhere. You can become a hero in one place and the same act, twenty miles further, can brand you as a criminal."

At this point, the eagle-like prison official approaches, now controlled and composed, and signals Moreda to step aside. The beak of his nose looms above an attempt at a conciliatory smile while they talk. When Moreda returns he answers our inquiring looks. "Nothing important," he tells us. "Just wanted to excuse himself for his outburst. Claims he has to maintain discipline, etcetera. . . ."

Ruiz, who joined us a while ago, now makes this comment, "I think that prison official anticipates seeing you again presiding over your High Court in Barcelona. How insecure can these reactionaries be?"

Tonight, when time comes for taps, the swarm of prisoners falls angrily upon the mound of quilts and pallets. The noise and confusion are maddening. Perhaps the events of the day have stirred life in this beehive. Clouds of dust and lint rise from the rancid bundles of our pallets. After a battle of kicks and jabs each one finally settles in his assigned place.

In the new distribution of pallets recently established, I form a kind of human square with three other men, one of them a gaunt peasant who has tied a black rag around his face. He is nursing a colossal toothache.

"How's that tooth?" asks one of my companions, a young fellow, member of the CNT, the National Federation of Workers.

"The same. But that's not important. The important thing is what happened today." There is a semblance of a smile as the peasant raises the rag to show his face, disfigured by swelling. There he is, suffering considerable pain, but the thought of a possible Republican victory as suggested by the visiting Madrid planes is acting on him as a sedative. Still, he doesn't seem anxious for conversation, so the young laborer turns to the other man in our square to comment on the big event of the day, the "bombing" and Moreda's admirable stand in the face of panic.

"Hey, how did you like the Magistrate's courage? What a guy! That's the kind Spain needs to lead the people. They say he's an atheist."

"All the better. Lots of murdering priests should be as decent."

By the conversation I can tell they are young members of the Atheneum of Rioja, many of whom are rabidly anticlerical and known to talk endlessly about the subject.

The hour of the "saca" is getting close. I spread my blanket and shut my eyes behind my dark glasses, trying to isolate myself from this sorry reality. The day's turbulent happenings begin to fade. I feel stifled by the poor ventilation, by the stench of the sweaty, unwashed humanity surrounding me. I think of the fields not far from here, gilded by sunlight in the daytime and dark and humid in the limpid night. The wheat stalks await the severing caress of the gleaming sickles that will reap at dawn. There are the trees, too, heavier at night with the dew clinging to the fat ripe fruit. And above all, there is the inviting fresh water of the river. Ah, to sink my weary body in it. . . . Who goes down to the Ebro for a swim now? At this moment of conscious dreaming a grotesque picture crosses my mind: the town's falangists, standing on the rocks, giving the fascist salute with their stretched arm before diving in. But the vision disappears and I see the river lone and deserted as it must be now. The war and the jails have done away with the swimmers. The girls? The girls never go down to the river alone.

Am I still dreaming? My watch has stopped. I light a cigarette and look around. No one sleeps; everyone waits for the "saca." As always, the tragic moment arrives. Fermín of Nájera reads the list from the old red curtain at the entrance of the court. One of the names sends a shiver up my spine and something cold seems to flutter past me. Death has just gone by. The young worker who showed concern for the peasant's toothache stands up and steps out. His face is colorless, already like a ghost's. He joins the other nine victims waiting at the soiled red drape.

Angel the pastor and Bello the anarchist play checkers after lunch. They sit on some rickety chairs that someone managed to wrest loose from under the loges. With pieces of cardboard, old nails, bottle tops, and other discarded materials, the prisoners have fashioned a collection of table games which, considering the circumstances, seem like objets d'art to us. My two companions rest the checkerboard between two suitcases, forming a bridge. Despite the incessant noise they are abstracted in their game. I stand by, watching them play as I smoke. There is no place to go. Time is endless and it makes no difference how we spend it. There is nothing to do but wait and wait in this crowded, overgrown coop.

"We're almost finished," Angel says when he notices me, pointing to an empty space near a stack of suitcases. By way of providing a collective activity, they go on to tell stories and jokes about prison life.

We are approached by a prisoner who carries a crate full of books. In his normal, "outside" life, this man earns his living by selling books in the street. I remember once having bought something from him as he passed in front of the café Los Leones. Now he tells us about his arrest. They rifled the books he was holding on consignment, but his wife was able to salvage two suitcases full of them, the ones he is now peddling to the prisoners. It has taken him several requests for permission and a severe censorship of his wares to be allowed to see them in jail. I leaf through the books. Nothing but biographies of saints. Angel buys one and the man goes on to seek other customers.

"My library too was ransacked," Bello tells us. "First came the usual when they arrest you: insults. Then that farce of looking for bombs under the bed. They searched the garden and came back furious into the house. My wife trembled as they opened cabinets and drawers and threw everything on the floor. Well, I live a frugal life and books are my only luxury. One of the policemen went over to eye a bookcase.

'You have many books, anarchist,' he said.

'Sure. They are my bombs. Perhaps nowadays these are considered more dangerous than the ones you couldn't find.'

'Don't get fresh and keep your tongue, or maybe we'll take your woman too.'

'This lady has nothing to do with all this and it wouldn't be fair to involve her.'

'This will teach you to respect authority!' He dropped his billy on me and I fell unconscious. They told me later that he tried to beat me some more while I was out on the floor, but the others stopped him. At the end, one of the policemen took my best books. Probably to sell them or to decorate some corner of his house, because I doubt he'll read them. It's the same old story, friends. The moment they feel strong they start to abuse and destitute the helpless."

"Power and authority can turn good men into bad ones and bad ones into worse," comments Angel the pastor.

"If we're going to talk about that," I say, "I'll tell you I'm more inclined to agree with Voltaire: Men are neither good nor bad, but a mixture of both."

"Whatever they are," Bello continues, "their mission is to control the worst in themselves. At any rate, those who don't shut themselves up in a shell of selfishness as a rule wish to reform the world somewhat. The pastor here with his religion, you with your democracy, and I with my anarchism."

A young fellow who is reported to be an anarchist comes over to give us news of the Basque front. The advances of General Mola toward the coast, although not impressive are continuous and becoming a source of alarm. Many believe impossible the fall of the city of Irún, considered just short of impregnable because of its military forts of Guadalupe and San Marcial.

I never get another chance to talk with Bello. This very night he is "taken" with nine others. I see him leave from my pallet, only a few yards from his. He walks straight to the door, his expression neither arrogant nor sorrowful, but dignified, as if accepting without rebellion the certainty of an irrevocable destiny. (Later we are told that his attitude was the same in front of the firing squad.) As I see him disappear under the red curtain, I think how in normal times a man of his convictions and fortitude could have kindled a general strike in the province with a gesture.

Bello's death is a terrible blow to his friend the pastor. In the morning we see him withdrawn in silent introspection, taking occasional refuge in his Bible. Some of us feel it our duty to stay close to him. Then, late in the afternoon, as Ruiz and I are walking the treadmill, we are approached by the Andalusian petty officer.

"Tell the shepherd without flock, that friend of yours, that there's a woman outside claiming his pal's belongings."

We go over and give Angel the message. He picks up a parcel he has ready and a suitcase and brings them over to the petty officer at the end of the court. A heavy silence falls on us. Part of the group disbands quietly, leaving only Ruiz the postal employee, Emilio the student, and myself, to comfort the pastor.

"Bello knew what awaited him," he tells us softly when he returns from delivering the baggage. "I remember his words of a few days ago. He believed that even if there were a turn for the better on our battle fronts he and I wouldn't be here to see it. He said he abhorred physical violence, although his political ideals had taught him to accept certain sacrifices. I, on the other hand—he insisted— had had a clean, easy road. Still, although for different reasons, we've both bred the same hate in our enemies, and that hate will have the same consequences for both." The pastor stops for a moment and then adds in a small voice, "My greatest regret is that I was unable to bring him close to God before his end."

"Line up!"

It's the petty officer, shouting from the entrance. His assistant corporals echo the order through the compound, sending us to our feet. Several falangist officials are coming to inspect us. Their visit is brief. Just a summary snooping. Or gloating.

Later, as I walk the treadmill, alone with my thoughts, I meet the Nalda group, now reduced from eleven to four. The last victim was

Juanón. I try to avoid the Nalda survivors. They remind me of the death of uncle Matías, and now of the death of massive, optimist Juanón. Just a few days ago, noticing my reticence to eat the abominable stew, he nodded to me with a formidable arm.

"You have to eat, man!" he said, beaming enthusiastically. "If not you won't have strength to pick up your gun when the time comes."

PRISON STORIES

There are several rows of orchestra seats pushed against a wall of the court. Heretofore they have been forbidden to us, but now that a new increase of prisoners again is crowding the Avenida jail, the ruling is relaxed. Fermín of Nájera and I often sit there. He tells me amusing stories of his days in Madrid as a young buck, one of them about his short-lived romance with an aging, eccentric marquesa. At first, dazzled by the lady's title and the luxury that surrounded her, Fermín didn't find her so old. Neither did he realize he had fallen into the arms of the type of female he calls "a hot cunt." He tells me about the tricks and excuses he resorted to in an effort to break up with her. He even tried to pass her on to a student friend, a kind of modern Cyrano whose disproportionately large nose was the cause of the marquesa's rejection. "Finally, I got so tired of that fucking old woman I left Madrid in a hurry without a clue to my trail," he says.

Another one of his favorite tales is about ancient coins and illustrious bones buried in a little plot of farmland he owns in Nájera. Some priest friend had told him that those plains were the site of a battle between the pretender of the throne of Castile, Enrique de Trastamara, and his bastard brother king Don Pedro the Cruel. And that information was enough for Fermín to hold on to his dusty findings and resist tempting offers for them.

This morning I see him sitting there, this time leaning forward on the next row of seats, his head buried in his hands. At first I think he may be taking a snooze, but a certain throb to his shoulders tells me different. I come closer and give him a slight nod, and when he raises his face I see tears in his eyes. He hands me a snapshot he's been holding, the picture of a pretty, young girl. "My daughter. Today is her sixteenth birthday, a great day for us at home in other times. Now, something tells me I'll never see her again."

I try to say some words of comfort and encouragement. "Come on, Fermín. Things are not that bad. We can't lose hope now."

"Do you really think there is hope for us in this place?"

Trying to distract him from his misery I drag him to the treadmill. We find several men leaning over a pallet where a prisoner lies between two ragged blankets, a thick black beard sticking out. The color of his cheeks and his glazed eyes indicate a high fever.

"It's high, all right," says Blanco, the volunteer male nurse, as he reads the thermometer. "If he's no better by tomorrow I'll ask the prison doctor to transfer him to the hospital. There's nothing I can give him here. Not even an aspirin."

Magistrate Moreda reaches into his pocket, produces a little bottle and hands two pills from it to the nurse-orderly. "Here, give him these." As someone runs for the water cup, Moreda whispers to me, "I wonder how much violence these unfortunates will vent on the nation when they return to normal life, if we ever get out of this alive."

That particular unfortunate never got a chance to avenge the injustices done to him. His transfer to the hospital was his last trip, as we were told in a few days.

I am losing my friends. Pepe Mato was transferred to the provincial jail, where his brother Alfonso is being held. Don José, the prison official was taken to the Civil Government one afternoon. Two days later we learned he was executed. And then Ruiz the postal employee, and Magistrate Moreda, were sent to the dreaded fort of San Cristóbal in Pamplona to be executed.

One of the new inmates, a bricklayer called Josechu, tells us about the truck used for the "sacas." The falangist authorities rent it from a sausage factory and it is lined with zinc. Josechu has seen them wash the blood stains only last night, while the truck was parked in Salmerón Street, one of the city's thoroughfares. We agree that, if true, the macabre public spectacle can only be part of a plan to instill further terror in the people.

Lice become widespread and join the rest of the fauna plaguing the jail, probably brought in by some of the men who have been hunted down by the patrols in the mountains. Rats have increased considerably, thriving on the leftover cold stew. The worst is the invasion of ticks and bedbugs that take residence in the mouldy straw filling our pallets. Our sense of smell is accustomed to the fetid odors of the place, but not so our visitors'. From my wife and outside friends I learn that the offensive stench reaches the streets surrounding the Avenida building. In the middle of the summer days a heavy vapor clings to the walls of the old ball court, producing a mirage as in the desert. The foul air is overwhelming and brings protests from men and guards alike. A sergeant allows a back door to remain open for a couple of hours at sundown, but a severe directive comes to put a stop to this.

There is scant possibility for the sick among us to be transferred to the provincial hospital. Every day the number of wounded from the war front increases, especially those from the Basque front, the nearest to us. Beds and medics become totally engaged in caring for them. In a few days only those near death are allowed to leave the Avenida jail for the provincial hospital.

We get several prisoners from Low Rioja and one of them is assigned to sleep next to me, José Luís, a very thin young chap. During his first days here he's extremely nervous and concerned and seems to suffer greater fear for his life than the rest of us. Suddenly his tense expression disappears and he is all jokes and laughter. I ask him the reason for his sudden change of mood and he looks cautiously around and signals me to follow him under the tier of boxes. He takes out his wallet and extracts a crumpled letter. "You're one of the best here," he says winking an eye, "so I can confide in you. I can tell you I've been terrified since they caught me among the caneshoots near the Ebro, as I told you and the others. But before they took me away from Calahorra I was able to entrust a cousin who is a Carlist Requeté with a letter for my aunt. She is mother abbess of a convent and is on fine terms with the bishop. I told her of my arrest and transfer to Logroño. Well, my cousin is now in Logroño, too. Came to volunteer to join one of the brigades marching to the front. He made a round of jails until he found me. He came to visit me and brought me some cigars—terrible, by the way—and this letter from my aunt. Here, read it."

Unable to see well in that poor light, I give him back his letter, which he reads almost by heart, looking more at me than at its contents. The mother abbess was informing him of her visit to the bishop. The prelate promised to help, but he also advised her to be calm and patient. After all, nothing would happen to her nephew. The glorious Movement was not vindictive, much less in the case of a stray youth. The jailing would serve as a lesson and the just punishment of God for having joined the Socialist Party. After an affectionate farewell, the lady advised her nephew to take good care of the blessed medal of the Virgin she was sending therewith.

Pointing to his inseparable companion, a reedy youth reputed to be an expert marksman, José Luís adds, "With just a dozen like him we could have taken care of all the falangist and Requetés of Calahorra. But we had no rifles. . . ."

I ask him about César Andrés, the mayor of Calahorra, an old friend of mine. He assures me Andrés is safe. After hiding for several days, peasants helped him follow the course of the Cidacos river. He reached the province of Soria at the town of Enciso and finally, after crossing the province, joined the Republican lines at Sigüenza. José Luís had been told by his visitors that the mayor spoke on the radio the day after he reached Madrid. He announced the formation of a brigade composed of riojanos, those living in Madrid and the few who have escaped from the Rioja section. In an effort to broadcast news of their safety to their families, the mayor named those who had reached the Republican lines.

Within a week—whether through negligence or for lack of influence on the part of the bishop to whom his aunt appealed—José Luís is taken one night with his medal and his marksman of a friend, and led to the execution wall.

We follow the alternating turn of events of the fighting in Navarra and Guipúzcoa in the newspapers that wrap our gift parcels. General Mola, chief of the insurgent forces in the north, considers that reaching the coast of the Cantabric is vital to the operations entrusted to his command in that sector. Attacks have been intensified along the road from Oyarzun to Irún. The capture of the frontier city of Irún would further separate France from the loyalist provinces of the north, and also open the way to a new supply port. Up to now, the rebel fascists in the north have been supplied by their German and Italian allies through the port of Vigo, with considerable disadvantages of distance and transport difficulties. Some years ago I worked on the land survey of the province of Navarra, under a contract granted by the provincial government to the company I was with at the time. With my instruments and equipment I had walked much of the area that is now a field of war. Knowing the topography of the region helps me follow—or imagine—the attacks and clashes of the fascist advance over those rivers, hills, pueblos.

In an assault on a hill near Oyarzun my relative, Captain Jalón, dies fighting on the rebel side. The news brings to my mind the last time we met, at the entrance to the iron bridge over the Ebro, when I found him dressed in full military regalia, wearing the large red Carlist beret. I am told that he tried, indirectly, to help me get out of jail.

The Germans have sent a considerable number of planes to the nearby Recajo airfield. At times they fly quite low over the city and buzz the rooftops. Accustomed to the small slow crates which in normal times fly overhead in practice flights, the people of Logroño are impressed by the speed of the foreign machines. Soon they begin praising Nazi prowess to the high heavens. We hear that, as a German squadron was passing over the city, a group of fascists boasted about the military strength of their new foreign friends. Someone standing nearby commented, "Madrid has planes like those by the hundreds." A voice among the falangists replied angrily, "Listen you, Madrid has nothing. Nothing at all, you hear? People like you who try to demoralize the glorious Movement should be in jail. And that's exactly where I'm going to take you right now." And that's exactly what he did to the bystander.

Another curious arrival at the Avenida is Bergasita, a relative, no less, of the well-known industrialist of Logroño who owns the movie house and jai-alai building now converted to our qualified jail. He tells us of his arrest. In the months preceding the fascist uprising it was evident that the reactionary forces were bent on creating tension and terror, just as evident as was the government's lack of energy to curb them. The attempts against the lives of Largo Caballero and Jiménez Asúa, together with the assassination of an officer of the Assault Guards, were the culmination of a series of tragic incidents.

Leftist extremists responded with equal violence. Among the victims of the retribution from this side was Calvo Sotelo, former minister in the Primo de Rivera dictatorship and the principal figure in the events leading to the rebel military uprising of July 18th. When news of the assassination of Calvo Sotelo reached Logroño, several young men were discussing the issue at a well-known bar in town. Passions rose to such a point that Bergasita, who was among them, decided to avert a fight and proposed, "Forget it. Let's have our drinks in peace. This round of beers is on me." A falangist employee of the place accused Bergasita of *celebrating* Calvo Sotelo's death by inviting everyone at the bar to *expensive wine.*

"As you can see, those few beers cost me plenty," he says now as he talks of his arrest. Bergasita has been saved from the execution patrols by his influential wealthy relative, who is well-liked and respected by all in town.

While receiving one of the brief and rare visits granted me, I observe from the visitors' hall a strange induction of a new prisoner, a peasant. He is asked the customary entry questions by the sergeant at the desk. Name, town, origin, and . . . political affiliation. Without flinching, the man answers, "Carlist."

"You bastard," the sergeant says furiously, "go and make jokes with the whore of your mother. This is no place for them," and turning to the guards, he orders them, "Throw this son of a bitch in the coop before I kick him in myself."

It takes the peasant a week to make contact with relatives in his home town and prove his political identity, which couldn't be closer to the glorious Movement. It is true, he is a Carlist! The error is corrected and the man goes free before his name comes up in one of the execution lists. That's how some carelessly and capriciously arrests are being made every day.

Other talkative groups come to replace the never-to-be-forgotten one headed by the deceased magistrate Moreda and Ruiz, the postal official. I begin joining one usually attended by Poli the lawyer, Emilio the student, and the mayor of the town of Briones. Guillermo, a young labor leader who works as a mechanic in the Cénzanó workshops, joins us too. He follows me everywhere, always respecting my long silences but asking me all kinds of questions when he senses that my mood has changed. Soccer is his favorite subject, and he listens quietly as I talk about players, teams, famous games, and other aspects of a sport in which I have been somewhat prominent. Guillermo paints: horses, flowers, anything that comes to his mind, all with a certain charm, despite the meager tools and soiled paper he's able to find. (Months later, when I return for a second period of incarceration at the Avenida jail, Guillermo is not there. One of the veterans in the prison tells me he has been transferred to the Alfaro jail and another assures me he was executed around the end of November, both leaving me in the dark about the true fate of my artist and soccer fan friend.)

After three weeks in this sewer of a jail I feel as if I had been here ten years. I've lost my appetite. My face is white and pasty. The smoke and the fumes of disinfectant keep my throat raw and parched. My health, not good at the time of my arrest, has become worse. I begin to feel the familiar back pain.

We learn that many of the guards are civilians dressed in a variety of uniforms, volunteers enlisted in the three main parties of the rebel forces: Falange, Carlist, and Monarchist. Soon members of these fascist militias take to marching and singing toward the jail in order to stand at the entrance and hurl insults at the prisoners. At the slightest favorable news—favorable to them—from some war front, we are paid one of their hostile visits in which imprecations are mixed with inharmonious singing of fascist anthems, all of it suggesting brawling and cheap wine. As they pass in front of the jail their voices and fists are raised toward the windows. From our pitiful first aid room I am able to see one of those parades. Beaming among them, dragging his saber, is one of the group of falangists who only a few weeks ago came to visit me in jail and offer their protection. The rowdy celebration is usually accompanied by much pealing of church bells. This in turn causes the prison population to sink into a dismayed silence, since we associate such joy with a possible Loyalist defeat on some war front.

Some time later I learn that when I had been at the Avenida less than a month my name was included once among the transfers to the dreaded San Cristóbal fort in Pamplona and twice in the list of nightly sacas. I was excluded from the transfer list at the last moment by Captain Alonso Martínez, and from the saca lists by Pernas, the town's new fascist mayor.

During the first months of the Civil War, the executions of thousands in the zones held by the rebels was a matter of chance and whim carried out amidst disorganization and confusion. Any man could be included or erased from a death list by people of influence in the new regime. Someone's presence—or absence due to illness, for instance—at a particular moment could decide whether a man was to live or die. The one responsible for my being included in the execution lists was one of the Herrero de Tejada brothers.

"If Escobal is alive it is not my fault," Josechu Herrero de Tejada was heard to say repeatedly at the meetings of the Círculo Logroñés, the town's club. I've never found an explanation for his feelings toward me. There was no unpleasantness between us. We were not special friends, but we often exchanged greetings when we met, which was often, in the street and at the club.

The Herrero de Tejada brothers, retired artillery captains, now were members of the secret tribunals known in Spanish jails as the White Cheka, established in every province held by the fascists. Accuser, judge, and jurors often were the same persons. There were no witnesses, and the only proof involved was anonymous accusations. At the end of the Civil War, as an award for the thousands of death sentences they signed, one of the Herrero de Tejada brothers was made governor of a province near Madrid, and another Director in Chief of Spanish prisons.

With 900 users, the latrine installations often get clogged and break down. One afternoon, as I am sitting on a mound of bundles, half asleep, watching the ragged curtain of the entrance through a haze of dust and smoke, several municipal laborers come in to repair the latrines. Their faces are familiar to me because the plumbing services are part of the city's water supply department which had been under my charge. Since any incident, however small, arouses the men's curiosity, a triple line forms around the workers as they begin to repair a pipe. I try to stay in the background, thinking it could embarrass the laborers to find their former chief observing them under these far from normal circumstances. Although they are experienced plumbers, in a few minutes one of them drops his tools and exclaims, "What a stench! It's impossible to work in this place."

When at last the job is finished I stand on a suitcase and greet them as they walk past me on the way out. "What would you boys say if you had to live with this stench twenty four hours a day?" I ask.

"You are right, Don Pedro," says the one who dropped his tools. "In comparison to what you are going through we have no reason to complain. . . ." They gather around me and begin asking me questions, but a guard approaches and gives them a look that sends them scurrying out the old red curtain.

The hero of our sanitation force is Macario, the dedicated peasant who labors with his two assistants in that inferno of the latrines. He inspires kindness and consideration in everyone. Today Poli and I meet him in the courtyard, and the two of them talk about mutual friends in Macario's home town. Poli asks him about his arrest.

"A bastard, that's all you can call him. A bastard friend of mine landed me here," answers Macario as he darts quick looks everywhere with his vivid eyes. "But he's getting his, too. I'm not a churchgoer, you understand, but I am very devoted to Saint Macario, and he grants me everything I pray for."

"What has a saint got to do with all this?" Poli asks laughing.

"Plenty. Ever since they brought me in here I've been praying to him at night. Now I hear the bastard who accused me is very sick. If I know Saint Macario, he's going to die soon."

"But that's absurd! To pray to a saint for the death of someone."

"What he did to me is more absurd. Imagine, accusing me! Me, who saved his daughter's life!" And in his picturesque language, with much meandering detail, Macario describes the countryside of his home town, surrounded by orchards linked by a dusty road. Once, at the end of a day, on his way home with his hoe on his shoulder, he met up with two carts full of gypsies followed by a flock of ragged children. Sitting between two fierce characters in the last cart was his friend's daughter.

"They had bewitched her, those gypsies. I stopped the carts and raised my hoe and told them off. Finally, afraid of my shouts and threats, they let me have the girl. I ran with her and took her to her father."

One of the men who has gathered to listen to the curious tale, stops Macario. "Idiot. It's a known fact by now that gypsies steal chickens, not children."

"That's right," Poli says. "Gypsies have enough children of their own to worry about."

"And what do they do when they get sick?" Macario insists. "Where do you think they get the fat for their cures? They're not going to cut up their own kids! Listen, plenty of children have disappeared from my home town, taken away by the gypsies."

A petty officer calls him back to his job and stops Macario from telling us more about this old peasant belief—that gypsies steal children to get body fat for medicinal purposes.

All in all, Macario deserved the Golden Scarab of ancient Egypt for his efforts to keep us, if not immortal, at least reasonably alive. On his birthday, he received the visit of a lady, friend or relative, who brought him a double gift: an impossibly colored scarf and news of his impending freedom. Beaming with joy Macario made the rounds of the entire prison, modeling the scarf and announcing the good news which, by the way, took some time in becoming a reality.

It is well into the month of August 1936 and the maddening heat has not let up. I long to lie under the green poplars by the river, where on the hottest day there is always a breeze singing through the branches. Nostalgia for the outside world and particularly for nature becomes an obsession in these leaden hours.

After briefly allowing us to buy soft drinks, their sale is again forbidden. Once again we must quench our thirst with the warm cloudy drinking water which not only leaves a greater craving for something clean and cool but also upsets our stomachs. The economy measures recently taken up by the prison administration rule out the purchasing of new brooms. The old ones become worn and thin until, like in a Chaplin film, we see the orderlies busily sweeping away with mere sticks.

All these details of our small hours suddenly are blurred from memory by an extraordinary "saca" that calls for double the customary number of victims. A lash of terror shakes the prison and no one sleeps that night. Fear and speculations invade our thoughts and conversations. In the morning, every man asks the question: Will the same happen tonight?

After visiting hours, Poli rushes to us with news that lifts our wilted spirits. According to his visitor the capture of Saragossa by Republican troops is a question of a few hours. The Aragonese front has been broken in two places and the fascists have had to send two troop trains from Logroño to stop the Republican advance. True or false, any news sends us into frenzied bouts of discussions and conjectures.

Avoiding the maze of clothes that hang from hooks and nails, I walk along the wall to a corner of the court where several men have spread their blankets and sit leaning against the wall as they smoke and talk. Among them I find Emilio the student; Santiago, a cavalry noncom who still wears his insignialess military jacket; a school teacher; a few socialist workers. . . . "If they take Saragossa the fascist demoralization will be general and in a matter of two or three days our people will be here," the teacher is saying.

Santiago, the cavalryman answers, "We've heard that before. In fact, this is the third time we've had that news, and as you can see, it hasn't happened yet."

"Sooner or later it's bound to be true," says one of the socialist workers. "Don't be such a pessimist."

"I'm not, I just don't want to start hoping until I see something that confirms the news!"

"A hell of a lot you're going to see from this hole," says Emilio, the student.

"We can't doubt the ultimate failure of the fascist Movement," the teacher tells him. "Why shouldn't Saragossa fall? Without money they can't buy armaments, and without armaments they can't win the war."

"Don't be a fool," says the cavalryman. "I am a Republican soldier, that's why I'm locked up here. And I know things are not so simple. In June, for instance, the Republican government concentrated its best planes in Madrid with the excuse that they needed checking and adjusting after a certain number of flight hours. Actually, the reason for that measure was the rumor of a military insurrection. So, on July eighteenth the fascists had only six old planes at the Recajo airfield, right here. Now? There are dozens of first class planes at Recajo! So many that there are not enough hangars for them. Why, only yesterday we heard about the German pilots being given a banquet at the offices of the military governor. And it's no secret that new Italian and Portuguese planes have arrived for the fascists. They may not have much money, but they certainly have plenty of armaments, and good ones. Two days, you say, and our people will be here? Don't make me laugh. If the government forces ever reach Logroño they'll have to award us posthumous honors, because we'll be stretched out under ground, with a cypress planted on our belly."

Silence falls on the group after this funereal allusion, until we hear the approaching insults, songs, and laughter that accompany the marching of the fascists to our jail.

"Here come those goddam 'maricones,' " says the old man. Poli, Salvado, and the pastor join our group. We all strain for the pealing of church bells, supposing, as always that the fascists are celebrating the seizure of some new town. But soon the orderlies come around and pass on the real reason for the rejoicing. A Republican plane was shot down on the Jaca front and its charred remains are being paraded through several towns. The noisy procession has now reached Logroño and does us the honor of passing in front of the jail to display the glorious trophy.

"Those idiots and their demonstrations," says Salvado the veterinarian. "It's all the same to them whether they march with a plaster image of a saint or with a maze of twisted iron. I'd like to see them sing and shout when worse comes, like mass death and starvation. Mark my words, there's much more ahead to mourn in this war."

Old Joaquín and the school teacher agree that in all this boasting is a sign of dwindling morale in the fascist rearguard, otherwise there wouldn't be such elation at the capture of just one enemy plane. "If they were doing as well as they claim they wouldn't bother with this ridiculous display," they say.

Later on my pallet I remember the incident of the captured plane, and I ask myself, "What am I doing here?" I brought about my own misfortune by returning to Logroño. I should have stayed in Madrid to fight for a cause for which I feel deeply, with all my heart and soul. But it's too late for self-recriminations. Time doesn't turn back. I remain still, thinking about it with eyes closed—the best guarantee of isolation, since it is an unwritten prison law to respect a fellow inmate's merciful sleep.

Wholly preoccupied by memory and fear, distracted by the frequent talks and political discussions with my friends, I've given little thought up to now to one of the most serious problems that inevitably plagues a human hive of mature males: sexual repression. In this crowded, improvised compound, the depressing and congested conditions preclude any kind of physical release. The minute space allotted us makes it impossible for a man to take a step without colliding with another, and the shortage of sanitary installations, the poor sunlight and ventilation, accentuate the nervous tension produced by insecurity and terror, leaving the body weak and limp as a soiled rag. In this state of filth and immobility some prisoners lose every vestige of decorum, a few even making unsightly spectacles of themselves. I witness a brazen case from my blanket one afternoon.

A while ago I looked for an empty space in the midst of the daytime confusion and found enough to stretch my blanket and sink into sleep. Now I am awake. It's near dusk and the holes in the high transoms are beginning to turn a dark grey. As I yawn and stretch I notice some suspicious moves on the pallet next to mine. When I start to stand up I see a funny little dark man with the face of a monkey, who, penis in hand, is concluding his solitary amusement practically on my blanket. The ugly sight so revolts me I can't control my indignation. "Hey, you. . . ." I hiss, shaking him hard. "Can't you find a better place for such things?"

With incredible cynicism he informs me that the prison director is studying a plan to bring women for us at night, and meanwhile prisoners are authorized to gratify themselves. That only makes me angrier. My indignant words and gestures attract attention and a few men come over. Seeing the evidence at the foot of my blanket, and knowing the habits of the monkey-faced man, they understand immediately. Demetrio, an electrician, exclaims furiously, "You pig! Go to the latrines when you feel like doing such filthy things."

"That's exactly where we're going to dunk your head next time you exhibit yourself," says another one. "In the toilet!"

"Why, this is the third time this son of a bitch has done it in front of everyone!" Demetrio adds.

"I don't give a damn," says the little man defiantly. "I do what I please with my body." And as the others keep up their threats and imprecations, he rolls up his blanket and walks away whistling the Marseillaise.

Between transfers and "sacas" and new arrivals, the prison population is kept stable, but of the original 900 men only some 90 veterans are still around. The old guard, I call them, those with whom every incident can safely be discussed.

Because of a supposed conspiracy to set the jail afire and escape with the help of outsiders, we are punished by being held incommunicado for three days, at the end of which I receive an unexpected visitor: a cousin whose husband, although not active in politics, always keeps in close touch with the town's reactionaries whose ideas and opinions he definitely shares.

Visitors at the Avenida are received in a large room at the entrance where there are always guards and spies keeping a close eye. When I reach the room I am surprised to see my cousin. After all, it's more than a month since I was arrested and I haven't seen or heard from her till now. Her sorrowful expression tells me something must be wrong. To disperse any doubts I may have, she proceeds to make a terrible scene of tears and hysterics. Between sobs and hugs she manages to hang on my neck an outsize scapular with the image of some saint. Freshly blessed, she assures me, only this morning, by a priest who is a family friend. It seems that through her husband's fascist contacts she's learned that my situation is hopeless, and since according to her all good souls go to heaven and all bad ones to hell, she finds it necessary to come to make sure I have a passport for the right place before it is too late.

I am so depressed by her visit and behavior—which can only mean it is our final meeting—that the thought of my impending execution takes precedence over everything else. Absently I return to my jailmates with the enormous scapular hanging on my neck. My friends receive me with jokes and laughter and ask if it was the bishop who came to see me. I am left with the problem of how to get rid of the blessed scapular. Fearing dangerous interpretations of sacrilege or disrespect, and intending neither, I wrap it carefully in a piece of paper and drop it in a refuse can on my way to the latrines.

Naturally, during the next nights my nerves are on the verge of shattering every time they read the execution lists. Then, after one of the frequent summer storms of the region, there are several small floods in the compound and my pallet gets drenched. Dampness, nervous tension, and lack of food put me in the worst possible condition to withstand a cold. One morning, after taking my pulse and temperature, the volunteer nurse gives me a strong dose of epsom salts.

"You've got a high fever, but this medicine is strong enough to cure a horse. You'll be rid of your temperature before morning."

By nine thirty that night, when the sea of beds is spread over the courtyard, I am still burning with fever. I lie on my pallet in its new position, at right angles to a corridor between a line of beds. Not far across there is a heap of theatre chairs which have been torn from the floor and piled up to make a wall between guards and prisoners. Before I get under the blanket I knot a handkerchief at the corners and put it on as a cap, a precaution against the increasing spread of a scalp epidemic. But I don't get a chance to rest this night. This is to be a very special night.

THE SINISTER NIGHT

Each of the past three nights I've turned my wallet, watch, and small property over to Poli, who promptly returns it all to me next morning, saying, "See? Back to you, not to your wife as you thought." But tonight, the premonition that I'm going to be called for the saca list obsesses me.

I try to keep calm. Why would this be the night, necessarily? My thoughts, incoherent at best because of the high fever, skip at random over a hundred scenes. I hear the sound of distant trumpets. I hear them, it can't be my imagination. The rifle butts slipping from the hands of dozing sentries keep marking time irregularly. Suddenly I feel a breath near me, then a certain flutter passing by, and my heart takes on a strange new rhythm. I can't stand it any more. I open my eyes. The Andalusian petty officer is facing me, signaling me to get up as he calls my name.

Every man has his limit of fear beyond which a plateau of serene resignation awaits him. As I reach mine I keep my mind fixed on one thought: to die with dignity. The best attitude will be a serene one, without signs of rebellion but firmly rooted in the validity of my convictions. I put on shoes and jacket and stand in the corridor. Hundreds of eyes follow my movements, I feel them boring through my face.

"You are going to the Civil Government," says the petty officer. I begin to walk and climb the ramparts of the theatre chairs separating us from the soldiers. Two security guards await me on the other side of the ragged red curtain. One of them with handcuffs ready. Automatically I stretch my hands and receive the cold clamp of the bracelets. I can't see the face of this guard under his visor cap, but the other one has several days' growth of beard darkening his. "Let's go!" he says. "Walk ahead and don't try to escape. We have orders to shoot at the first strange move."

Under the indifferent look of the soldiers at the gate I walk out of jail. It is a clear night and the fresh air fills my lungs and revives me. Despite my fever and illness I walk firmly. I know because I can hear my own steps fall rhythmically on the sidewalk. There are voices and laughter coming from the windows of the Círculo Logroñés, the social club. The route is the same one I walked thirty eight days ago in the opposite direction.

Only one thought is in my mind now: the White Cheka. How does it function? Is a defense at all possible? Its members are known to me as they are to most of my friends in jail: Captains Benlló, Conde, Purón, Martínez Alonso, Bolumburu, and Herrero de Tejada representing the military and falangist mayor Pernas and the chief of police sitting in for the civilian side. As I walk under the ring of trees edging the town's Glorieta park, the bearded guard steps ahead toward a parked car and talks to the driver while I and the other guard wait behind. When the bearded guard walks back to us past the lamppost I see the buttons on his half-open jacket shining like evil stars.

At the entrance of the Civil Government building, Carlist Requetés and falangist militias chat with the idle chauffeurs awaiting orders. A guard sits on a stool near the door and cleans his rifle by the light of a lantern. He gives me a sly smile, and I can't help but remember his solicitous greetings of four months ago, when I visited this building several times in the company of the now murdered mayor of Logroño, Basilio Gurrea. There is a great bustle inside. Men in uniform are everywhere, coming and going with folders and briefcases in and out of every door. I am led through two corridors, across a vestibule, and pushed into a large room I know is used as an office in normal times. Two secret police agents sit at a desk to the left, facing a large inkwell and a larger ashtray brimming with cigarette butts. To the right there are twenty men lined up against a wall, frozen on the spot. I suppose they await their last hour, for their marble-like faces take on an added sadness when I am unshackled and ordered to join them. Totally oblivious to our plight and presence, some fierce-looking blueshirts are carrying on a lively conversation in a corner of the room. A door in the back has been left ajar, and through it I see a roofed patio where a group of ragged prisoners sleep piled up on the floor. Must be peasants caught in recent razzias through the villages, those who like my uncle Matías go from provincial arrest to the cemetery without the intermediate stop at jail.

Several times guards come and take prisoners from our file against the wall, the police calling the victims' names firmly, looking right at their faces. After a while, all activity ceases and the falangists in the corner simmer down and begin talking normally. They are discussing the Somosierra front to which they apparently will march at dawn to relieve others, commanded by their platoon leader, a fat one whose childlike innocent face contrasts strongly with the ferocious countenances of the others.

A young blueshirt, seeming to bend under the weight of heavy shoulders, bursts in and slaps an automatic on the table. "What pretty pictures I am taking tonight with my camera," he exclaims, pointing to the weapon. "We're both ready for more, as you can see!"

Apparently such jokes are common in this place, for the police at the desk don't even bother to acknowledge this one. Only some of the falangists in the corner snicker slightly.

Knowing as we all do that the execution patrols often ransack the dead after performing their duty, I've again given my wristwatch to Poli and left my wallet and a note in my suitcase whose key I've kept in my pocket. Poli will see that everything gets to my wife eventually. The lack of a watch and my high fever make me lose track of time. Perhaps some thirty minutes pass as they sweep off half of my companions from the line against the wall. I watch how tightly they bind their wrists and thumbs behind their backs. The expressions on the faces of those condemned men remind me of Madrid's slaughterhouse. I had a friend who was an auto mechanic, chief of the crew in charge of repairing the meat delivery trucks in the capital. Whenever my car needed attention I brought it over to him. And once, to pass the time while he did minor adjustments, I accepted his invitation to visit the slaughterhouse, unfortunately, just at the time the slaughtering was taking place. I never forgot the steers' eyes as the attendants hacked away their front hoofs in preparation for the final blow. The eyes of these men facing me now as their hands are bound behind their backs have the same desperate gleam of ultimate wonder.

The night seems endless. A guard is authorized to escort me to the toilet. I know the man. When we get to the men's room he doesn't allow me to close the door, but looking cautiously around, he whispers to me, "Some important new orders from Burgos have just stopped everything. Maybe you'll be lucky tonight."

When we return from the bathroom I meet a procession of ghosts who march resignedly to their end. They are the last of the peasants who slept in the covered patio, those whose fate apparently was decided before the important new orders from Burgos came to "stop everything." Among them, two little old men resist timidly, bleating softly like lambs. I can't pay much attention to them. I'm being shoved back into the large room and I am worried about my own fate.

The fascist militias have disappeared from the corner. There are seven men still waiting on the line against the wall. The police drowse on the table. After a long silence there is action again. I witness two betrayals from the prisoners in our dwindling line. The first one steps over to the desk and tells one of the police agents, "Listen, I can volunteer important information and also prove my innocence. I must talk with someone in the courtroom. It's very important."

The agent gives him a disdainful look and signals to his companion, who writes a few words on a sheet of paper and gets up slowly to pass the note on to an orderly. Two security guards come in a moment and take away the man who wants to talk, together with all the others in the line but me and one other. Now the police chief comes in and sits between the two agents at the desk. They mumble something among themselves and then call my companion. The chief asks him about events immediately prior to the outbreak of the Movement in his town. Before the man can answer, I am ordered to wait just outside the room, between two guards. At first I cannot hear what they say inside, but as the conversation progresses, they talk louder and louder until the guards and I can hear it clearly.

"Yes, your brother, your brother. . . . With his subversive ideas! He's been a menace to the peaceful people of your town. We know all about his organizing strikes and distributing firearms. Why, in 1934 he was arrested for keeping a cache of pistols! Your brother. . . . I don't need further details. We know he tried to cross over to the Reds and couldn't make it. He returned to your pueblo and has been hiding ever since. You'd better think it over before you answer. Your life depends on it."

"Sr. Comisario, I never approved of my brother's activities. I joined the Socialist Party only to keep peace at home. But I never distributed firearms or even attended meetings. I had nothing to do with the strikes my brother organized. Like the rest of the family I've always attended church. Why, not long ago I had a fist fight with my brother; everyone in town knows about it. And since then we've been estranged. After he failed to cross over to the Republicans he went into hiding at the hut of a shepherd called Eulogio. That's all I can tell you. That and the fact that other shepherds brought him milk and food. He was still in hiding when I was arrested; I haven't heard a thing about him since."

"That's old news. Eulogio and the other shepherds have been punished already. If that's all the information you can give us it's not substantial enough to save yourself."

"But that's all I know, and I'm ready to collaborate with you in every way. Perhaps if you let me go back to my village I could find out a lot more. I've changed; I'll gladly help now. . . ."

The betrayals continued with the mention of other names. One I heard repeatedly was that of José, apparently the town's pharmacist. To save his own skin the man is willing to help capture his brother and also implicate others in his town. I lose the rest of the conversation when the guards are ordered by someone to take me upstairs.

The room where the White Cheka meets is at the end of a long corridor. From that supreme court without appeal come capricious and arbitrary sentences passed between much drinking of beer and cognac. Now I can see the empty bottles outside the door. The guards first halt at a small room, handcuff me again, and give me a slight shove into a larger room.

Captain Conde is sitting at a table strewn with a disorder of papers and notebooks. For a few minutes he pays no attention to me or simply fakes being very busy. At last he raises his head and launches into a lengthy and hazy questioning of my political activities, my "firearms," and the convents "I have set afire . . ." each accusation followed by the suggestion that I give information about it so it can be entered as a favorable factor in my case. It is easy to refute the charges. The accusations have been made by people already assassinated: Gurrea, Ulecia, Rupérez, Erce the chief of the Urban Guards, others. . . .

"I am not immune to fear," I tell him. "But I cannot invent stories and accept accusations which are as stupid as they are impossible to confirm. This is the second time they have confronted me in this place with the same ultimatum. You've mentioned only dead informers. Why don't you give me a chance to face a live one and let me prove false these outlandish charges?"

He looks at me steadily for the first time. "Escobal, since the start of the uprising you've been heard making sarcastic and demoralizing remarks, knowing as you do the danger entailed in taking that attitude. You've refused to raise your hand and give the salute of the new Spain. And you can't deny you've always had leftist ideas and important friends in the Left."

"In the first place, since the outbreak of the rebellion I've been free only four days. I've hardly had time or inclination to make sarcastic remarks, especially in the light of the seriousness of the situation. I have said in private that I don't believe in the victory of your Movement. I have not raised my arm to give your salute because that gesture is unknown to me and I cannot make it unless I become a hypocrite. As for close friendships, I've had them everywhere, including some among those who now wear blue shirts, as you well know. I will never deny my personal opinions. I've always had an open mind, open to all kinds of ideas, and I refuse to believe that ideas can justify sending a man to his death."

"You are wrong. We don't execute men for their ideas, but for their deeds."

Just now an orderly walks in and hands Conde a note. He leaves the room. Another long wait . . . ? I try to keep calm and put my thoughts in order for the second part of the mock trial which may well await me in the next, the largest room. But everything is destined to be a surprise on this night. The guards at the door order me to follow them. I go down the stairs of the now almost deserted building, and when we reach the door, they push me toward a black car parked at the entrance.

There is a falangist militia sitting next to the driver and a guard in the back seat, all three of them smoking large cigars. Another guard, standing by the door of the car, touches his pistol to my chest, places me next to his companion, and closes the door.

The car starts down the Saragossa highway toward the Recajo airfield. Through the car window I see the last houses of town in the distance, under the first light of dawn. With them disappear my last hopes. The good black earth of the orchards will receive my last, prone embrace. After all, here I was born, here it is fitting that I die, too. And she, my anguished Teresa? Will she know where to find the place? I can almost see her mournful, black-clad figure, carrying flowers to her dead. But no, it can't be possible! This cannot be the end of life and love! How could God allow such injustice? Waves of hot and cold sweat seem to flush my being alternately.

My life runs through my mind in a wild race. Childhood . . . the first escapades down to the river . . . the Jesuit boarding school . . . student days in Madrid . . . dear ones . . . the ecstasy of first love. . . . Those and a hundred other brilliant images contest in my brain, like pictures vying for a place in the album of my life about to be closed forever.

I am only a burden which these fiends in uniform have to unload somewhere. The old stories of the Carlist wars are becoming a new reality in my land. How often the black beast of reaction has bathed these fields in blood!

The car proceeds slowly, lights out. With every puff, the driver's cigar throws an infernal point of light on the muzzle of the falangist's rifle next to him.

The will to live is replaced by a cold resignation which overtakes me completely when the car screeches to a violent halt. We are at the entrance of the bridge over the Iregua. My actions anticipate the orders of my executioners and I make a move to get out of the open car door. It is best to end the ordeal before desolation breaks me down.

Amidst the laughter and jokes of his companions, one of the guards shoves me back into the car. "Not tonight," he says laughing.

Up to now no one had said a word and all was incomprehensible to me. Later, when I review the details of this night, I arrive at the conclusion that it must have been a diabolical punishment, perhaps for not having revealed the secrets they thought I was keeping from them. Whatever it was, I remember having felt nothing but a total relaxation on the fast ride back, as if the wiry spring of my nerves had suddenly changed to supple wax.

Quickly, we reach the Civil Government building where another team of guards takes over and escorts me back to the Avenida prison. I am made to wait at the entrance until an orderly brings my pallet and suitcase. They free me of the handcuffs which I have forgotten to the point where they seemed a part of me. I heave the baggage on my back. The day is rising as I and my escort proceed slowly to cross the short distance between the Avenida and another qualified jail, the Industrial School. Without stopping for entry formalities, I am led through a courtyard to a room on the ground floor.

When I hear the key turn in the lock behind the heavy door, I collapse on my baggage.

℘ **Part II**

Solitary Confinement and
the Industrial School Prison

Let us imagine a group of men in chains, and all condemned to death, and every day some are strangled in sight of the others, those who remain read their fate in the fate of the condemned; they eye each other with agony and without hope, awaiting their turn. This is the image of man's fate.

Pascal

THE GEOGRAPHY
CLASSROOM

A feverish state of shock has left me faint and limp after last night.
I regain consciousness, only to feel my head heavy as lead. Weariness overtakes me and I fall into a deep sleep.

When I wake up the reddish sunlight reflected on a half-closed
window and the dish of cold chow on the floor tell me it must be
late afternoon. I have no watch, and I still have not learned to tell
time by the bells of the nearby church.

I look around. I am in a large room that must have been the
geography classroom of this school. The enormous only door com-
municates with one of the courts packed with prisoners on the
ground floor. The teacher's desk is still on the platform. The students' benches have been piled up against the side walls all the way

up to the ceiling. Between two windows crossed with iron bars and heavy wire, there are several pallets rolled up and tied with string. Among them I see a great number of suitcases, tags dangling from their handles. There are maps on the walls and two globes with sextants, mounted on varnished wooden stands. The floor is littered with the remnants of past meals, with cigarette butts, papers, dirt, and dust.

It's some twenty hours since I had anything to eat or drink, and although I am not very hungry, I tackle the piece of bread and the water jug left by the guard on the floor during my sleep, together with the inedible plate of chow. I can't digest the cement-like mass of ill-baked bread and water, and the violent effort of vomiting leaves me exhausted. It also disturbs my old back injury. Soon the pain becomes unbearable. Gnawing stings like those of a dentist's drill upon a sensitive nerve begin to pierce my back at short intervals.

When I can't stand the pain any longer I drag myself to the door and kick it with all the strength I can muster. An orderly opens and allows a doctor and his aide in. The expression on my visitors' faces tell me how terrible mine must be. I refuse to take the bromide they offer unless they first give me morphine to ease the pain. In a moment I get my first shot of morphine. There are medical supplies in this qualified jail. Two physicians drafted among the prisoners help the chief doctor, together with several mates who have volunteered to serve as aides.

Soon the effect of the drug takes over, and as pain subsides I fall into a state of semiconsciousness, dreaming with eyes open, as if enveloped in fog. I can move my arms and not feel their weight. My body seems to float in space. A multitude of old and recent memories passes through my mind as if none of it had any association with me. All seems simple and pleasant in this realm of awakened slumber. Nothing matters; I am not locked up. I could leave this place, but I don't want to. The hum reaching me from the courtyard sounds like the murmur of the distant sea one hears in a seashell. The maps on the walls invite me to travel. I fix my eyes on Asia, over the immense region of the great steppes and imaginary enormous moons. Siberia, the Aral Sea, the rivers. . . . The Ob and the Yenisei extend their thick black arteries toward the blue Arctic Ocean. Memories of lessons learned in childhood pour as an avalanche over my mind. Those rivers sleep most of the year in their snowy beds, but in the spring they break up their icy swathings and flow impetuously downstream, crunching and crushing gigantic icebergs and all that crosses their path, like the inexorable torrent of life and death. In the race, tall powerful spruces are demolished like caneshoots by the fragments of stones and boulders broken after the long winter freeze.

In the silence of the great solitary earth I hear the roar of the stream lashing the rocks. I can even see the foam bursting on them. Innumerable tree trunks float in the brilliant white whirlpools, their roots and branches wrested from the mountain slopes. How many men in the same way have been wrested from their homes! Imagination takes on tremendous power when the brain is stimulated by drugs. The foamy whirlpools blinding me change gradually to rosy tones, growing in intensity to a bright red. Some part of my subconscious has not been put asleep by the drug, and in my state of quasi-indifference I seek analogies with the bloody combats and abominable excesses that form the river of "the glorious Movement."

The door opens and Teresa appears. For a moment I think she too is part of the dream. How did she manage to get here? Vaguely, I notice signs of tears in her eyes. The visit is short, since it is unauthorized and has been possible only as a personal favor granted by a security guard. Her lips touch mine just before she leaves, and drugged as I am, I cannot feel the warm kiss of the beloved I haven't had in my arms for many weeks.

Save for very few times, during the next fifteen days that door opens only to let the revolting chow in and to let me out when I go to the latrines. I am living almost exclusively on water, cigarettes and morphine. Matches are forbidden to prisoners who are incommunicado, but a mate out in the courtyard manages to pass me a few under the door on a piece of cardboard. Later I am told how dearly he paid for that gesture.

In my state of detachment, I still do not hear the church bells. The hours pass but I have lost my sense of time. Near dusk the door opens again and a guard enters like a silent shadow and leaves the food plate, water jug, and some cigarettes on a bench. The thought of how much Teresa must have had to pay or plead to get those cigarettes into my cell spoils the joy of receiving them.

My physical exhaustion is so great that after the effect of the morphine, despite the persistent pain in my back, I fall into a restless sleep heavy with nightmares. The stifling air of the cell becomes populated with monsters, their large heads with protruding eyes climbing all over walls and ceiling. Among them I see the faces of people I have long forgotten. The enclosure swells and with it the grotesque apparitions begin to shrink and finally fall upon me on my pallet. I must be going mad. Facing the mysterious threshold of lunacy I try with all my strength to cling to one idea: Perhaps madness is not as horrible as it seems to the sane.

I am left trembling on my pallet after those attacks of frenzy. Exhausted by the fever, I see the room turn like a Cyclopean wheel around my head. My thoughts magnetically return to the night of my "saca": Faces, words, and events have remained engraved on my mind. The driver puffing at his cigar, the stop at the bridge over the Iregua where I almost died. A little further on, the place where I had learned to swim as a child, and the four houses that make up the village of Varea that—according to the historians of the café Los Leones—was the river port where the fat ships of the Caesars loaded wheat for Rome.

The light of day slips through the top frame of the window. I see the mound of suitcases and read the names of their owners on the tags, some of them friends who have been executed. I suppose the others came to the same end. My fate seems to be written here. On one of the tags I find the name of Erce. The suitcase is unlocked, and as I put my hand to it I wonder if I have the right to rummage through the belongings of a dear friend. But the thought that I may find something useful spurs me to open it. I find a change of clean underclothes, a dry lemon, shaving things, and a letter: "Dear M, although I will make every effort to get this letter to you, I am not sure it will reach you. My situation is hopeless, but I am proud to give my life for a just cause. When I went into hiding I thought my nephew would help me for a few weeks until the government took command of events. But his help stopped in five days. I could have managed to survive, if only by eating rats which abounded in my hiding place. But it was thirst that beat me. I even drank from the sewer, knowing I was only exchanging bullets for typhus. My health became so poor I could hardly stand on my feet when I gave myself up. I know you will take care of our children, give them my last kiss. This is the hour of truth. In spite of everything I've loved you and my last thoughts are for you. Yours. . . ."

Erce was the chief of the Urban Guards, a confirmed Republican who had sown much hate among the reactionaries of the town. We became friends during my permanent stay in Logroño. He was a strong, vivacious man, always in good humor. He had one great weakness: women, so his marriage had not always been a happy one. When Logroño fell he took refuge in the basements of the houses near the river, in the old section of town. Seen from the opposite shore, that terrace of houses on the right bank of the Ebro give to the landscape a picturesque, postcard look. But through its maze of basements and dungeons the sewers flow down to the river estuary. That dark labyrinth known only to a few inhabitants of Logroño is an ideal place to hide. With a minimum of outside help someone could hold out there for weeks, perhaps months. Erce attempted it, but help failed him when his nephew was arrested and there was no one to bring him food and water. In my recent interrogation at the Civil Government, Erce was named by Captain Conde as one of my accusers. I did not believe it then. It seemed too vague and improbable. Now, after reading this letter, I am convinced that a man like him, even broken and demoralized by his ordeal, could not have committed such an outrage. I put the letter in my pocket, hoping to forward it to his wife somehow. Sometime later I was able to pass it on to the outside.

The bells of the church of La Redonda play a musical background in the long silent nights. I have always associated those peals with death. I remember one of the first songs I learned as a child: "Bells which sound the alarm of fire, bells which toll for those who expire. . . ." Perhaps those bells, in part, cause my somber thoughts to become even darker with the sound of their funereal peals.

It must be just past midnight when I hear heavy steps approaching. The key turns in the great lock, the door opens, and the warden walks in with a stranger and two guards. In the dim flashlight their faces seem ominous. At this time of night the visit of this portentous delegation can only mean one thing: My time has come. Automatically I stand up from the pallet and reach for my jacket. It's only a ten-minute ride to the execution wall behind the cemetery.

I can keep myself together that long, especially after the training I had two nights ago; still, as I tell myself that, the same gun pellets seem to distend my dry throat when I try to swallow. I make a move to start out the door.

"Who told you to get up?" shouts the warden.

"I thought. . . ."

"Don't think yet," the stranger in the group tells me, a sly smile revealing his black teeth. "Everything will come in time."

They examine the locks and windows, they check with the flashlight under the benches and among the suitcases, and they leave.

What kind of an inspection was that? They know there is a team of guards just outside the windows, which alone precludes any thoughts of escape. . . . Maybe it wasn't an inspection at all. Maybe it was just another touch of sadism to remind me of my impending doom. "Everything will come in time," they said. . . . For the first time in my life I contemplate the idea of committing suicide.

The bell of La Redonda just gave a lonely peal. It's one o'clock. A multitude of ticks travel from the rancid straw filling my pallet up my limbs. The most daring ones attempt to reach my face, but the smoke of my cigarette discourages them. In this state of desolation and hopelessness only the mind seems to remain fully alive. The body feels like a trunk of uncut cork, alive but numb. The wind brings me sounds of cars parking and cars starting from the nearby Civil Government building. Soldiers and falangists shout slogans to each other. Smoking, anticipating the quarter hour, then the half hour, then another hour, I follow the bell of La Redonda until dawn.

At six I hear the bustle of morning, awakening with the sun, out in the gallery on the other side of the door, in "the world." The prisoners begin the daily cleaning, reminding me of the Avenida's morning rush to the latrines. Conditions must be far better here, I think. I stand up and call at the door. No one answers. I try again. Nothing. I am alone in "this world." Unless I kick up a rumpus—beyond my strength, at this point—they won't open the door. I decide to urinate in the farthest corner of the room.

My cigarette supply is dwindling and I am out of matches, although I stretched the ones I had with some improvised wicks I made out of the pallet-filling. I wait and then pound the door again. There is no answer although, up to now, some prisoner loitering on this side of the gallery has given me a sign of life. In a moment I try again when I hear steps shuffling near the door. Surely, some jail-mates must be only a few inches from me behind that door. I get on my knees and look through the keyhole. The small range allows me to see only trousers and shoes, which disperse and disappear from sight the moment I call again. Why do they run from my signal? I speak, shout, pound, but my noise and voice get lost in the uproar of the gallery.

Something unusual must be happening. I stop my attempts to get attention. But in a while the desire to smoke compels me to try again, this time by inserting the cigarette through the keyhole. Quietly I wait several minutes. No one seems to notice my SOS. At last, someone lights my cigarette with his, and as I retrieve mine he taps softly on the door. With my ear pressed against the keyhole I hear his husky low voice: "We can't give you a light when the guards are looking this way, compañero. The one who gave you the matches was placed in solitary. If you feel like smoking, do as you did now and be patient, I will light it if I can."

I sit on the teacher's platform and smoke several cigarettes, one after the other, while the thought of the prisoner who passed me the matches hovers in my mind. A little before one o'clock Medrano the medic and one of his assistants come in with the chow. After taking my pulse, the doctor tells me it is very weak, but he assures me it will become normal when I finish the meal. He orders his assistant to give me a cupping treatment, and after promising to see that I get a bucket for a privy, he leaves the room, smiling. That enigmatic, almost imperceptible smile probably has no significance, but it intrigues me, just the same. I eat with considerable effort. In ten minutes I vomit what little I had swallowed, in the corner that serves as a latrine.

Two volunteer nurses come to see me at midafternoon; one of them had come in before with the doctor. Later I learn that both are creeping parasites who've won the warden's confidence and some privileges by licking his boots. They remove the cups and equipment from a box and quickly apply the treatment to my back.

"Can you stand cupping?" one of them asks.

"I don't know," I answer. "I've never had it done."

They could skin my back and I wouldn't feel it. I feel nothing but the persistent pain. As they finish the treatment I remind them of my bucket. Whether by orders of the warden or because of an oversight, the doctor's promise is not fulfilled.

Next day they begin to take me out at night to a small latrine at the end of the gallery. An orderly comes in and cleans the corner I've used up to now, with sawdust and disinfectant.

I have no means other than my imagination to see myself through this situation. I think of the past, of things I could have done and never did, of battles I could have fought, of fantastic adventures. Those unreal meditations are my defense and help me keep one step ahead of desperation. Thus, weaving the hours to the sound of the church bells, I live through a succession of days marked only by the freak thoughts that inhabit my mind.

I know every detail of the room: the exact position of the suitcases, the cracks in the wall, the stains on the ceiling. . . . I can almost tell the atoms that form this small universe.

Every two days I get a supply of cigarettes. And I no longer have any problem lighting them. Although at times I have a long wait, I seldom take an unlit cigarette from the keyhole.

At times I get close to the door and try in vain to hear the conversations taking place out in the gallery. But my thirst for news is not quenched by a half-heard phrase caught at random. As I learn later, new prisoners have filled the gallery to the point that some pallets have to be placed close to my door, something heretofore strictly forbidden. From then on the sounds and bustle of life that reach me through that door lend some human warmth to my lonely cell. Once, during a lull out in the gallery, I put my ear to the keyhole and hear a mate whispering to another, "You know who's locked up in there? The municipal engineer. One of these nights they're going to take him. . . ." In other circumstances the overheard phrase would have increased my worries, but in my present mood I am not reacting to words. This forced silence has changed the meaning of all sound.

One of my windows is shut tight, but I can look out the other and get a glimpse of the street if I press my face to the iron bars and steel mesh. There I spend long moments inhaling fresh air and straining to see something of the world. That has always been a lonely street, and now I can only see some stray dogs, the guards, a few passersby who walk past darting dark looks at the building. If I could open the other window my field of vision would increase considerably. I know, for instance, that I could see the offices of a newspaper that was razed by a fire, a small workshop, and a large thoroughfare that crosses at right angles to the Civil Government building.

At the end of my first week of solitary I live through another night of unbearable pain. In desperation I shout and kick the door with such violence that the guard bursts in furiously. The moment he sees me his rage subsides and he orders a soldier to summon a volunteer nurse. In a few minutes I get my second shot of morphine.

I wake up to the chant of distant roosters who never fail to join the church bells in the morning. In one gulp I empty the water cup, trying to rid my mouth of the flavor of tar. The pain is gone; there is only a slight discomfort in my spine. For the first time I feel the immediate effects of the drug: an intense cold concentrated in my head as if my brain had been frozen. I attribute it to a slow flow of blood due to nervous tension and the excitement produced by the alkaloid.

The wheel of my thoughts turns and turns again around recent events. All of them lead me to the same conclusion: Everything happening now is part of a previously designed plan to break me down. They have to degrade and debase and twist us before they murder us. Those who survive will be only shreds of human beings, broken in body and spirit, incapable of offering the slightest resistance to the new imperial Spain which is the falangists' hollow ideal. "One Spain, a great Spain, Spain free! Arise, Spain!" is their cry. The part about free Spain sounds like a sentimental, patriotic farce, what with the country divided as never before, a half million men in prison, and foreign troops everywhere in the land. As for a great Spain, it is an open secret that the deluded falangists—and the Carlists, whose ideas are tuned to clocks that stopped over a century ago—plan the reconquest of America and of part of Europe, with Cataluña and Gibraltar as a launching point.

What kind of a revolution is this, carried out by perjurers bathed in innocent blood? And assuming that they win the struggle, what manner of civilization, art, or culture can they build? The will to abolish human inequality has spurred men to achieve great things through revolution, but these men are fighting to perpetuate inequality and injustice.

Every night, at the change of guards, they continue to take me to the latrines as if I were a dog. As we cross the galleries the prisoners lift their blankets to look at me, and by the light of the flashlight swinging in the guard's hand I see the eloquent sympathy reflected in their eyes, wistfully attempting to make fleeting contact, projecting their silent wish to talk to me. If they only could. . . .

The ramblings of my fantasy continue into the second week, but the enforced immobility helps me recover and I am able to retain some food.

A kind of inward paralysis is overtaking me as if I were a vegetable gradually losing sensitivity and turning to stone. Perhaps the process accounts for my increasingly chaotic recollections. If this solitary lasts a few more weeks I will reach a state of madness or idiocy from which, if I recover, I won't be able to reconstruct a thought. It's no use trying to tell the passing of time by the shouts that reach me from the gallery, by a few words overheard through the keyhole, by the features of the jailer who silently brings my food —a different one every time. Worst of all, I have no pencil or paper to help me pass the hours.

I try some effective ruses to help sustain my spirits. I have discovered some notches scored on the wood at one side of the teacher's desk. The shallow lines indicate they must have been scratched with the fingernail. Between the groups of lines I notice some deeper marks made with a sharp instrument, a belt buckle or perhaps the metal ferrule of a shoelace. When I experiment myself I realize they have been made with a ferrule. The groups consist mostly of two or three strokes. One of them goes on to six and then one more, a horizontal stroke binding the whole. As I study the improvised calendar I see only one instance where the grouped lines indicate more than two weeks. Since the number of suitcases exceeds the marks, I conclude that not every one of my predecessors in this cell has bothered to annotate the days spent here. It takes me several days to decide to keep track of my internment. After scoring a mark every morning I remain lost in my wanderings, trying to associate each suitcase with an individual and imagining the life and last moments of each man who has left a sign of his presence in this cell.

Despite the distraction provided by the arrival of the volunteer nurses with their cupping equipment, I discontinue the treatments which have succeeded only in irritating my skin. As for the morphine, I can get a shot with little trouble if I need it badly enough. They've given me two more this week. Still, the combined action of the needle stab to my spine and the reflex contraction of my chest is as painful as anything I've ever felt.

Whenever I feel up to it, I take one thousand paces around the room, a kilometer, I figure, in something like fifteen minutes. The promenade invariably ends at the teacher's desk, terminal station of all my travels of late.

By past associations, this classroom takes me back to another one, where the blackboards were crossed by colored chalk lines in the shape of cones and cylinders and other symbols of one of the hardest subjects I had to pass in my student days, descriptive geometry. The memories bring to mind faces of schoolmates I have long forgotten. Now, seen from the depth of this tomb, my years at the Central School of Industrial Engineering take on a simple charm in retrospect. I see myself flinging the chalk crayon smartly in mid-air with a final flourish at the end of my electrotechnical test, the main subject at the end of my difficult studies. I recall my sense of pride and optimism when I graduated as an engineer. Disillusionment soon replaced my cocky self-assurance. There was widespread unemployment in the technical field then, and I found myself going up and down the stairs of ministries and office buildings hunting for a job. In the incessant parade of faces returning to my mind, I spot those of women who had some significance in my past. As always, at the end of my reminiscences I am left with the same gnawing question: Why this prolonged stay in solitary confinement? If I am going to be executed, what can they be waiting for?

For several days—and for reasons unknown to me—packages are not allowed into the prison. I have exhausted my supply of cigarettes. Almost two days without a smoke! Finally, by offering to pay a high price for them, I am able to wangle three packages of "mataquintos" from a jailer. It is the worst, and now the most expensive tobacco I have ever bought. I have to spread the mixture on a bench and sort out stems and sticks before I roll my cigarettes. Actually, the lowly brand tastes heavenly to me.

By the end of the second week an extraordinary event shakes me out of my lethargy. Suddenly, breaking out of its methodical schedule, the church of La Redonda begins pealing without end! It is soon joined by other church bells of the city. And in a few moments I can hear voices and chanting coming from the front of the school building. I can hardly wait for the door to open and let the jailer in with my ration. When at last it does, I ask the reason for the commotion.

"We've taken San Sebastián," the jailer tells me with obvious satisfaction. I cannot get another word out of him. Once I am alone again, I tell myself that surely such a defeat must be the result of some betrayal, for the northern industrial zone is in the hands of the Republic, its resources are considerable, and its people determined to fight. I didn't know it then, but the well-defended field of Oyarzun, the forts of Guadalupe and San Marcos with the frontier city of Irún had already fallen to the insurgents. And again, when I learn of the new disaster I cling to my theory: There must have been some pretty serious betrayals within the military commands of the Republic. Isolated as I was then, locked up in that room with the suitcases of my murdered predecessors, I was unable to learn until much later that indeed, there had been a betrayal, but not from the military commands. The betrayal was perpetrated by the International Committee of Non-Intervention. Witness how David Lloyd George described the infamous committee to the House of Commons on October 28th, 1937: "The fact is, and I say this deliberately, that the Committee of Non-Intervention is the greatest and most base fraud perpetrated by great nations upon a weak people."

News of the fall of San Sebastián, succinctly told to me by my jailer, leaves me pondering sadly the possibility of our defeat. Still, after much speculation, I conclude that the incident is only a transitory retreat. It can't possibly impede the final victory of the Republican cause.

Two days later, around midmorning, a medical orderly comes into my cell accompanied by a short stocky corporal. Without bothering to look at me, the corporal announces impersonally, "Orders from the Civil Government. Your solitary confinement has been lifted. Gather your belongings and follow us."

As I pick up my suitcase and blanket, I take a last look around and mentally say farewell to my faithful companions. The desk, the maps, the globes. . . . Now the corporal, the martial edge gone from his voice, informs me that I have been authorized to take a shower if I wish. If I wish! I am to be transferred to the arithmetic class-room in the first floor.

THE INDUSTRIAL SCHOOL

This modern school building has adequate sanitary facilities. Its present sorry state is due to poor regulations. Actually, one could hardly expect less, what with the crowded conditions caused by a sudden conversion from a school to a jail. The showers can be used only by medical prescription.

Right in front of the medical orderly and a guard, I take my shower. I only have a dirty towel and the almost unused piece of soap I've kept hopefully during my stay in solitary. But I am in heaven, feeling as cleansed and exhilarated as if I were luxuriating in the thermal baths of Caracalla. The physical sensation of well-being increases when I comb my hair and brush my teeth. It does not diminish when I put on the same dirty, wilted clothes. When I join my new jailmates I am unable to answer their barrage of questions with more than a few random words. After being silent for so long I find it difficult to speak, and jokes and conversation bewilder me. But it doesn't take me long to return to the normal communicative mood of most prisoners.

There are two windows in this classroom; one of them, in the rear, is tightly closed. The other one is next to a large table which is used as a double bed, the only piece of furniture in the room. The pallets are rolled up in two heaps during the day. At night we spread and place them in the inflexible order prescribed around the walls. There are twenty of us here. At times others come to join us, but the number of occupants never exceeds thirty. I know some of the faces around here, but the only friend I find is Eduardo Andrés, to whom I am distantly related. He is a greying man of fifty, always optimistic and cheerful. I owe him the few laughs I have in my new internment. Among the thousands of men I meet in my long pilgrimage through Spanish jails, I find few who remain steadfastly immune to the general terror that prevails. Magistrate Moreda, I remember; Eduardo Andrés here at the Industrial School; and later Santolaya at the provincial jail. None of them believed in the possibility of being executed, an optimism which proved to be false in the case of Moreda. I detect a certain preoccupation in Andrés' eyes at night, but I soon learn that his concern is for my fate rather than his. The fact that I've been punished by solitary confinement is no guarantee of future security. He knows of men who have completed the same temporary sentence and then been put on the "saca" lists, days and even weeks later.

Andrés is a veteran here. He knows the rules and habits, he has already sized up the men in this cell. He warns me to beware of the spy among us. Our stool pigeon is a goodlooking young fellow, Manuel, from the town of Ausejo. The mates hold him responsible for several executions. "The rest of them are pure gold," Andrés tells me with a reassuring wink.

Manuel was arrested because of his leftist affiliations. But shortly after he arrived he began encouraging political discussions in which, to everyone's astonishment, he wedged comments like, "A horde of rowdy rabble are not going to defeat the courageous army that represents law, order, and justice." The abrupt change is what gave him away. It smelled of convenience rather than conviction. Andrés tells me how the men simply turned their backs on him. Some show him open hostility, but most of them continue to treat him at least civilly. "It's as dangerous to annoy a bee as it is to pet a snake," Andrés adds with another significant wink. "I am with the majority, of course. But I always keep an eye open."

Other companions in this cell are Gómez, a tailor; Monterrubio and Damián, bakers from the town of Nájera; Barrera, a railroad engine stoker; an old man called Pascual; Sesma, an aide to the guard; Marino, a young teacher who limps slightly; Júdez, an office clerk; Rafa, a cabinetmaker; Félix and Víctor, a couple of youngsters. Not quite seventeen! The rest are peasants from nearby towns.

Understandably, most of us would prefer to join the prisoners who are kept out in the gallery, rather than be confined in this classroom. Out there the sun floods in through the great windows facing the patio. There, too, one has as much contact with the outside world as can be expected in this jail.

Next morning, Gómez the tailor, the two bakers from Nájera and I sit quietly on our pallets and hear Eduardo Andrés tell one of his adventures from his youth. It is a simple, unimportant tale, but after my long isolation the steady flow of talk sounds fascinating to my newly awakened ears. It doesn't take long to make good friendships among prisoners. The common misfortune weaves bonds which in normal life would take months and even years to develop.

Barrera the stoker hails from Huelva. His witty Andalusian accent remains typically sassy despite many years in the lands of Castile. He has been making a pencil drawing of a locomotive on a greasy sheet of paper. When he learns of my profession he shows it to me proudly.

Gómez the tailor, tall and gawky, suffers from nephritic attacks which leave him prostrate for hours, his face tense and livid from pain. During one of his worst crises I suggest that he request to be taken to the infirmary for a few days. "Don't worry," he tells me with a wry smile. "I'm used to this illness by now. The pain goes away after a while and leaves me in peace for a few months. I don't want to go to the infirmary. It's full of spies and orderlies. Lousy company for a man like me!"

Damián, one of the bakers from Nájera, is always brimming over with energy, a short dark and very hairy man of thirty. He spent most of his childhood in the orphan asylum, until one day a relative came to claim him. Before reaching the age of twelve he went to work as an apprentice in a bakery. His life is one of unending toil and struggle. Still, despite his harsh background, he developed into a fine, tactful, cordial individual. He behaves with a quiet dignity that wins him our respect and esteem. He has held a position of some importance in the local chapter of the provincial Socialist Party. One night, a week after my admission to this new cell, he is taken together with a newly arrived peasant to be executed against the cemetery wall. Of all the men I have seen leave on their way to death, none did so with Damián's aplomb and courage.

"I wish you all better luck than mine. Long live the Republic!" he pronounced firmly from the door. By the guard's flashlight I witnessed the expression of his face, fearless, hopeless too, but without a trace of envy toward the fortunate ones he was leaving behind. It takes us some time to recover from the grief of losing him. Then, three days later, the cabinetmaker suffers the same fate, but without displaying Damián's ultimate fortitude.

Communications with San Sebastián have been resumed, and now several families who were caught by the revolution vacationing in the summer resort, return home to Logroño. Rumors not exclusively spread by the returnees tell of their having been forced by the "Reds" to labor with pick and shovel in the construction of trenches, all under the whips of Russian foremen. It is part of the tactics of the fascists to breed hatred by encouraging rumors, however false.

Don Pedro Lozano, the prison chief, is a retired Civil Guard officer who was recalled to service with the advent of the rebellion. He is a medium size man with eyes of a reptile and a slanted gash for a mouth. Despite his fierce expression, we hear he is quite susceptible to flattery which explains why our spy, Manuel from Ausejo, is promoted to the chief's personal guard. In a few days Manuel moves his belongings to the rooms adjoining the administration office. From then on he rarely puts in an appearance at our cell. We see him, pistol in belt, making the rounds with his Don Pedro. When he is granted his freedom, he enlists as a volunteer to fight at the Madrid front.

A few days before his departure, while drawing a bunch of keys from his pocket by our door, Manuel inadvertently drops a wallet on the floor. It's the one he has rifled from a prisoner who was taken from the main floor and executed. Only a few days ago he showed it to us with wicked pride. Now, when one of the peasants in our room finds it and announces he will return it to Manuel, the tailor blurts out angrily, "Are you crazy? Why give it back to that bastard turncoat? Throw it away or keep it for yourself."

Wasting no time to heed the counsel, the peasant throws the thing into a refuse can. Several times the spy comes around looking for "his" wallet, sure that he has dropped it in our room and implying that one of us has kept it.

"Stop crabbing about that fucking wallet," the tailor tells him. "If you think it's been stolen, why don't you notify your darling pet, the chief, so he can order a search of the prison?"

As soon as Manuel scurries out, the stoker says, "This reminds me of the German story. The one about the fellow who complains because someone has taken the sausage he took from the cat who took it from the miller's wife."

We laugh and end up recalling the time the spy cut out from a magazine a picture of Franco taken when the Caudillo was elected chief of the glorious Movement, and the city of Burgos put on a pompous celebration in his honor. Thus the portrait showed him with chest thickly studded with medals and decorations.

"They should've presented our spy with a picture of Franco without pants," the tailor muses.

"What a thought!" we exclaim. "What the hell for?"

"Idiots! So he could kiss his ass as often as he wants."

There are two floors to this rectangular building. Half of the prison population is held on the ground floor, where I spent the days of my solitary confinement, with the front wing reserved for the guards to use as barracks, offices, and storerooms. The other half of the prisoners are kept here, on the upper floor. This front wing, too, over the guards' quarters downstairs, is used for infirmary, dispensary, and offices and living quarters for the chief and his aides. There is a small hall which serves as a visitors' room. On both levels the prisoners occupy the patios, galleries, and classrooms at the rear of the building, with smaller classrooms designated as solitary cells. Since the Industrial School is adjacent to the artillery barracks where our chow is prepared, the kettles reach us before the contents lose their welcome warmth. Bad as the stew is, it has that one point in its favor. But the bread they give us is hard and heavy, better suited for a camel's stomach. And, as in the Avenida prison, there is a nightly "sacas" call, except on Sunday. New prisoners come to fill the places of the executed.

Female prisoners, some ninety of them, are quartered in the right wing of this floor, separated by a special guard and an iron grill. Of the four major classrooms at the rear of the building, the largest is the chemistry hall, together with its accompanying laboratory. Sixty

prisoners are being held there. Counting the women, the prison
population consists of twelve hundred inmates equally distributed
between the two floors.

THE MOOR OF VIGUERA

One grey morning a tall, slender man in his mid-forties joins the
prisoners in the gallery outside our classroom. His ragged clothes
and unkempt beard indicate he has been caught while hiding in the
mountains. I know him. His dark, imposing looks have won him
the title of The Moor of Viguera—his town—but his name is
Florentino.

As a youth he emigrated to Argentina, where wealthy relatives
awaited him. When he failed to make a fortune in America he returned to Spain and took up residence in Logroño. He often climbed
the road up to his town of Viguera and visited his family. He was
quiet and circumspect, but much given to visiting the cafés of
Logroño late at night with his inseparable friend, Doctor Vallejo. I
was better acquainted with Vallejo, a man of unusual courage who,
despite his lack of political affiliations, had no qualms about voicing
his anticlerical opinions and his sympathies for leftist causes. I have
been told that at his execution in the first days of the revolution,
Vallejo was offered the last rites by the attending priest. His answer
was to spit on the floor. "Never mind," he said. "My gods will judge
me." A moment later he fell to the volleys of the firing squad, together with his "saca" companions.

When Florentino the Moor recognizes me, he throws his arms
around me. "I thought you were dead!" he tells me warmly. "I'm
hungry," he repeats. "I'm starving." I give him the last of my personal provisions: two ounces of chocolate and some crackers I've
been keeping for emergency in my suitcase. We watch him eat, in
solemn silence, his eyes shining with a deep dark brilliance. When
he finishes, he goes to the washbasin and cups his hands to drink
avidly. He returns to us and sits on a blanket.

"It was hunger that forced me to give myself up," he tells us. "The morning I saw our situation lost, with the fascists in power in the city, I left for Viguera, not alarmed, just sure that I could wait there for developments. You know my leftist sympathies. I've been as anticlerical as our departed friend Vallejo. But I was never involved in political parties, and I've never acted against the clergy, although I mistrust them and despise them. But I was worried about getting in trouble with one or with the other. After all, they work hand in hand in this revolt."

"What happened when you got to Viguera?" I ask him.

"It was almost time for harvest and people should have been working in the fields. But everyone was terrified by the rebellion. An old friend of my family told me he had never heard of so many assassinations, not even in the stories of the Carlist wars. By the fourth day after the outbreak of the rebellion, just before dusk, several men in falangist uniform came looking for me. I hardly had time to get a glimpse of them through a window! I escaped through the backyard and crouched my way to the forest. It was easy to reach the sierra; you know our pueblo is surrounded by thick woods of oak, beech, and chestnut trees. It was dark but I know the area. I've tramped it often enough since I was a child. I remembered a cave where I used to take cover from the rain and the windstorms when I went hunting. It's about half an hour's walking distance from the pueblo. When I finally got there I picked up a sheaf of branches and dried leaves and tumbled on them. I was nervous. It took me sometime to fall asleep. The light of dawn and the birds woke me up."

The men are listening quietly all around him, encouraging him to continue. "I spent the day taking sips from a nearby brook to fill my empty stomach. I didn't dare walk in broad daylight, but as soon as it got dark I started back for the pueblo. There was no one at the family house. After wandering the streets for a while, I decided to knock at the house of some friends. They opened the door with terrified faces. All the men in my family had been arrested and taken to Logroño, they informed me. The women followed in a passing truck, thinking they could help them. That's why there was no one in my house. My friends gave me two blankets, a large loaf of bread, and some cans of sardines. They also promised to help me further if my family did not return from Logroño. In that case, we agreed, it would be less dangerous for all concerned if I did not go into the house, but instead picked up what provisions they could leave for me in a window facing the backyard. They warned me about the patrols who searched the hills looking for escapees. Disheartened by the difficulties now facing me, I picked up the food and blankets and returned to my cave. Next day I looked for other hiding places so I could sleep in a different one every night.

"By the fifteenth day the provisions left by my friends at the window dwindled considerably. Part of my family had returned to the pueblo, but terrified by the situation and knowing nothing of my whereabouts, they left again. One night, when I stole to the pueblo, hungry as a wolf, I found nothing at the window. I had to return to my lair empty-handed and . . . empty-bellied. I was desperate, thinking how easy it would be had I a rifle with me. You know I'm a good hunter. But I had to manage by picking greens and fishing patiently in a rivulet. At the end of the fourth week I decided to start for Madrid. I walked all night till dawn, toward the sierra of Viniegra. I reached a little hamlet and found a rickety, abandoned house. The sun was beginning to rise, I thought it would be dangerous to go on. I jumped over the fence and got in through a hole in the crumbling shutters boarding a window. I dragged myself to a corner and climbed on a heap of dry grass, leaves, and branches. There I fell asleep, dead to the world.

"Just about noon I heard steps outside. I had just time enough to sink into the pile of dry grass before they came through the door. It was the ones with the red berets. They began searching in the dark. One of them reached the pile of stuff where I was hiding and poked it with his rifle. The muzzle almost brushed my forehead! After a couple of minutes another man came shouting through the door. 'What the hell are you fellows doing? Stop wasting time! We know where he is and also that he is not armed, as the shepherd said.' I realized they were looking for someone else. One of them asked the one who seemed to be leading the patrol if they could stop to rest and smoke a cigarette. 'Maybe you're right,' the leader answered. 'We've got a half an hour's walk yet. All right, take five.'

"I saw their silhouettes leaning against the door. One of them took out his cigarettes and passed them around. From their conversation I learned they had been ordered to shoot escapees on sight. The chase was relentless. It extended all over the sierra, with the patrols linking one pueblo to another. When they left I told myself it was foolish to go on. At nightfall I retraced my steps, eating green chestnuts and drinking from every pond and brook in my path. By dawn I reached the spot from where I had started. I slept all day, waiting for night to return to my pueblo. I couldn't stand hunger any longer. I decided to throw caution to the winds and call back on my friends. I got on my knees and begged them for food. They gave me a loaf of bread, chocolate, some cans. . . . But they asked me to keep away and stop involving them. They couldn't help me any further. Their lives were at stake."

(One of the most severely punished "offenses" in those days was to help a Republican hiding in the fields. When one of them got caught, the patrols would search his pockets, and if they found bread crumbs or any other trace of food, the man would be tortured until he revealed his source of help. His benefactor would be arrested and paraded through the streets to the beating of a drum. The intended public disgrace invariably was followed by execution, usually in the town square. Later, when the murders were better organized, the sentences were carried out in the provincial capitals, under the fascist code which proscribed *collaboration*. The terror spread by such measures was so effective that no one dared help an escapee, however close his friendship or kinship to the hunted.)

"You've had it, Florentino," I tell the Moor.

"I held out another three weeks," he adds. "I called on other houses, but all I found was the threat of being denounced. Finally famished and desperate, with all doors closed, I decided to give myself up to the Civil Guard. They put me in a car and brought me to the Civil Government. There I spent the night alone in a cell facing the patio." He stops and lowers his head before he mumbles, "The last days I was in hiding there was a full moon shining on the valley. I was already thinking of giving myself up, telling myself that maybe all I'd heard was exaggerated. After all, I had done nothing. What could they claim against me? If I had had a companion with me I would've tried to reach the Republican lines, even if we had to eat raw roots on the way. I was a coward and a fool to give myself up. But . . . hunger and loneliness beat me. Now I expect the worst."

This very night his sinister premonition is confirmed.

Across a narrow, lonely street, the rear of this building faces an empty lot owned by the municipality of Logroño. There is only a tool shed on the lot, used to store lumber and all sorts of construction materials. The stock is watched at night by an old City Hall employee and his dog. The day I arrived here at the arithmetic classroom, I was told that the dog whines and howls during the "saca" in proportion to the number of victims. At first I didn't pay attention to the story, it seemed so incredible. But soon I had unquestionable proof of the animal's accurate timing. It hasn't failed since. His sinister howls start with the departure of the truck and last until the shots are heard from across the river. Then they subside and stop, not to be heard again until the next night.

By now the common graves of the ponds of La Granjera and Lardero have been filled with the fallen, so the execution patrols have to carry out their orders in front of the cemetery wall. When the wind is blowing in this direction we can hear the shots from our window quite clearly. We wait for the faint echo to disappear, and then most of the inmates fall asleep. Only a small, less stoic or perhaps more sentimental group stays awake a little longer, paying a kind of posthumous farewell in absentia to the mates who lie in a puddle of their own blood on the dry brush near the Ebro.

The night they took Damián, the courageous baker from Nájera, I joined the vicarious funeral cortege. Silently, glued to the one open window in our cell, we stood awaiting the wind's doleful message. Once the burst of simultaneous shots was heard, our tailor pronounced the ritual R. I. P.:

"They have been killed."

Without further commentary, we walked to our miserable beds, dropped on them heavily, and sank into sleep.

A MYTHOLOGICAL DREAM

There is an hour in the morning, during the change of guard, when the watch in here is somewhat relaxed—the one outside always works like a clock. I take advantage of the slack when I return from the latrines and walk into a room facing the gallery which is often kept locked. It is here where they keep the clothes of the men who have been executed, mingled with the teaching materials from the classrooms now converted to collective cells. Among the stools and drafting-boards, barometers, precision scales, test tubes, and other lab equipment, there is a collection of sculpture brought over from the art pavilion. The statues sport all sorts of apparel, giving the place the look of a bizarre museum. There is a plaster Venus with a dirty raincoat thrown over her shoulders like a cape. Hermes wears a brand new straw hat and looks at Venus with empty eyes. A bust of Hercules is crowned by a soft cocked hat, a multicolored knapsack slung from his shoulder. Filthy handkerchiefs hang from the plaster acanthus leaves and branches nailed to the walls. On the floor, broken plaster masks and moldings mix with nondescript bundles.

I mention this abandoned room because of a dream I have tonight. . . .

I am in a hall illuminated by a purple light spread from lanterns atop columns of gold and lacquer. Venus walks over gracefully, clearing with ease all obstacles before her. Her bare feet step over the objects strewn on the floor without disturbing them, while sparks of all colors burst from the bundles like a display of fireworks. She approaches a precision scale and sits on a stool, letting her white tunic slip from her shoulders to reveal her bare back. With a pair of pincers she plucks flowers from a basket and drops them on one of the plates of the scale. On the other she drops worms which she picks from a large box next to her. Hercules and Hermes and the other statues descend from their pedestals and surround Venus and the scale in a circle, while the masks hanging on the walls stick out their red tongues. Among the spectators at this mysterious scene is a man trying to elbow his way into the circle. He wears a blue mechanic's overall and two pistols at his belt, all the time smoking an enormous cigar. His features, unmistakably, are those of Pedro Lozano, the jail warden.

A giant hand stretches out from the wall and slaps the cigar from his mouth, while an ugly, gawky statue shouts, "No smoking here!"

Don Pedro's eyes turn glassy with anger as he reaches for his pistol. But he's not given a chance to use it. Hercules takes him and crushes him between his fingers like a cockroach. He then shakes his fingers over the basket and I see one more worm fall into it. The pyrometers, test tubes, and thermometers begin to dance and jump in their cases, and a jungle-like tom-tom reverberates throughout the hall. Displeased by the uproar, Venus raises her arms to stop it. She then leans over and picks up a worm with the pincers, and when she drops it in the plate, the weight tilts the scale. A voice says, "There are too few flowers left. No weighing can be done unless we get some more."

Now all the statues repeat in unison:

"It can't be done, it can't be done. . . ."

I am awakened by a jarring shove. Dawn is breaking and Andrés is looking at me with amazement. "What is it that can't be done?" he asks. "You must have been dreaming how impossible it is to get out of here. Right?" he asks smiling.

"Yes," I answer. If I tell him the dream he'll think I'm going mad. I can't interpret it myself.

During the dictatorship of General Primo de Rivera, an engineer called García Pardo drew up a master plan to modify and enlarge Spain's utilization of water resources. The coordination of several watersheds was called the Hydrographic Confederation of Rivers, and was expected to enrich the crops considerably. The confederation of the Ebro was one of the principal phases of the plan, the Ebro being the largest river running its full course within Spanish territory. The Ebro's second dam was in Ortigosa, a little town in the province of Logroño. On several occasions the project was halted for lack of funds, but shortly before the outbreak of the Movement, work had been resumed on a small scale.

On July 18th the workers took over the town of Ortigosa, armed with sticks and vintage shotguns, and cut off communications with Logroño. The local Civil Guard detachment remained passive, so for almost two days the workers ruled the town without causing a death or an arrest. In the afternoon of the second day truckloads of armed falangists and Carlist Requetés began arriving, while the Civil Guard shook off their indecision and joined them. The workers were easily disbanded. Only at the crossroads with the main highway did a small group of workers exchange a few shots with the falangists before retreating to the sierra. As soon as the falangists took over the town, the mass arrests started. Many of those who had escaped fell prisoner or were executed during the searches organized from the pueblos. Some were able to reach the Loyalist lines of the Guadarrama front through the pine forests of Soria. The majority, who remained confidently in town, were arrested and sent to the jails of Logroño.

It so happened that when the Ortigosa workers had cut communications with Logroño, one of their patrols stopped the car of Dr. Medrano, a physician. Save for the inconvenience of having to wait a few hours for authorization to proceed, the doctor suffered no harm or humiliation. But he didn't forget the incident when he was appointed physician of the Industrial Prison. Upon taking over the infirmary at the Industrial School he vented all his cruelty on the Ortigosa workers imprisoned here. A tall, fair, hefty man who sleeps out in the gallery is one of them. Several times Eduardo Andrés and I try to get him to tell us the Ortigosa story. Sesma, the corporal's aide, and another inmate tell us that the man was wounded by a Mauser shot. His name is in the list of prisoners we've received from the provincial hospital. He's always avoided talking about the subject, and keeps much to himself. But this afternoon he breaks his silence. He tells us he believed Medrano is responsible for the execution of several of his co-workers. He knows one of the men in the patrol that had detained Medrano's car. His friend assures him that Medrano's attitude during the incident had been hypocritically cordial with the very men he later denounced.

"We were a few dispirited men jailed in a small cell at the Ortigosa City Hall," the hefty blond man tells us. "We were waiting our turn to be transferred to Logroño, not knowing what was happening, or how we could best help ourselves. Suddenly, between the bars of the open window, a stone dropped in our cell with a note tied to it. 'The Movement failed in Madrid, Barcelona, Valencia, Bilbao, and other cities. The forces of the Republic are advancing from Sigüenza and will reach Piqueras at dawn. Courage! If you can escape in this confusion try to do so before they take you to Logroño. Very few get there alive.'

"Heads together, by the flame of a cigarette lighter, we read the note. It was from Marichu, the sister of one of the men in our group; we knew her well. The escape was planned for that same night, late, when security was lax. The outside door could be broken down easily. Our only worry was the armed patrols watching the streets, but they'd be drinking at the tavern by then, and with luck, it would be too late to catch us by the time our disappearance was discovered. Around eight, when the jailer came in with our supper, we were ready for him. In no time we had him gagged and tied. Quietly we stole out into the corridor. There was no need to force open the outside door, we had taken the key from the guard who brought our food. But despite our speed and quiet, we were discovered by the guard's nephew. The youth screamed so when he saw us that everyone in the place was alerted. Before we could get out of town the patrols were shooting at us. At the outskirts of the village we split in two groups. Three men turned left and dropped to a ravine of brush. Another fell wounded at my feet. I kept running in zig-zag fashion toward the woods. Some fifty yards away a path led to them and on to the hills. It was my only hope. I felt a buzzing in my head, not knowing whether it was the bullets hissing past or the throbbing of my heart after the chase. Suddenly something hit me on the back of the neck and I fell. When I woke I was in bed at the Provincial Hospital with a kilometer of bandages around my head. Look," he tells us now, bending to show his bull neck. He has a fresh round scar the size of a two-peseta coin.

"The funniest thing is that the bullet came out my mouth without even chipping a tooth! My mother says it was a miracle."

The bullet's course certainly backs up his mother's words. It made its way out without touching a vertebrae, an artery, or his palate. Not even a tooth.

THE CHEMISTRY HALL

It faces the artillery barracks, across a narrow street from this Industrial School. It is connected with our "classroom" through the gallery, separated by several small rooms used as solitary confinement cells. It is the largest, cleanest, and most comfortable collective cell in this qualified jail. Tile floor, sunlight, several sinks formerly used for chemical experiments. . . .

I find many friends at the Chemistry Hall; two of them, Adolfo Alvarez and Rafael López, keep their pallets close to one another between two large windows. Rafael is a young teacher at the Normal School. I think the brutal prison life offends his sensibilities so much that he seeks a form of protection from the environment in Adolfo. Adolfo Alvarez is the only inmate allowed to possess a book here, after passing the customary censor. It is a volume of the works of Shakespeare and I've had it in my hands several times, unable to concentrate enough to enjoy it fully because of the constant noise that surrounds me.

Not far from here, near the living quarters of the prison Chief and his aides, there is a large room used as a dispensary. It is also a hangout of the orderlies, those favored by Don Pedro the Chief and, accordingly, the most hated by the inmates. The orderlies are the ones in charge of receiving our gift parcels at the main gate, the mornings when the privilege is allowed. If some unsuspecting or as yet unnotified relative brings a package for a man who has been executed, the orderlies keep it, organize a dinner from its contents, and invite the guards.

There seems to be a tacit understanding to avoid dramatic scenes at the front door. Thus a package is accepted even when the recipient is already dead. Usually, the second time it is refused while the donor is informed with an inhuman, mocking, "He doesn't need it any more." The method only serves to stave off the inevitable tragedy once more; the result is the same at the end: the wife or relative broken by sorrow at the prison gate, crying or cursing, while the now useless gift parcel is returned to their trembling hands.

A member of that repulsive flock of orderlies is called Ignacio, a degenerate from Navarra, a bully and a glutton. As if to conceal his moral decay, he carries dangling from his neck a number of religious medals and scapulars. He is one of Don Pedro's favorites, and according to rumor, has taken advantage of his relative immunity to seek "personal" favors from the women—friends, relatives, or wives—who come to visit and bring parcels to the men. He is an enthusiastic consumer of the gift food destined for those already executed. People who know him and his family say that his father is a well-to-do landowner who disowned his troublemaking son after having several fights with him. Ignacio boasts of being a great ball player, and even of having played soccer at some time. Perhaps that accounts for his attempts to make friends with me. When I must go to the dispensary to get my medicine, I see him there, breaking into beaming smiles for me.

We are not often allowed to walk from our arithmetic classroom to the Chemistry Hall, but I take my chances, attracted by its cleanliness and by the friends I have there. One afternoon Ignacio sees me sitting there as he comes in to fill a water jug. He takes a quick look around and departs. Little do I know he is running to the Chief to squeal on me. He has seen me reading an old newspaper, the kind occasionally brought into the prison wrapping someone's gift parcel.

As I start back to my classroom a voice behind calls me to a halt. It is a petty officer, sizing me up with an angry look. "Where is that newspaper you were reading?" he asks.

"It's just an old sheet I found among the parcel wrappings. I left it on a table at the Chemistry Hall."

"Let's go and see," he says incredulously, and luckily the old sheet is still where I innocently left it, on the table.

When I return to my cell I have to answer the questions of my curious jailmates, and I let them know what I think of that hypocritical Ignacio. . . . The incident didn't seem to reach warden Don Pedro.

There is a long-nosed sergeant in charge of distributing the chow. He watches carefully as the kitchen helpers pour one ladleful in each plate presented by the prisoners formed in double file. The stew is still unbearable (though warm), and to make matters worse, there has been a temporary suspension of gift parcels. I don't know why that long-nosed sergeant has become such a good friend of Eduardo Andrés, the contractor. Every time it's Andrés' turn in the file, the sergeant smiles and asks the kitchen helper to pour two or three ladlefuls in his plate.

"This is a good one," the man winks, urging the helper to fill the plate. Poor Andrés! Nowadays the stew is so scorched and dreadful that he has no recourse but to throw most of it carefully in one of the refuse cans. One day the sergeant catches him. The tuberous long nose flamed to a red pepper.

"You ungrateful bastard," he shouts lunging at Andrés. "If I ever see you throw food away again I'm going to stretch your balls and tie them around your neck!"

Terrified, Andrés tries to utter some words of apology, but he is unable to make a coherent sound. When we return to our cell Luís Gómez the tailor is laughing heartily.

"It's the logic of the canary," he tells Andrés, still laughing.

"And what the hell has a goddam bird got to do with all this?"

"I don't mean a canary bird. I mean a man from the Canary Islands who went to live in Cuba. One day, walking in the jungle, he reaches a sugar cane plantation. There he sees a mulatto hard at work cutting cane. The mulatto stops chopping for a moment and greets the stranger, the canary, 'Hello, friend.' The canary starts to think: 'Friend. . . . Man's best friend is the dog, and the dog is the cat's worst enemy. The cat eats the mouse, who in turn eats cheese which is made from milk. Milk comes from cows and cows have horns. Ha! This character just called me a cuckold!' Whereupon, the canary pulled out his own machete and attacked the poor mulatto."

"Don't bother me with your shitty stories," Andrés tells him. "Can't you see I'm still nervous from that bout with Long-Nose?" and turning to me, he adds, "Did you see what the sergeant's protection almost cost me? Why, if I eat all that scorched crap he piles up on my plate, I'd wind up with stomach ulcers!"

"Love can kill at times," says Judit, winking.

Antonino Judit is a little guy, funny and thin. He's only thirty five, but he is pale and worn out and bald-headed, he looks older. The times he has enough tobacco he goes around puffing like a volcano. He wakes up coughing, takes a cigarette, and . . . presto, the cough is gone. I've never seen a better medicine.

There is a pathetic case isolated in one of the small rooms between the arithmetic classroom and the Chemistry Hall. He is a tall, dark, slender greying man whom they call El Ciego, the blindman. In the first months after the outbreak of the rebellion, the favorite execution grounds used by the falangists—not counting the roadside—were the pond of La Granjera, the graveyard of Lardero, and the walls of the city cemetery. The executions were carried out in one of those three places until the first two became so full of bodies they had to use the cemetery walls exclusively. A special detail was in charge of carrying the bodies in a mule cart and burying them in the common pit. One night at the end of July, our Ciego had been taken from the provincial jail and executed with seventeen others. Next morning, when the sun peered behind the shadow of Mount Cantabria, the men in charge of burial found one body missing, according to their list. Soon they noticed a trail of blood across the road and into a narrow path that led down to the river. They found a prostrate body on the grass, and when they turned it over, they saw a mass of mud and blood for face. Only the nose holes gave it a remotely human semblance. Accustomed as they were to look death in the face, the men shuddered with horror at the sight. As one of them leaned to wrap the body in a sack, he noticed a slight tremor. His companions came to investigate and discovered that the heart of the cadaver was still palpitating feebly.

"We won't bury a body that's still alive," they insisted. Still uncertain, their chief went across the highway and telephoned the proper Civil Government office. An ambulance came in due time and took the bleeding mass of flesh and mud to the provincial hospital.

Two months later, recovered but blind, the man was transferred here to the Industrial School and placed in an isolated cell. He fell ill with some intestinal disturbance which kept him calling for someone to lead him to the latrines. The men always sent word to the administration office, and Don Pedro would then order a guard to take the blindman out. But as soon as he was better, they began taking him out to the latrines only at night and before sunrise.

One rare day I see him being led by the guard. The sight leaves me paralyzed. The noon sun streaming into the gallery floods his pale face like an insult, accentuating the contrast to the deep dark empty holes left by the eyes. I shall never forget that scene.

A table near one of the windows in our classroom has been used up to now as a double bed by two small peasants, one of whom is called one night on the "saca" list. The survivor now fights with Sesma, the corporal's aide, about the window we all wish to leave open all night; the room is small, and crowded with so many unwashed bodies that we cling fiercely to any means of increasing the scant ventilation. I end the argument by proposing a change: I will take the exposed place by the window. With Sesma's approval and the inevitable notification to the prison office, I occupy the combination table-bed.

My new place is near El Ciego's cell, just on the other side of a boarded door. His footsteps reach me in the dead of night. I even hear him sing softly, sad songs that sound like the plaint of a wounded bird. His voice is soft and pleasant. Who knows what forms and colors are behind those sightless holes, what love and sorrow he may be trying to express with that soft hum. . . . ? I thought I had seen the nadir of misfortune, but now I realize there are still some depths unknown to me. What is my plight compared to that of this eyeless, solitary man? Some of my jailmates who have managed to exchange a few words with him, assure me he seems quite optimistic and thoroughly convinced he soon will be set free.

I never learn the outcome of the case. All I know is that much later, when I am transferred to the third jail in my tour, El Ciego—Cayo Sagasti is his name—is still living in strict solitary confinement in the same cell.

There is another example of inhuman cruelty perpetrated in this jail; the case of the legless hunchback. This man is in his middle thirties, and dark thick eyebrows shade his narrow face. Whether since birth or by accident, his lower limbs end at the thigh, just above where his knees should be. He propels his half body on a platform mounted on a chassis which runs on four small iron wheels. The device looks homemade, but quite sturdy. He straps himself to it with a set of greasy belts crossing his shoulders. The cart is set in motion by hand; he pushes himself with his long arms, using two thick wooden wedges like a pair of crude gloves. His name is Antonio Llorente and, like so many prisoners here, he was born in Calahorra. For years he has held some job at the Municipal Welfare Department where he terrified the nuns with his blasphemous swearing. Still, some of them were moved by compassion and took his side against the majority who kept trying to fire him from the job. I never get to ask him why he was arrested. He sleeps in a corner of the court, almost in front of the Chemistry Hall. When I visit my friends I see him there, sittling like a Buddha on his cart, surrounded by small piles of tobacco and cigarette paper books, all spread out on his blanket. He keeps busy manufacturing cigarettes which he sells to the men. He must be quite an expert, for even Don Pedro the warden orders his cigarettes from him, supplying his own favorite tobacco. Llorente is a soccer fan and likes to talk about the game. I give him food from my gift parcels. Once, I intercede for him in some dispute, and Andrés tells me later, "All right, he is an invalid, but he has a tongue like a snake's. I wouldn't be surprised if someone knocked his teeth out some day." Behind the bustle of the gallery in the day time or in the silence of night, one can hear the creaking and squeaking of his cart rolling by when he has to go to the latrines.

An event that is somewhat associated with the legless hunchback creates quite a stir in town. A man who had just been informed of his brother's execution went into a tavern to relieve his shock with wine. Upon leaving the place he saw a Civil Guard officer, and distraught with grief and rage, he took out a knife and severely wounded the officer in the chest. He himself was cut down shortly after, right on the spot, by gunfire from a falangist patrol.

The incident is decisive in the fate of Llorente, for in the ensuing investigation the authorities discover he is related to the aggressor. It is a perfect opportunity to charge the tragedy to a conspiracy, and the falangists are not going to waste it. Quickly, the attempt on the officer is construed as part of a plot at the Industrial School jail, in which Llorente is accused of being involved together with several other inmates.

A few nights later, the regular "saca" is increased by another one of nine men supposed to be implicated in the imaginary plot.

Llorente sleeps soundly in the corridor, with the heavy sleep that overtakes many of the prisoners after the "saca" hour. By the moonlight reflected on the gallery windowpanes, or in the darkness blanketing the cells, hundreds of sleepless men question tomorrow's destiny. These are the moments of the last nervous snickers, when conversation subsides until every man retreats into his own disquieting inner monologue.

All activity seems to have ceased for the night. Llorente is out there, off to a quiet sleep, believing that his miserable condition alone exempts him from further misfortune. Suddenly the flashlights glare around his bed, and the guards' boots kick him awake. At first he jumps, startled, but he is soon paralyzed by terror. One of the guards tries to avert a scene and tells him the call is only a question of a statement he must make to the Police Chief at the Civil Government. Since the hour of the "saca" has passed, Llorente believes him. He mounts his humped half body upon the cart, adjusts the straps, and propels himself with his two wooden wedges, surrounded by the guards. But upon reaching the end of the gallery the ruse is exposed. Llorente detects the tense, pale faces of the other condemned awaiting him to join the extra "saca," and he breaks into alternate waves of pleading and screaming, neither of which moves the impassive guards. Tears turn to rage and his insults and blasphemies fill every corner of the building. When they attempt to tie him he fends them off like a wild beast, biting and striking every hand with his wooden wedges. Finally, one of the guards thrusts a cape over him. The others quickly tie the human bundle and bind the hands behind it.

One of the men who sleeps at the end of the gallery drags himself quietly and is able to see the guards carrying the bundle down the stairs toward the gate where the death truck, motor running, awaits to transport the entire detail to the cemetery walls. The jail is shaken by the information relayed from one inmate to another. Here in the classroom we are all awake, whispering in the dark, shocked by the screams and the commotion.

The tailor's voice is heard saying, "If they've taken that pitiful half man . . . what hope can there be for us? If we had any balls at all we'd start a revolt and die fighting, like men."

"I've heard that before," Andrés says. "Listen, Gómez, if we just stood up from our mattresses now they'd cut us down like flies, and I remind you we don't even have pins with which to carry out your revolt. Come on, the war is not lost, and that alone checks the "sacas" somewhat. They are afraid of reprisals later, when we win. They know damned well not one of them will come out alive. Granted that our situation is serious, but we still have the hope that our number won't come up in the list."

"He's right," echoes Antonino Judit.

As a counterpoint to the terror that spreads over the jail, the watchman's dog across the street keeps up his barking and whining long after the death truck starts down the road.

Next morning we learn that not all the guards have a stone for heart. One of the soldiers of the detail that helped put the bundle of the legless hunchback on the truck had to be excused from duty for the rest of the night and sent home on sick leave.

RESCUES AND EXECUTIONS IN HARO

The Chemistry Hall was a convenient source of news and com-mentaries, perhaps because so many of its inmates were educated men. One of them was Benigno Marroyo, ex-principal of Logroño's Junior College and a retired professor. Despite his almost seventy years, he was able to withstand that purgatory for a long time. But he died shortly after being granted freedom.

Among others held there were the Azpilicueta brothers, wealthy planters from Fuenmayor whose wineries were well known all over Rioja. There was a marked contrast between the brothers. Félix, the eldest, was of heavy build and quiet temperament. The other one, Patricio, was short, slender, and restless. He had the habit of strolling in the courtyard, head bent, hands clasped behind his back, repeating a phrase that made him famous in that part of the build-ing: "How deep we are in this!"

When the Franco authorities found it necessary to seek funds and foreign currency to support the war, they began sending emissaries and secret police agents from the Civil Government to our jail, try-ing to start negotiations with some of the well-to-do prisoners, offer-ing them freedom for a sum. There was much coming and going of that sort with the Azpilicueta brothers. Patricio, from the start, wanted to negotiate at any price. But Félix counseled moderation and kept up dickering and bargaining. Finally they agreed on the sum of 500,000 pesetas. The money was drawn from a foreign bank and both brothers were set free. As a parting gift to their friends they left behind a substantial cache of food they had been hoarding as a protection against possible restrictions.

We read the flowery account of their release in a local newspaper that passed from hand to hand on our floor:

'The Azpilicueta brothers of the town of Fuenmayor have made a splendid donation of half a million pesetas to the common defense of our cause for the glory of the new Spain. Let their generous deed be an example to others who, being able to do as well, try to evade or reduce their contributions to our crusade.'

Three wealthy planters held in the main floor also were able to purchase their freedom. A different case was that of a young man also being held at the Chemistry Hall. He was the son of an important member of the Leftist Republican Party, Cervera, an educator, who had managed to escape to Madrid. As a retaliatory arrest, his son—who had no political affiliation—was jailed instead. He was a tall, handsome young man, the picture of courage and health. Perhaps for that reason he was granted his freedom and . . . sent to the war front in Aragón.

Another veteran at the Chemistry Hall—veteran in years as well as in Republican struggles—was Bonifacio Aldana. This man had four sons: one, a journalist, and another, an Assault Guard, were away in Madrid; the other two were employees of Logroño's Municipal Public Works. Aldana occupied a place at the Chemistry Hall right next to a window. Near him there was a retired fireman and I never saw them far from one another; they were each other's shadow. I remember their anxious faces as we talked about the war. The retired fireman kept a batch of old newspapers hidden in his mattress as if they were priceless old documents.

Little did I know that one day in New York I would meet Aldana's journalist son and be called upon to tell him what I knew of his father's death. Aldana and his fireman friend had been taken from another cell, but next morning their mates spoke of their last moments. Aldana had walked out in quiet dignity, but the fireman lost control of his legs and had to lean on the guards escorting him all the way to the death truck.

Toledo has been taken by the rebel army of Africa, thus ending the siege surrounding the Alcázar, the Infantry Academy where the fascists had entrenched themselves. As usual, the fascist victory is celebrated with the pealing of bells. For some reason—perhaps because of the fascist victory news they feature—some newspapers reach the Chemistry Hall and we read the official Franco version. Marino brings in two newspapers and, while two mates keep an eye on the gallery, we gather in the classroom and leaf through them. There is a photo of Colonel Moscardó, commander of the besieged forces, on the first page. The information is almost identical in both newspapers. The liberating forces were commanded by General Varela, but the contact with the fascists barricaded in the Alcázar was made by Lieutenant Lahuerta with a company of Moors on the night of September 27th. There is one episode pertaining to the siege which causes many comments among us: the interview of Colonel Moscardó with Vicente Rojo.

Major Rojo belongs to the small group of officers who have remained loyal to the Republic. He is a straightforward, honest, and extremely capable soldier, professor of the College of War. Marino reads us a description of one of the negotiation attempts in which the Republic proposed the capitulation of the Alcázar at the start of the siege. Major Rojo, officially representing the government, walked into the room that was serving Moscardó as headquarters and said, 'At your orders, Colonel.'

"That's a lie!" exclaims Antonino. "No one would address a traitor rebel like that."

Marino reads on. When the negotiations failed and time came for farewells, some young rebel officer proposed to Major Rojo that he remain with them in the Alcázar.

'I can't,' Rojo replied, according to the newspaper. 'If I stay with you my wife and children will be shot tonight in Madrid.'

"That's ridiculous!" Antonino exclaims again.

"Maybe all this is a bunch of lies," the teacher tells him. "But the fall of the Alcázar, of Irún, San Sebastián, and Badajoz are not lies. And there'll be more defeats until we build our army." To that, no one objects. After a thorough reading of the newspapers we talk for hours about this new fascist victory.

The siege began around July 20th, 1936. It is doubtful that the fortress could have been defended by the cadets, since the academy was closed for the summer and its director and most students were away on vacation. Only a small group of pupils and instructors of the School of Gymnastics—of which Colonel Moscardó was chief—

were present. The principal defenders were the Civil Guards from the surrounding small towns, who abandoned their posts, took refuge in the fortress and there joined the rebels.

Another episode that has two versions:

According to the fascists, the chief of the Republican Militia, Cándido Cabello, telephoned rebel Colonel Moscardó at the Alcázar and offered to save the life of his son, Luís, in exchange for the surrender of the fortress. When the father rejected the offer, his son, who was Cabello's prisoner, was executed. If certain details to the contrary are taken into consideration, the episode becomes a myth. It is said that Luís Moscardó was nowhere around Toledo in those days. And it is a mystery how a telephone conversation could have been established between the fortress and the city when the water supply and the light and power lines had been promptly cut off at the start of the siege.

Among the 570 women who took refuge in the Alcázar were the wives of the defenders as well as the hostages taken by the rebels when they had to retreat into the Alcázar forced by the advance attack of the militias sent from Madrid. Those hostages, among them families of prominent Republicans of Toledo, were taken by the rebels into the Alcázar at pistol point. The deaths and sufferings of this defenseless group during the siege throw a shameful shadow on the military glory of the feat. The greater part of the credit belongs to the Civil Guard garrison because of their tenacity, discipline, and blind obedience to the commands.

It is inconceivable that Moscardó was unable to give his wife and two children the same asylum and protection he gave to the families of the defenders of the fortress, for under the circumstances, no one could doubt that if the rebels held Republican families as hostages in the Alcázar, the Republicans would do likewise with the fascist families left behind in Toledo.

In one of the small rooms facing our gallery, there is a prisoner in solitary called Iscar who enjoys the reputation of being the finest auto body mechanic in the province. He is fair, strong, and quite impulsive. We've tried to make contact with him, but only once have we succeeded in passing him some cigarettes, matches, and a little food, all thanks to a dispensary orderly who has befriended Antonino. Iscar has been held incommunicado for so long that there are rumors that he may be verging on insanity.

As on every morning, this hazy autumn one brings us news and comments regarding last night's "saca." Antonino, who has been called to the main gate to receive a gift parcel, tells us the rumors he picked up on the way:

Fifteen men were taken from the main floor, among them two from Logroño; four were taken from the nearby galleries, all from the town of Lardero. And . . . we lost Iscar, too. Antonino was told that he walked out firm and impassive, like a rock. "Heaven is full of bastards," he said with a venomous spit as he stepped into the death truck. "So, give me a ticket for some other place."

Iscar's son, recently called to military service, was doing guard duty in the jail last night. The officer of the guard managed to send him elsewhere on some pretext and save him the sorrow of watching his father depart in the truck of the condemned.

In a few days, Antonino Judit finds out that Iscar's son did not learn of his father's execution until the following afternoon.

The eldest among us in the arithmetic classroom is a vivid-eyed, slight man called Pascual. He is over sixty and wears his white hair closely cropped. Of all the men sent to this cell from nearby towns, old Pascual is the most talkative and affectionate. I often hear him speak of the assassinations that took place in his pueblo, but he never fails to sing the praises of a priest whom he says had saved his life. The priest was kind to other paisanos who never set foot in his church, he assures us. Unlike the other clergymen, who as Pascual says, behaved like hyenas.

The "saca" system has been organized to perfection by lawyer Olabuenaga, the warden's right-hand man. The mattresses we spread around the walls at night must occupy the exact place assigned to each prisoner, and each place must coincide with a number registered in the office files. Thus any change in the placement of the pallets must be registered immediately with the front office, usually by the corporal's aide in charge of the cell.

Two nights after they executed Iscar, the "saca" list includes two of our cellmates, both peasants. The macabre overture that precedes the "saca" is invariable: We hear the motor of the approaching truck, then the voices of the guards. Keys turn, locks open, then steps approach with much creaking of leather boots, and finally . . . the arrival of the patrols in the cells. Whether in the classrooms or out in the gallery, they click their flashlights on the pallets and count mattresses, and when they arrive at the place of a condemned man, they flood the flashlight on his face. If the man is sleepy or slow, they give him a slight kick at the same time that they say: "Up!" And once the man is on his feet, they verify his name.

Tonight, in the silence and anguish of our cell, they walk in looking for number eight, one of the peasants. Old Pascual lies next to him, and by mistake, the light flashes on his face. The guards realize their error immediately, and the light then moves slightly to flash on the right man. It is the first and last time that I learn of such a near-fatal mistake in the execution ritual, and it all happens right next to me, for old Pascual sleeps by my side.

As the guards disappear with our two unfortunate "compañeros," I think I can hear Pascual's heart pounding like a stalling motor about to choke and stop. I get up from my mattress and join three other mates around his bed. The old man lies convulsed, his mouth twisted in a horrible rictus, his few teeth chattering, unable to react or hear us.

Sesma, our corporal's aide, runs out to the infirmary for help, but they tell him it's too late to do anything tonight. There is nothing new about fear and shock in this jail, but if the old man is not better by morning, they'll notify the prison doctor.

None of us can sleep tonight, fearing that Pascual could die momentarily. In the morning, a medical aide and two orderlies bring a stretcher and take him to the infirmary. Without regaining consciousness, Pascual dies in a few hours.

I have another attack of back pain and there is no more morphine in jail. The wounded in the front lines need it worse. I get some other drug instead. It acts faster, but leaves the same sensation of freezing cold and as much lack of appetite as morphine.

Again gift parcels are restricted, and the only available food, the revolting stew, sets the men dreaming deliriously about succulent banquets of their own invention. Some of them try to get on the sick list, hoping to receive medical authorization for food parcels. But

Medrano, the prison doctor, tends to the line promptly and efficiently, saying no to the sick and the well, alike. I am the only one
granted a concession in the line: a bottle of milk at each meal in
lieu of the hated stew. None of my mates envy me the privilege. To
them, milk is only for the children and the aged.

As soon as the restriction is lifted, I have a chance to eat the best
potatoes I have ever tasted. Marino shows me a casserole his mother
has just brought him, urging me to taste its contents. To please him,
I take the wooden spoon and pick up a small morsel. From then on
he never has to urge me again. His mother is a gourmet cook and
her potatoes are a rare delicacy.

Our teacher is a music lover and he whistles quite well. Two of
his favorite compositions are excerpts from Borodin's *Prince Igor*
and De Falla's *Amor Brujo*. He also sings Aragonese jotas and some
popular songs. But our great flamenco expert is the Andalusian
stoker, Barrera.

One day I ask Marino about his friend, the mayor of Villamediana. All he knows is that the man was executed together with many
others of his town. I remember the mayor, always smiling. They
used to call him "the lion of Villamediana." The nickname has nothing to do with arrogance. He was a man of few words, but everyone
in his town knew he would always say the right ones. The mayor had
taken part in the uprising of Jaca in 1930, when the famous captains
Fermín Galán and García Hernández attempted to proclaim a republic and succeeded only in bringing about a state of repression
and their own execution along with thousands of arrests. The mayor
of Villamediana was jailed in Madrid's model prison, where his open
manner and excellent ball-playing made him popular. One afternoon
he was playing with Don Fernando de los Ríos, the eminent professor and distinguished Spanish socialist. Suddenly the mayor noticed a pair of well-shaped legs on one of the seats facing the jail
court. Some woman visitor was watching the game, and the mayor,
enchanted, forgot everything else. Suddenly he heard Don Fernando's imperious voice calling his attention: "Mr. Mayor, watch
the ball, not the audience!" This became a favorite story of the intel-
lectual Republicans who patronized the café Los Leones in Logroño.

Marino is one of the most cultured and educated prisoners in the arithmetic classroom, and in our conversations with our fellow inmates of the Chemistry Hall he often talks about the considerable progress in education made by Spain during the Republic. With Don Fernando de los Ríos as Minister of Education, ten thousand new schools were built in urban centers, and the traveling theatre of the university, "La Barraca," brought Spanish classic theatre to remote corners of the nation under the direction of poet Federico García Lorca. We often talked of Federico. . . .

The repression has been particularly bloody in Granada. Its Socialist mayor, Montesinos, Federico's brother-in-law, was among the first assassinated in Granada at the outbreak of the fascist Movement. A few days later, at the peak of his career, the young poet, too, was murdered. All of Spain knows about this despicable crime by now, and Marino still can't reconcile himself to the irreparable loss.

The progress and culture brought about by the Republic has been a source of particular resentment among the reactionaries: the new freedom in public education, the many provincial cultural atheneums that have been established, the founding of "La Barraca." As a consequence, the fascist rebellion has been very severe with teachers and professors. There is hardly a cell in this jail where two or more of them are not being detained. And there are dozens of them out in the gallery. Marino himself is convinced that his profession rather than his political views was the cause of his arrest.

I lost sight of Marino when I left the Industrial School jail, and months later, when I returned to the Avenida prison, I heard he was still one of the survivors in our arithmetic classroom.

In one of the galleries close to our cell there is a railroad worker called Lucas, a man of herculean strength and proportions. His robust constitution withstood the tremendous beating he got when they arrested him. He still has the marks of the rifle butts on his back. One afternoon we gather out in the gallery and hear Lucas tell of the executions that took place in Haro, his home town. The chief of the execution patrols there was Acedo, a well-known ex-soccer player. We had traveled together to play in the Olympic games in Paris in 1924, as members of the Spanish team. I found him insincere and boastful, so he was the only man on the team with whom I didn't become friends during that trip. Thus, when I hear Lucas mention his name today, I stay with the group and listen to his account of Acedo's subhuman cruelties. One of his games was to bet the rest of the execution patrol that his bullet would pierce his victim's right or left eye, his mouth, or some other part of his anatomy. The wager was the coffee or wine bill, or cigars, or even money, placed amidst much laughing and joking in some tavern.

If for some reason the executions would stop for more than a couple of days in the town of Haro, Acedo and his gang of murderers would march to the City Hall or the Civil Guard headquarters, and make their demands to the tune of this ditty: "Acedo and his band are hungry and need fresh meat!"

Lucas was executed shortly after I left the Industrial School jail.

The German and Italian air forces that made their appearance at the start of the rebellion, are joined in our region by broad contingents of infantry and mechanized artillery. As provisional billets for such large foreign reinforcements, the falangists have had to use several small pueblos and even some cities of the north zone, just as they did a few months before in the south. The German division of volunteers, the "Condor Legion," set up headquarters in Burgos and Salamanca. One of the prisoners of the gallery elicits much laughter among the men when he tells us that the German High Command has taken over two of the principal whorehouses in Burgos. This new inmate has been transferred to Logroño from Burgos, and he tells us an emergency infirmary had to be set up at the foot of the stairs leading to the rooms of the whorehouse, where a Nazi sergeant of the medical corps immunizes the German soldiers against venereal diseases with a shot. The foreign volunteers are thus equipped to fight their first combat: in Spanish beds.

One of the barbers smuggles in for me a note from Fermín of Nájera who is still at the Avenida jail. The letter abounds in flowery exaggerations and praises me to high heaven, leaving me half amused, half embarrassed. The month of October is here and the pueblos and cities of the province have already paid their tribute to the war, with the bulk of their manpower in jail, executed, or sent to the fronts. But the local falangists are not satisfied, and soon they fall upon Logroño, demanding the lives of whatever citizens of the small towns are imprisoned here. Among them is Fermín. I hear about it from a prisoner recently transferred to this jail from the Avenida. Fermín has been in charge of reading the nightly "saca" list, and one night as he was performing this duty his eyes came upon his own name. Right at the entrance of the court he fell prostrate with a heart attack, the accursed list crumpled in his hand. Still unconscious, he was carried into the death truck to join the rest of the victims of that night.

The barbers come every two weeks. There are four of them working constantly in this jail and it takes them all that time to get around. They are good at their job. They also lend themselves to pass messages from friends and relatives. But we can't get a word out of them about the war. One of them tells us the reason: They are put in jail and their tools are confiscated if they dare give us any news regarding the military situation. Since many falangists have sworn to let their beards grow until they can take Madrid, we have decided to grow a mustache instead. But since we get a shave only every two weeks, there are certain days when beards and mustaches are indistinguishable on the faces of prisoners and jailers alike.

The Chemistry Hall so far has escaped the presence of a spy or a stool pigeon. All cellmates there are known to one another, thus war news can be discussed freely, something we don't always venture to do out in the galleries or in other common cells. A new prisoner arrives there, Emilio, an old playmate of mine during childhood, before I left Logroño and went to live in Madrid. He wastes no time bringing us up to date about developments. A new Basque offensive is being launched upon Vitoria, he tells us. The Republican troops are only some twelve miles away from that city, and in the outskirts of Logroño one can hear the cannon boom, echoed by the mountain-rise of Peña Cerrada. On the Aragonese front, Republican forces are close to Teruel and only a few miles from the city of

Huesca. Huesca is surrounded, and its only pass, to Jaca, has been closed by the artillery fire from the Catalonian troops. The fall of Huesca is expected momentarily. The entire first floor of the jail rejoices at the news which everyone undertakes to spread around.

THE JESUITS

The Jesuits, anxious to save the souls of those about to be executed, launch a religious campaign in the prisons. It appears that the executioners, besides having plenty of time to make their peace with God, are assured of a place in Heaven because of their participation in the holy crusade. One afternoon, we are forced to fall in around a platform erected in one of the halls. A diminutive figure mounts the dais and introduces himself as follows:

"Look at me. These robes deceive no one, and almost all of you undoubtedly know who I am. I am a Jesuit, a modest disciple of those giants of our Company of Jesus, Saint Ignatius and Saint Francis Xavier. Our mission in this world is to save souls. From the very first moment, we have been gravely concerned about those who died without the last rites of the Church. For reasons beyond our control, we have been unable to begin this noble mission before. Now that the obstacles have been overcome and with the full consent of the legal authorities, we commence the preparatory work with this lecture. The disastrous policy followed during the years of the Republic has undermined your religious traditions, and many of you here have long since forgotten and abandoned the Catholic practices which Spanish mothers always try to inculcate in their children, almost from birth."

He goes on to outline the series of lectures and the matters to be dealt with in each of them. Catholic teachings will be mixed with a little religious history and reflections on Christian ethics and morality, to end as soon as possible in confession and a general communion when "the proper time" comes. In view of the lack of time and the magnitude of the topics to be discussed, it is impossible to expand on the subject at proper length, but he offers his help and advice about any doubts which might arise. If we so desire, anybody, "theoretically," can discuss the points dealt with in the lectures. At the end of the lesson, which lasts some thirty five minutes, he leaves, apparently convinced of the effect of his words and of our gratitude. If he knew the truth, I don't know whether that priest would leave laughing or crying, for the comments of the prisoners justify either reaction. A week later, the sermon is repeated by another priest.

Adolfo Alvarez is a young man of medium height, dark and powerful. Together we have practiced skiing in the neighboring peaks, and played tennis and other games in which his skill is outstanding. He had left for London, and later Germany, after his father's death, some years before. When he returned to Logroño, he spoke both English and German. Now a married man, he earns his living mainly by giving English lessons.

One afternoon, in the café Los Leones, we were discussing Hitler's rise to power in Germany and the conversation degenerated into disdainful mockery of the Fuehrer. Adolfo Alvarez, who had only recently arrived from Munich, interrupted with words which were to prove prophetic:

"That man is no laughing matter," he said. "His influence over the German people is immense and the youth look upon him as a Messiah. Out of curiosity, I went to one of his meetings and I have seen tens of thousands of people electrified by his words. If he remains in power, I am very sure that the peace of Europe will not last very long."

"But, who thinks about war nowadays?"

"With that mustache, he could never get anywhere except in the circus," etc., etc.

Another of the occupants of the Chemistry Hall is a middle-aged schoolteacher named Ruano, who was forced by the Fascist revolution to postpone his wedding. During the first burnings of convents, Ruano offered hospitality and protection to two Jesuits who had taken refuge in his house.

The Republic was proclaimed April 14th, 1931, in an orderly manner and amidst the greatest popular enthusiasm in the country's

history. Nevertheless, the panic in the first few days was considerable and a group of Monarchists fled to France. The peaceful course
of subsequent events convinced most of the refugees to return. This
rightest group, together with the more numerous right-wing elements
who had stayed at home, immediately launched a conspiratorial
campaign against the new regime. The first Monarchist demonstration was held in Madrid in the middle of May. The meeting took
place in a house in Alcalá Street near the Plaza de la Independencia.
The windows were left open, whether because of the heat or to
attract attention, and the cries of *"Viva"* and *"Muera"* reached the
street, accompanied by the strains of the *Royal March*.

The reaction of the masses gathering on the sidewalks was to
assault the premises. Most of the people attending the meeting made
their escape over the rooftops, and only a group of nine fell into the
hands of the rioters. The police quickly arrived at the scene of the
disturbance in time to save their lives. Nevertheless, they were in a
sorry state when they were driven away in one of the patrol cars of
the General Division of Security. Popular passions flared and a few
hours later the burning of the convents began, spreading the following day to the provinces. All the priests and nuns managed to find
refuge in the private homes of friendly families and there were no
personal casualties.

Of the two Jesuits who sought refuge in Ruano's house, one was
sent to a mission and the other rejoined the Order elsewhere, later
on. The schoolteacher's confidence in his Jesuit friends' efforts on
his behalf is so great that he not only hopes to recover his liberty
but also to be restored to his post, so that he can get married. The
reality is somewhat different, and one night. . . .

After the shooting of Ruano, the "sacas" are concentrated in the
halls of the lower floor. The upper floor contributes three workers,
and two peasants from Navarra who sleep in a hall far from our
quarters. The following morning I learn that those two peasants
defended themselves like cornered beasts, and one of them went to
his death with his jaw broken by a rifle butt.

With the exception of the towns close to the Ebro, the Province
of Navarra was always resistant to liberal ideas, so there were very

few members of left-wing parties. Yet the number of people executed in Navarra probably exceeds fourteen thousand, including those transferred to Logroño who suffered the same fate. The number of executions in the province of Logroño was almost the same, and all these figures were exceeded in populous provinces like Granada, Málaga, Seville, Saragossa, Badajoz, and many others. When one remembers that almost all the 49 provinces suffered the same treatment, and that Robespierre's famous terror in Paris during the French Revolution claimed no more than a thousand victims, the cruelty of the Spanish Civil War can be gauged with some accuracy.

The alleged plots in the Industrial School prison reach their maximum intensity, and the entry of packages is frequently discontinued. Prisoners with relatives at the front begin to figure prominently in the "sacas." In this atmosphere of terror and distrust, vigilance is carried to incredible extremes. One day I receive, during a visit, a few packages of cigarettes, the gift of a friend. The guard on duty, known among the prisoners by the nickname of "Fierce Wolf," seizes the packets and opens them with great deliberation and, after breaking each cigarette in half, finally hands them over to me. When they are permitted at all, many packages are subjected to similar forms of inspection.

Luís Pereda is a taciturn fellow who sleeps in a hall near the arithmetic classroom. I met him there only recently, but when I was a child, his father, then a well-known oculist, cured me of an eye infection. Perhaps that's why I like him and speak with him frequently. Some of the prisoners avoid him, for he is a man of sour character and few words. I am with Sesma in the courtyard one afternoon, when Pereda, who has just received a visitor, approaches us. In his outstretched hands he carries a box of cookies and a few broken cigars. As he opens the box to offer us cookies, he exclaims:

"Cookies taste the same when broken in half, but these cigars. . . . What do these sons of bitches expect to find inside a cigar?"

During one of the frequent inspections, Don Pedro enters our classroom and orders an assistant to open my bag. Without conducting further searches, they leave the arithmetic classroom. This singular inspection sets me wondering if, as a result of some denunciation, I have appeared to be mixed up in the alleged plots which they continually claim to exist in the prison.

About this time, I again feel excruciating pains in my back and chest which interfere with my digestion. My wan complexion and the 40 pounds I lost make me look like a ghost. But I manage to keep my spirits up. The Republic controls almost all the country's economic resources and cannot lose the war. That chimera is my consolation.

It is almost impossible to receive news from the isolated women's section. Most of the female prisoners come from nearby towns, but there are several local cigar workers. One of them is shot around this time. Arrested in their homes, they were taken to the dungeons of the local Municipal Building amidst the insults and occasional stone-throwing of spitting crowds and street urchins, whose cruelty is greatly encouraged by the authorities. The second part of their Calvary consisted of purging with castor oil, cropping of the hair, and transportation to Logroño.

Also assigned to the Chemistry Hall are the concierge of the local Republican Left headquarters and one of his sons. The concierge endures his imprisonment with great equanimity. Some months later, he is released, at the same time that his son is drafted into the fascist army.

Lusa is the son of the only Protestant pastor in Logroño and another of my friends in the classroom. A slender youngster, with a very pale face, he earns his living playing the violin. A single glance at his kindly features is sufficient to convince anyone that violent words and actions have no place in his character. As in the case of Ruano, his wedding has been delayed by his arrest. Perhaps because of his age, Lusa's father was not molested, but his chapel was completely destroyed.

The violinist was a great admirer of the philosopher Ortega y Gasset, and still more of Rabindranath Tagore, of whose work he knew many lines whose beauty moved me to the point of subsequently reading many of his works.

JUANITO AND
DON CRISANTO

There is a rowdy sixteen-year-old boy in one of the nearby galleries who has become quite popular because he's always laughing and joking, always ready to scurry around with messages, outwitting the guards, which seems to give him great pleasure. Together with other teenagers, he participated in the burning of convents, some months ago. His companions have joined the falangists and enlisted as volunteers. Before leaving for the front, they made Juanito a parting present: a denunciation with every kind of incriminating detail. When the youth was arrested and taken to the Civil Government for questioning, his defense could not have been simpler: "I only burned a wooden bench," he kept repeating for an hour. Weary of that monotonous litany, the tribunal ordered the guards to take the boy out of the room. According to prison gossip, the order was executed amidst some well-aimed kicks to Juanito's tender backside.

Everyone believes that the boy is out of reach of the execution patrols, if only because of his youth. Months later, I have the sorrow of being informed we were quite wrong. Juanito was executed.

Roberto, a young teacher from Soria, joins the group headed by Adolfo Alvarez at the Chemistry Hall. He attributes his accidental arrest in Logroño to denunciations made by some of his colleagues.

The province of Soria was held by the Republicans for two days, until the Navarrese column of General Escámez crossed the mountain pass of Piqueras. The Civil Governor and the chief of the Civil Guard made a gentlemen's agreement to respect each other's lives and help one another flee, depending on the turn of events. The chief of the Civil Guard kept his word. Before General Escámez reached

Soria, he took command, proclaimed the province in favor of the rebels, and helped the Civil Governor escape to Madrid.

This afternoon teacher Roberto joins us in reminiscing about the advent of the Republic in 1931.

"I used to live in Madrid then," he says. "But I would often go to Soria to visit my mother. As was everyone else, I was elated by the change of regime, particularly the improvements the new government began making immediately in the field of education. One of those visits to Soria happened on my mother's birthday. We celebrated it with a big dinner and invited some relatives, among them a distant uncle of mine. He was a person of renown and importance in the local parish. During the dinner I talked with enthusiasm about the new large national budget for education, the new schools, the increased number of teachers, all of them matters of professional importance to me. My distant uncle interrupted me.

'What we need in Spain is *good* children,' he said. *'Not* cultured children.'

"I think I would've thrown the soup bowl at him if my parents hadn't been present."

Now Roberto tells us a story about an old teacher, an anecdote he heard from one of his young colleagues.

"Don Crisanto was one of those old-fashioned teachers whose method consisted of wielding a strong long ruler like a magic wand. That ruler had the extraordinary power to pound into his pupils' heads all sorts of things: numbers, letters, lessons, patriotic songs, Christian doctrine, etc. Don Crisanto's great weakness was his love of culture. He was ready to make any sacrifice to spread and defend it. In the small town where he lived and taught, everyone knew that his was the largest and best library for leagues around. Often he would point to the books stacked neatly on the shelves and tell his pupils, 'There, among books, you will find your best friends and your spiritual nourishment when you grow up.'

"The great champion of culture would enrich his library with new acquisitions he purchased to commemorate historical dates. The price and quality of the volume depended on the importance of the date. The year before the advent of the Republic, for instance, in 1930, Don Crisanto celebrated the king's birthday by ordering from Madrid the complete works of the Spanish classics, attractively bound in imitation leather. The purchase left its mark on the old teacher's savings, but no matter. With one supreme sacrifice, bursting with joy and pride, he made the most important acquisition of his life: the forty-eight-volume Espasa Encyclopedia, profusely illustrated with maps, engravings, drawings, in the opinion of Don Crisanto the greatest monument to Hispanic culture and civilization. That purchase had exhausted his savings, brought him no end of privation, and even prevented him from marrying. This last sacrifice was the greatest. At times Don Crisanto thought about a young woman who now was the wife of a rich merchant of Segovia. . . . But no matter. With one look at the neatly stacked forty eight volumes of the encyclopedia, Don Crisanto would regain his peace of mind. Since his life was dedicated to culture, he could have done no less. On the other hand, possession of that monument to knowledge— the only one for leagues around his pueblo—brought Don Crisanto such satisfaction he doubted he could have found its match in married bliss.

"In those volumes of the encyclopedia he had human knowledge at his fingertips. There he could find the answers to the questions his devilish pupils often would throw at him hoping to trip him; there he found the answer to his own questioning doubts. If the exact date of some remote event in Spanish history kept him awake at night, all Don Crisanto had to do now was put his cape over his nightgown and walk into the library only a few steps away. The famous encyclopedia never failed to send him back to bed comforted with the answer, now ready to sink comfortably into sleep.

"After the outbreak of the fascist Movement, the turn of events placed Don Crisanto's little town quite close to the front lines of Sigüenza, so when the old teacher saw the fascist columns of General Mola marching triumphantly through the town's street, he was seized with patriotic fervor. At last the Spain of El Cid and the great conquistadores was surging like the phoenix from its ashes, he exclaimed. He ran to the basement to fetch the faded flag of the old regime, ran up to the school balcony, and raised the monarchist banner on the mast, as he used to do in other days on every holiday. As the troops passed by the schoolhouse, Don Crisanto applauded rapturously.

'To Madrid!' cried the enthusiastic officers as they led the soldiers, brimming with pride and hope under the glaring sun. 'We are going to take Madrid!'

'Make a great Spain, and don't you forget to build schools!' cried back Don Crisanto, much like a teacher tells his class.

"Two days later those very troops that had marched deliriously through the little town, reappeared in total disarray, running disbanded as they cried, 'The Reds are coming! The Reds are coming!'

'The Reds?' asked Don Crisanto. 'What Reds? I don't understand. . . .'

'The Marxists, the savages! They'll cut your head off! They'll kill everyone!'

'Then, this is the end,' exclaimed the dismayed teacher. 'Good-by culture, good-by civilization . . . !'

"The troops recovered from panic, and once discipline was reestablished, they entrenched themselves in the town. Don Crisanto ran to take cover in the house of friends to await the worst. The combat started, with the fascists well barricaded at the town's gates and able to resist the heroic attacks of the militias. Next day a voice was sent to spread the news all over town: The militias had received substantial reinforcements from Madrid and now were ready for a formidable assault. The town shook with fear.

'What will happen if they pass the gates?' Don Crisanto asked a sergeant assigned with his soldiers near the door.

'They'll raze everything with blood and fire. They won't respect anything. Life, property, honor. . . . They'll destroy the church, the school, they'll burn the books.'

'Not the books!' cried the teacher. 'The books are sacred, and I'll defend them with my life! Culture should be above wars.'

"A few hours later the Republican forces pressed ahead. The outer defense began yielding, and the fascists had to retreat to the center of town. The captain ordered a concentration of all forces behind barricades constructed from whatever could be found in the town. The platoon standing near the school ran into the building. There was no time to lose, the enemy was already in command of several accesses to the town. In a few minutes, furniture, desks, books, etc., went flying out the windows. Meanwhile, Don Crisanto, at the home of his friends, was worried sick. "Maybe the Reds are here already. My duty is to go to the school and make sure they respect the rights of culture.' His friends tried to keep him there with them, but Don Crisanto escaped and ran out of the house.

"He gasped with rage when he reached the school and found it a shambles. He was ready to face those savage Reds and accuse them of ravaging the school and all that meant culture and knowledge. He looked at the parapet they were building up in a frenzy, and saw the fascist troops obeying orders from a sergeant and filling gaps in the barricades with volumes of his cherished encyclopedia.

'Cannibals!' the teacher cried pointing an accusing finger at the sergeant, who, busy with the immediate business of building the barricades, paid no attention. Don Crisanto could not restrain himself. He climbed up the parapet and tried to pick up a few volumes. When the sergeant looked up and saw that madman exposing himself to the enemy, he called, 'Imbecile! Can't you hear that barrage of bullets above you?'

"Just then, Don Crisanto fell inside the barricade, his forehead bleeding, his arms still embracing a few books.

"When at last the militias took over the town, one of the prisoners told them about Don Crisanto and his last desperate gesture. Moved by the story, the Republican soldiers picked up what books they could find and returned them to the school. Then, they laid Don Crisanto in the town square, with a sign that said:

'Killed in defense of Culture and Civilization.' "

Roberto finishes his story and sinks into the prisoner's customary post-narrative silence. A few days later he is transferred to Soria. Some say to be executed there. We never learn his fate or hear from him again.

THE LITTLE BURRO
OF SEÑOR JUAN

Sesma, the corporal's aide in our cell, is a sober man, a good person, and a fine cellmate. He likes to keep everything in order and follows the cleaning regulations relentlessly. His fastidiousness arouses some critical comment among the men in the arithmetic classroom. When he senses a bit of tension, he tells us a funny story out of the endless supply of popular lore he knows so well. In one of my last afternoons in this prison, Sesma tells us an old traditional peasant tale.

Señor Juan was a kind, witty villager, married to Señora Fabiana. Fabiana was the answer to Juan's dream: a fine wife, a good woman, always ready to accede and concede. Theirs was truly a happy home. Juan used to like to travel to other towns to attend yearly festivals and open market days, often in quest of gypsy traders, among whom Juan was well liked and very popular despite being an outsider, thanks to his wit and generosity.

Once he took his nice little burro, Rayo, to a festival, and some gypsies fell in love with it and wanted to buy it. Señor Juan had no intention of selling his fine little jewel, his only means of transportation. But the gypsies insisted so relentlessly, that Señor Juan said he would think it over and return next day after consulting with his Fabiana.

Next day Juan tucked five silver peso coins under the burro's saddle, close to the back. The money was so placed that, by pulling the burro's tail slightly, a peso would slide out and fall to the ground. Señor Juan went to meet the gypsies, and after telling them of the inexhaustible treasure hidden inside the little burro, he said he would sell it for two thousand pesetas. Of course, the gypsies didn't believe him. And . . . who was going to spend two thousand pesetas for a burro, however cute and sprightly? But that of the treasure was something else. Still wary, the head gypsy came closer and pulled Rayo's tail, and accordingly, a peso silver coin dropped to the ground. After a second try, with much haste and in fear that Juan would change his mind, the gypsies quickly closed the deal and took home their little walking silver mine, while Juan just before parting, recommended that Rayo be given the best possible food, put to sleep on sheets and covered with good blankets, for he was prone to catch cold.

When señor Juan got home he told his Fabiana the story during dinner, boasting of the joke he had played on the gypsies. Fabiana didn't laugh, however. She was terrified at the thought of the terrible revenge that sooner or later the gypsies would plot. But Juan paid no mind. "Don't worry, dear. It'll all be straightened out with another joke. You'll see."

The gypsies' house became a wreck. The five silver pesos had been spent and no more were coming from the burro's belly. Meanwhile the burrito had eaten all their food and torn their sheets and blankets to shreds. In desperation, the gypsies took Rayo to one of the meat markets near the Moderno Theatre and . . . sold him to a butcher.

Now . . . revenge! On they went, looking for Señor Juan, to kill him with their knives. But Señor Juan had the other joke prepared. He had two identical white rabbits, one of which he took with him to the café across the street, while the mate remained in the house with Fabiana. Everything was ready when the gypsies arrived looking for Juan.

"My husband is not home," she told them quietly. "But I will send this little white rabbit for him. That's what we have him for, as a messenger." Fabiana took the rabbit out of his cage, told him to go and fetch the Señor pronto, and . . . she let him out the door.

As soon as Juan, across the street, saw the white rabbit dash out of his house toward the field, he simply walked to his house, holding the other rabbit in his arms. "That's a good boy," he said to the rabbit as he walked into his house full of gypsies, and looking at Fabiana, he asked, "Here I am, dear. What do you want?"

The gypsies were fascinated.

"We had come to kill you, Señor Juan. But if you sell us that magic rabbit we'll forgive everything and give you two thousand more pesetas."

After hemming and hawing, and professing a great love for the white rabbit, Señor Juan accepted the offer. The gypsies left delighted, with the rabbit tightly tucked in the chief's arms. Needless to say, in the first test, the rabbit ran to the fields and was never seen again. The gypsies damned their stars. Two brazen frauds and the loss of four thousand pesetas! This would be the end of Señor Juan. Exactly what Fabiana told her husband. "This will be the end of you, Juan. They will kill you and I will be left alone in this world of thieves."

"Don't worry, Fabiana. Nothing will happen so long as I can keep playing jokes on them."

And when Juan went past his balcony and saw the gypsies coming up the street, he quickly closed the door, took a wine boot and filled it with thick red wine, and then put the boot down Fabiana's wide blouse. "Hold it near your heart," he warned her.

"When the gypsies walk in I'll stab you with the knife in the heart, that is, in the wine boot, and the blood will spurt out and you will drop to the floor. Agreed?"

"Agreed. I'll die as well as María Guerrero, our great actress. But make sure you stab the boot and nothing else."

"Don't worry, darling. One more thing: As soon as I play the guitar, you will arise slowly, resuscitated by the music, agreed?"

"Agreed. There they are. Open the door."

Juan opened the door to a pack of raving men with brandished knives.

"I know you've come to kill me," Juan said dramatically. "But before I die I will kill my wife and save her the indignities you no doubt have in store for her." And running to Fabiana, Juan pulled out his knife and sank it into her. Immediately gushes of "blood" began spouting from her chest as she dropped to the floor. The gypsy clan was terrified.

"Don't anyone despair," Juan announced, raising a hand. "I kill my wife any time I feel like it, but I have this guitar to bring her back to life. Watch."

He strummed and struck a few chords on the guitar, and Fabiana began to give signs of life until she stood up to a glorious crescendo. There was no doubt about it, the guitar was a miraculous, enchanted object. Again the gypsies told Juan that all would be forgiven if he consented to sell them the guitar. But Señor Juan was feeling magnanimous that day and decided to give it to them as a gift. He also invited everyone to a conciliatory glass of wine.

As soon as the gypsies got home, they stabbed their wives and immediately after raked and racked the guitar . . . to no avail. The women did not budge from the puddles of blood on the floor. This time the fraud was too much and the gypsies simply broke into Juan's house, put him in a sack, and took him down the road toward the Ebro river.

"Good-by my Juan," Fabiana cried disconsolately at the door. "Good-by forever."

"Never mind," Juan shouted from the sack. "I'll see you tomorrow. And make sure you have cod with tomatoes for lunch."

The gypsies carried the sack down the road, but before reaching the river, they stopped to cool their parched throats with a glass at a little wine shop, first leaving the sack well tied to a large tree outside the shop. As soon as the gypsies went inside, Juan began shouting, "I don't want to marry that woman! Help, somebody! My brothers are taking me in this sack to force me to marry some ugly rich woman!"

A shepherd happened to pass by with a flock of goats, and hearing Juan's wails and laments, proposed that they change places: He would get in the sack, marry the ugly rich woman, and Juan could keep the goats. They agreed. The shepherd untied Juan, Juan stepped out of the sack, helped the shepherd in, and tied him, all the time congratulating him on the fortune he was going to make by marriage and also thanking him for a bagpipe that the shepherd, moved at the last minute, added to the gift goats.

When the gypsies came out of the wine shop, they untied the sack from the tree and continued their way down to the river. There they threw the sack as far as they could into the rolling stream, and while watching the poor shepherd drown, they said to each other, "Good riddance."

In a little while, they were walking on the road, back to town and presumably peace, at last, when . . . what a surprise! There was Juan sitting on a rock by the side of the road, playing the bagpipe to call his flock of goats.

"You've done me a great favor by throwing me in the river," Juan said to the astonished gypsies. "I found these goats, bagpipe and all, in the bottom of the river. There are millions of them down there! I just took what I could."

The gypsies ran back to the Ebro and jumped right in it. Just then the river rose and the great swells enveloped everyone and the whole tribe disappeared.

Señor Juan and Señora Fabiana, after attending the gypsies' funeral, left for the town of Lardero to celebrate their wedding anniversary.

꧁ **Part III**

Provincial Jail and
Transfer to the Avenida

"Revolts or submissions are alike written on the sands, merely to become the playthings of the wind. And yet, in this infinite universe, to feel that we have filled the fleeting moment with our existence, is surely something."

Georges Clemenceau

HOTEL FONTANILLAS

On a clear November evening, I lay back, half-asleep, against the rolled-up bedding, counting the slow passage of the hours, waiting. . . . Suddenly, the prison warden, Don Pedro, enters the arithmetic classroom, accompanied by two Assault Guards. The same harsh voice that shouts my name orders me to pick up my luggage—suitcase and blanket—and follow them.

I have made notes about the tales of the prisoners and the events which most impressed me, and I don't want to lose them. These notes are hidden in a hole under the table which has been my bed for almost two months.

Grabbing the little roll of paper, I wrap it in the blanket and leave the room, with the bag in my other hand, after a hasty farewell to my cellmates. They look on, puzzled and curious. They know as well as I that this is not the hour for "saca" or interrogation at the Civil Government building.

I hardly cross the threshold when I realize my folly. The search downstairs, before leaving the prison is very thorough, and there is enough dynamite in those notes, though disguised with impersonal references and symbols, to blow me into the future Valley of the Fallen. I am in a quiet panic. "Unimportant papers" have been the end of many a man in this jail. Those notes are my death sentence and it will probably be carried out within two days. Perhaps one! Perhaps this very night!

Nervous spasms contract the fingers that clutch the suitcase and my heart thumps violently. I almost stop breathing. The corridor makes a right-angled turn and the latrines are just around the corner. I react immediately and, hurrying forward, ask permission of the warden, on the pretext of an intestinal disorder from which I have been suffering for several days. My deathly pallor must have impressed him.

"Go and be quick about it. We've no time to waste."

And I lose none of it in getting rid of those papers! Never before have I left a lavatory so relieved.

At the foot of the main stairway, the sergeant of the guard opens the suitcase. The search is not as thorough as I had expected. Shortly afterwards, I get into a car whose bearded, blue-shirted driver exchanges friendly greetings with my guards. I think I hear something about the "Laguardia highway" and I venture to ask if I heard right. The older of the two guards mumbles gruffly:

"Orders are orders. You will know when the time comes."

It is useless to insist. I confine myself to peering through the windows of the car.

On the sidewalks, amidst a great crowd of Blue Shirts and Red Berets, groups of people are gesticulating excitedly. As we pass the Church of the Redonda, I see a portable altar. Everything points to the preparations for a fiesta. I refrain from asking again, in view of the previous rebuff.

Two kilometers beyond, the highway is crossed by a road which, on the right, leads to the Provincial Prison. When we reach the crossing and the car does not turn, but continues straight ahead, indifference changes to anxiety and uneasiness, those two old companions of prisoners.

Another kilometer on we are halted by four civil guards commanded by a corporal. The falangist driver gets out and hands the corporal a sealed envelope, exchanging a few words with him which I am unable to catch. Back at the steering wheel, he turns the car around with ease and drives back toward Logroño. My uneasiness vanishes.

The car turns left at the crossing and in a few minutes stops in front of the Provincial Prison, also known among the prisoners as Hotel Fontanillas. The prison is a brick building, entered through an adjoining structure with offices and guardroom on the ground floor and the warden's living quarters above. Since everything here is regulated by the penal code, he uses the title of "director," and not chief, as in the other prisons.

The office staff in charge of the reception of prisoners consists of several men seated in front of grimy tables. They proceed with the routine of registration and a very thorough search, from which even shoes are not excluded. The fear aroused in these officials by the circumstances and the strictness of their orders are the reason for such minute examination. After the formalities, a jailer takes me inside. A ditch with a double wall over twenty feet high surrounds the prison. In the outer wall there is a series of small stone sentry-boxes, strategically located and spaced, and manned by the military, independent of the internal administration of the penitentiary. The cry of the sentries, "Sentinel, alert!" at intervals during the night, will be my lullaby for several months.

After crossing the ditch, I enter a room full of soldiers and militiamen. A cloud of tobacco smoke obscures the last door leading to a roofed inner courtyard, in the center of which a glass cabin has an unobstructed view in all directions. It is there that my guide takes me. The officer on duty, a skinny little man, receives me with a grimace which may be a smile or the result of an eye irritation from the smoke of his cigarette butt. The galleries, laid out in a semicircle facing the glass cabin, are lighted by anemic little bulbs whose yellowish glow gives the whole courtyard a morbid aspect. By contrast, everything seems spacious, and my first impression is relatively good, compared to my miserable, small previous quarters. Almost all the prisoners are in the outer courtyard or in the cells. Only small groups loiter in the inner courtyard, giving an impression of ample room which is far from accurate, for this jail too is filled to four or five times its normal capacity. Some men I know greet me with signs but don't venture to come closer. Up a spiral staircase to the second floor, I follow the jailer to one of the dormitories.

After an affectionate embrace, Dr. Calvo, a long-time inmate and occupant of one of the ten beds with which the cell is normally furnished, makes room for me between his bed and a pallet. As soon as I am installed, two friends, Alfonso Mato and Manolo Alba, come over. After a brief talk with the prison official, they get permission to transfer me to their cell, about twenty yards away along the same gallery. There, I see a table made of suitcases skillfully arranged, and around it, a group of people, almost all of them known to me. I am stunned by the avalanche of questions. They want information on the war, the situation at the front, local gossip, and above all, news of relatives and friends being held at the Industrial School.

A broad-shouldered man, one of the few I'm not acquainted with, stares at me for a moment, and disappears into a small passage at the back of the room. After several days I learn the reason for that strange reaction: I was nothing but a skeleton wrapped in filthy, crumpled clothes, and the expression on my face and my general appearance had upset Jaime de la Calzada, a man whose sensibility is as great as his physical strength.

When I express my yearning for air and sunshine, the gathering moves to the outer courtyard. I take advantage of the last rays of sun, and spend the remainder of the afternoon in that same round of questions and answers.

The entire prison talks of only one thing: Madrid. The front lines are close to the bridges of the Manzanares; the loyal forces are short of ammunition. (Is it true?) The attack, headed by Moors, Italians and the Legion, began at dawn. The Socialist leader Indalecio Prieto, with his dynamism and fiery eloquence, organized the people's militia, composed of barbers, masons, bakers, etc., and prepared for anything. "No pasarán!" (They shall not pass!) To the rear of the falangist forces, everything is ready for the entry into Madrid: traffic patrols, police, officials who will take immediate control of the civil administration, caravans of vehicles filled with food, portable altars, and priests to recite the Te Deums of thanksgiving for victory. All this explains the festive air which struck me during my trip from the Industrial School a few hours ago. Where does this torrent of news come from?

When they close the outer courtyard, we return to the cell, where two surprises are waiting for me: a cot and . . . a note from Teresa! A common criminal who works in the kitchen, an ardent soccer fan supplied a cot. From now on, I need no longer sleep on the floor. I am never able to find out where he found that cot. There certainly is no abundance of them in this place. The guards make their rounds, herding the prisoners into their proper cells, and preparations begin for the evening meal. There is plenty of food and I realize that the restrictions on packages are lenient. The convicts sentenced for common crimes, a minority—about ninety—enjoy undisturbed nights, regular visits, letters, and other privileges denied to political prisoners.

I participate moderately in the feast and in the animated conversation of my cellmates. Before the lights are put out, I read again the explanation of my transfer in Teresa's letter, which she was unable to tell me of in advance. My exhaustion after the hectic day overcomes my anxiety and, for the first and last time, I fall asleep before the hour of "saca," which this night calls for three prisoners.

At dawn, a grey light filters through the bars of the window to pick out the details of the little room of three by four meters, which nevertheless is the best in the place, despite several leaks in the walls. Formerly, it was the infirmary, but the growth of the prison population forced the warden to use it as another cell. The door is barred from outside at night and opens onto a gallery with an iron railing, from which the spiral stairways lead to the inner courtyard. The cell has another, smaller door to a short passage with a barred window, leading to a tiny cubicle with a toilet, innumerable cobwebs, and a rusty bathtub—the only one in the entire jail. The lack of hot water makes it unusable in winter and its coating of rust uninviting in summer.

Five men including myself sleep in this cell, and in the short adjoining corridor sleeps "El Corbatas," a young sneak thief who for a few pesetas is willing to act as servant and errand boy. The light gradually increases until the faces of my sleeping mates become visible. Their twisted faces and postures reflect their restlessness, as if their dreams were terrible nightmares. Only Santolaya sleeps the sleep of the just. He is a fresh-faced old fellow, tall, methodical, jovial, and a vigorous snorer, fond of good wine in moderation. Next to Santolaya is Jaime de la Calzada, dark-skinned, of medium height, with uncommonly broad shoulders. His hearty, spontaneous laughter reveals big, powerful white teeth.

The name of the next sleeper is Alfonso Mato, tall and thin, with very thick glasses, considered the best lawyer in the province. The last of my cellmates is the agronomist Manolo Alba, whom we call the Prussian because of his serious character and iron will. This man is very skillful at all kinds of manual work, and thanks to his public spirit and love of cleanliness, the cell at times sparkles like a silver coin.

A noise like thunder rumbles in the distance, growing louder as it approaches. It is the officer on duty, opening up the cells. The protests of the rusty bolts reverberates in the silence of the corridors, so that even the soundest sleeper can't resist the racket.

El Corbatas always is the first to jump from his pallet on the floor of the corridor, to clean out the cell, make breakfast, and collect some package or note through the bars. Little by little, the others begin to get up, lawyer Matos and Jaime de la Calzada the last out of bed. We discuss the events of the night, if any, speculating as to places and persons, until the door to the corridor opens and our conjectures are confirmed or corrected by the occupants of the cells visited by the "saca." Afterwards, we descend to the outer courtyard which, though meager and narrow, seemed so spacious and beautiful to me the evening before and continues to seem so for a long time.

Soon the news reaches us from outside: "They haven't entered Madrid." The passion aroused by that topic is so intense that the taking of four prisoners from one of the dormitory cells hardly arouses comment. The morning greeting among the prisoners is not the usual "good morning," but "No pasarán!" The enthusiasm is so infectious that the common criminals adopt the greeting, which is general for several weeks.

Whenever I am out in the courtyard, it is sheer ecstasy just to look up at the sky. The weather is fair, with a bright sun in a blue sky and big white clouds swept by a strong wind. I feel almost free, despite walls, bars, and jailers. As winter approaches, the cold at night is intense. The prison guard on duty in the little glass cabin in the courtyard begins to use a brazier to keep warm. Every morning I watch one of the prisoners go through the elaborate ritual of preparing it.

The common prisoners occupy the jai-alai court from the early hours of the morning. Its high wall separates us from the women. At the height of one meter from the ground, one of the convicts has drawn with white chalk the horizontal fault line in the game. The balls are hard as stones and leave the hands of both veterans and beginners swollen and full of cuts. Our chief pastime is to walk, that is, to walk round and round, threading our way as best we can through the crowds that always fill the narrow courtyard. When the jai-alai court is clear, the complete circuit, following the outer wall, is of one hundred and nineteen paces, reduced to half that distance when the game is in progress.

In a corner at the entrance to the outer courtyard is the laundry washtub, which serves "El Bruto," one of the most popular convicts, as a pool when he finishes his ball games. That washtub is also Guerrero's favorite spot. Guerrero is a picturesque political prisoner who has been transformed by fear or madness into a mystical ascetic, and prefers that spot for his prayers and penitence.

Compared with other prisons, arrivals, transfers, and "sacas" are at a minimum; neither are we troubled with the supposed plots, which made the last days of my stay in the Industrial School jail such a nightmare. When the weather is bad, our meeting place and recreation center is the inner courtyard, damp and dismal. A few dim bulbs light the glass cabin and its cobweb trappings. Without those lamps, the darkness in the tiny inner courtyard would be absolute. There is no regular timetable for cleaning up in the morning. A cloud of dust rises from the upper gallery of cells facing the court, to hang suspended in the air for hours. One can almost chew the dust. The whole thing, seen for the first time, is like a fantastic ship floating in a mist.

On days when there are no visitors, the morning drags endlessly until midday, when most of the food packages arrive. Sometimes, skillfully camouflaged with the aid of the common prisoners, we receive messages from relatives and news of the war. During the visiting period, the racket is frightful. We are ushered into a kind of narrow cage, separated from the visitors by an iron grill that reaches to the ceiling. It is dark in there and the people on the other side of the thick metal mesh covering the bars seem like phantoms. Only by shouting is it possible to hold any kind of conversation.

The noise from the outer courtyard is deadened by the thick walls and reaches us like the sound of the breakers on the seashore. The visits are held in groups of twelve and last a maximum of fifteen minutes.

Compared to the revolting stew I was fed up to now, the food at Hotel Fontanillas is delicious: a plate of soup made from chickpea broth, and afterwards the chickpeas themselves garnished with a small piece of bacon and another of beef. By purchasing vouchers at a reasonable price it is possible to obtain a glass of wine with every meal. The concoction is cook León's secret. By profession he was an expert pickpocket from Madrid, where his mother works in a cigar factory. That man has such a flare for cooking that he always manages to give our stew the same tasteful flavor, despite the inadequacies of his kitchen and the excessive number of prisoners to be fed. Pacheco, the prison director, believes León capable of duplicating the miracle of the loaves and the fishes. The cook's influence in the prison is so great that it sometimes surpasses that of our jailers, the prison guards.

Chow is served in the outer courtyard in good weather, inside if it rains. Four kitchen boys serve the food to the lined-up prisoners under the supervision of a prison guard, while León, like some pagan high priest, pontificates benignly over the work of his acolytes. One of the good cook's special privileges is the monopoly of tobacco in the prison. There is gossip of a huge bank account in the name of his wife or mistress.

If, for any reason, permission for food parcels is suspended, we can make do with prison chow without great sacrifice. The prisoners' families, according to their economic resources, make great efforts to send the best they can. When the entry of food is authorized, we pool all our supplies on a collapsible table jointly purchased with permission of the director. The lively meal that follows aways ends with a brew made from chestnuts in lieu of coffee. Served by León, steaming-hot, it tastes like nectar to us.

The diners have formidable appetites and only Santolaya maintains his moderation. He says that a good cook is an old man's worst enemy.

Among our after-dinner visitors is the first prisoner I had met there, Dr. Calvo, a slight man, with grey hair and thick glasses.

Although a member of the Republican Left, he was not politically prominent. He enjoys great privileges because of his professional reputation. One of his patients has such faith in his ability that she has persuaded her husband, an important falangist, to obtain frequent permission for him to visit her at her home. Calvo's professional visits outside the prison are hedged around with all kinds of precautions. He always returns with the latest news and his arrival is anxiously awaited. Not long after this, Dr. Calvo is set free through the influence of friends and the payment of a huge fine.

Regular visitors from other cells include Celestino Ríos and Alonso Selgar, both discharged secret police agents; Práxedes Toledo, former municipal treasurer; Manuel Fernández, vice-president of the Left Republican political party; and José Arsenio, a fat, squat man with a childlike face, who owns a bakery. Many others join us occasionally.

Madrid is still the all-absorbing topic of conversation, on which all reports agree. After several assaults on the capital, which had lasted for two days, the Moorish columns were held by the people's militia, and their attempts to cross the bridges over the Manzanares River failed. Franco's army is temporarily in retreat, but, despite enormous losses, a new offensive is being prepared with greater forces and more powerful armament. The falangist local authorities believe the new attack will be irresistible. Consequently, they have given orders not to dismantle the portable altars, but to have the supply columns ready to leave for Madrid at a moment's notice.

Teresa visited me this afternoon and supplied details she had been unable to include in her letter of the previous day. She had hoped to get a special pass to bring my son, who is now almost four months old. I haven't seen him for some weeks. I found my wife very pale. (She had been ill due to difficulties with the feeding of the child, something I knew nothing about until much later.) A sentinel standing right up against the bars made it difficult for me to ask her questions, but I took advantage of every opportunity and was able to confirm that the first fascist assault on Madrid had failed.

That night, as if by magic, a map of Madrid province appears in the cell. While "Corbatas" sleeps soundly in the corridor leading to the dilapidated bathroom, indifferent to the progress of the war, we embark on a series of strategical games in which we exhaust the possibilities of attack and defense. Such is the passion we put into the game that we fail to hear the noise of the locking up of the cells preceding "lights out." The battle was cut short by darkness. Annoyed over the unexpected cessation of hostilities, we resolve to avoid any repetition of the incident. The following day, with wire and plaster smuggled in by the cook, we rig up a connection with the power lines. Alba covers up the hole in the wall with great skill, and from the outside it just looks like another moisture stain on the wall.

I soon learn the origin of other dark stains on the wall beside my bed. They were caused by dried blood absorbed by the plaster. It was at this very spot that Dr. Montero opened his veins with a nail. All sharp instruments are the object of special searches, and there isn't a single razor blade in the whole jail. On two separate occasions, when the cell door was opened and he heard his name read from the "saca" list, Dr. Montero tried to commit suicide. The first time he was taken to the Provincial Hospital. He returned, healed, only to be put back on the death list. On his second attempt, however, one of Sergeant Sánchez's assistants leaped upon him and tied his hands and wrists with the thin, hard piercing cord they have ready for the victims prior to execution. "If this son of a bitch thinks he's going to make another trip to the hospital, he's mistaken," shouted the guard.

Jaime, who witnessed the incident, tells me the story to the end. "Limp like a rag, bleeding to death, they took him into the truck and on to the pond of La Granjera, to be shot with four other men from this jail," he finishes.

Manolo Alba recalls an anecdote he heard about Dr. Montero. During a visit to a Jesuit seminary in the north of Spain, the Doctor was shown around the building. He noticed a group of novice priests in the courtyard, whose stupid expression contrasted vividly with the intelligent look of the others. Intrigued, the Doctor asked the Rector to explain the contrast. "That is one of the teams we are training to be missionaries or martyrs, as the case may be," was the reply.

Little did Dr. Montero know, as he told the story in the café Los

Leones, that he soon would be a martyr himself, without any training.

The uncertainty about the fall of Madrid disappears among us, and even the inveterate pessimists have adopted, as an article of faith, the famous Republican slogan, "No pasarán!"

THE PROSECUTOR
AND THE COURT CLERK

Of the men who were transferred to the fort of San Cristóbal during the first weeks of the Movement, some were murdered en route and others suffered the same fate in the midnight executions at the fort. These shootings took place along the winding approaches to the fort, which, together with the mountain pass of El Perdón, were the favorite places for executions in Pamplona. The remnants of these groups, decimated by the periodical purges, remained at the fort from two to five months, until a general order sent them back to their points of origin, to be distributed among the prisons of the Province of Logroño.

One morning, the portcullis is raised and some thirty men burst out into the inner courtyard in a noisy throng. In the midst of that group, clothed in rags and dirty blankets, with their bags beside them, are the former prosecutor Gilabert and the erstwhile clerk of the Provincial Court of Logroño, Antonio Ruíz, their faces framed in thick, tangled beards.

After an affectionate greeting, space is found for them in the second tier of the upper gallery. I remember that one day, in the Industrial School jail, we suddenly received the news that Antonio Ruíz and the prosecutor Gilabert had been taken from the prison at an unusual hour—two o'clock in the afternoon. "Those two won't see the sun tomorrow," had been the general comment. That evening, we learn from a visitor that a relative of Gilabert, an influential military man, had obtained an order from the Civil Governor for their transfer to Pamplona. New charges filed by lawyers and colleagues of Ruíz and Gilabert turned into accusers had made that protective measure necessary.

We are very anxious to speak with the newly arrived pair. León the cook has just arrived with the hot concoction we call coffee when our two friends appear at our cell. As the news spreads, people flock in from nearby cells, all moved by the same curiosity, until there is hardly room to move. Afraid to speak in front of so many, they reply evasively to the flood of questions, much to the disappointment of the audience. Little by little, the majority of the visitors return to the courtyard. About four o'clock after the outsiders leave, the prosecutor opens:

"We had just finished eating the meager rations of the Industrial School when Don Pedro the chief turned us over to a pair of Assault Guards, who handcuffed us and took us downstairs. A truck with its engine running was waiting in front of the exit. The driver and two falangists were seated in front. In the rear were three Requetés. One of them was a very small man, with a twisted face. "Let's go," said one of the guards laconically. We got in and the truck pulled away. Before we left, however, the two falangists moved to the back of the truck, to leave room for the two guards up front.

"We crossed the stone bridge over the Ebro, leaving Logroño behind. Soon they began to sing their songs, some obscene, some patriotic, while staring at us defiantly, until we had passed the town of Viana. One of the Requetés reached into a battered suitcase and produced a bottle of cognac, and they began to pass the bottle around. When his turn came, one of the falangists passed the bottle under our noses. The fool thought it made us sad or angry not to be able to drink with him. Suddenly, the eyes of our escort flashed, full of malice and hatred. I was sure that those criminals had orders to murder us in route. Several times, after whispering among themselves, they got up and moved about the floor of the truck. Then they resumed their singing, louder, now under the influence of the alcohol. Beyond Los Arcos, the other falangist, a fellow with shining black hair and dark rotten teeth, who was armed with a shotgun, asked:

'Don't you know this song? *Cara al sol. . . .*' He went on singing the falangists' favorite hymn. Since we did not answer, he thrust his face so close to ours that we almost touched.

'Didn't you hear me?'

'Yes, we heard you, but we don't know that song,' Ruíz replied.

'How is that?'

'We were arrested at the beginning and, as you know, they don't teach songs of any kind in jail.'

'You lie, penpusher,' exclaimed the falangist, laughing. 'As if you weren't tired of hearing it hundreds of times from outside your prison! Come on, you bastards, sing,' he added, shoving me against Ruíz.

The fat falangist interjected: 'It's very pretty and it may be your last song.'

"At this they broke into perverse laughter. Ruíz and I remained silent, with our eyes fixed on the boards in front of us.

'I always wanted to tackle a public prosecutor and a clerk of the Court of Appeals,' one of the fiends shouted.

"There was a peephole in the metal wall that separated the driver's cab from the body of the truck. One of the guards peered through it and interrupted, laughing.

'Let them alone, fellows,' he said, 'they'll soon have enough to worry about.'

'Now, that "saca" last night,' remarked the fat man, changing the subject, "was a really good one. By midnight, we had accounted for forty seven.'

When the truck stopped in Estella, the Requeté with the twisted face got out. A group of Red Berets passed and one of them threw a wineskin at the truck and all our escort drank from it. As soon as the truck started up again, the insults were resumed with renewed vigor.

'This white-collar scum is the worst. They should all be wiped out. *Maricones!*'

'They don't seem to think it has anything to do with them,' said the other Requeté. He spoke in front of us. And a large scapular hanging from his neck was visible through the open shirt. The scapular undulated in the wind, its flapping synchronized with the speed of the vehicle.

'Don't keep staring at those boards, you'll wear them out. Raise your heads a little. Do you see that straight stretch ahead? At the end, where the road turns, there's a little dell. Damn good spot for a picnic!'

"As it entered the curve, the truck suddenly stopped.

'Here we are,' shouted one of the falangists. They made us get up, and when we started to get out, giving ourselves up for dead, they changed their minds: 'Farther on,' they said. I'll never forget that trip from Estella to Puente la Reina. The same falangist who had shouted continually went to confer with the driver through the peephole. Ruíz whispered in my ear:

'It is stupid to suppose they would bring us so far just to kill us. You know it is customary to taunt and torment prisoners who are being transferred.'

"Shortly after this, the mock execution scene was repeated. This time they were not satisfied with making us get up. We had to jump down from the truck. It was a shameful farce. Antonio Ruíz could not control himself, and though he was as frightened as I was, he dared to say:

'You're a bunch of fiends!'

"The answer was a brutal blow in the back with the butt of a Mauser which left him stretched out on the ground beside the wheels. The same guard who had interceded on our behalf before, now spoke up energetically:

'For a joke it's gone far enough! We have no orders to mistreat them.' And turning to me, he added: 'You're going to the fort of San Cristóbal and you needn't be afraid. Our orders are to deliver you there, so nothing is going to happen to you.'

"They picked up Ruíz, who had to be lifted into the truck and tossed into a corner, where he spent the rest of the trip groaning, his face a mask of pain. There was silence during the rest of the trip. We reached the slope leading down from the pass of El Perdón, but I did not feel at ease until we arrived at the fort. As soon as we entered the prison courtyard, Ruíz was taken to the infirmary. He returned a couple of hours later, much better, with his back heavily bandaged.

"I doubt if there is another place as unhealthy, dismal, humid, and sad as this famous fort in the whole of Spain, or even perhaps in Europe. The "sacas" and the other incidents of prison life were the same as in all these places, and you well know how bitter they are. They've destroyed my faith in my career as public prosecutor. I used to believe that charges of brutality and coercion were excuses and pretexts on the part of delinquents, but now—well, not now precisely, but some time in the future—next time I hear in the courtroom: 'They forced me, they threatened me,' I'll know better."

"There were many common criminals mixed with the political prisoners. During the first few days, we were badly housed and closely watched in a big pavilion, where we were short of everything. Finally, they transferred us to the luxury pavilion, 'Preferred,' where some thirty six prisoners lived in a somewhat less humid environment, enjoying certain privileges which money could buy. The transfer to the pavilion of the privileged was the work of a friend of Ruíz, a man with influence in Pamplona who took an interest in us.

"I have a souvenir such as several of the group of survivors have brought with them." Dipping into his bag, he fished out a piece of tissue paper, folded with great care, and hidden in the last folds of the paper was a sliver of sausage the thickness and diameter of a five-centimo coin.

"These were our meat rations at the fort."

Ignoring the amazement in our faces, the Prosecutor continues:

"There were executive officials to whom these rations seemed an extravagance. One afternoon, the regional delegate for the northern prisons toured the fort, accompanied by the warden. We could see and hear through a half-open door. 'As to rations,' said the inspector-delegate, placing a friendly hand on the warden's shoulder, 'beware of sentimentality. Remember, everything is needed for the battle fronts.' "

The gaunt, emaciated figures of the entire group which just arrived are proof enough that the delegate's admonition had not fallen on deaf ears. In the days that followed, they speak of their trials in the fort of San Cristóbal. Among their fellow-prisoners there was an engineer from Alava, who was arrested in Vitoria and transferred to Pamplona.

"His brain," remarked Ruíz, "was like a radio synchronized to receive favorable waves. He believed the collapse of fascism was a matter of days, at the most."

According to the engineer's information, there had been no more than a couple of hundred executions in the Province of Alava. This figure would seem monstrous in normal times, but now it is only a fraction of those carried out in Rioja and Navarra. (A group of prominent Alavese, including several priests, courageously marched to Burgos to submit their complaints. They did not approve of the practice of transforming into death warrants the orders for "provisional liberty" signed by the Civil Governor. The civic leaders of the province considered such practice cruel and anti-Christian. Rejecting any compromise, they obtained a kind of autonomy, unique in rebel territory, by which the massacres behind the front lines were completely eliminated in Vitoria.)

Gilabert and Antonio Ruíz, linked in the past by their professions, keep up their close friendship in prison and frequently pay joint visits to our cell. One afternoon, Ruíz shows us a Pamplona newspaper with an early August date, which he keeps as documentary proof of the role played in the Civil War by the ecclesiastical hierarchy. The article, under the title *The Case of Spain, by the Archbishop of Toledo, Cardinal Dr. Gomá,* says:

"We must destroy once and for all a preconception which could have disastrous consequences for the future. A war against communism, like the one now raging, is not a war against the proletariat corrupted by communist teachings. It would be a calumny and a crime, the germ of a future class war in which religion would inevitably be involved, to attribute to the latter an alliance with the military to humiliate the working class or even perpetuate old abuses which should not have lasted until now. The workers need not fear, whoever they may be and whatever groups or unions they may have joined to improve the position of their class. Neither the Army nor the Church are their enemies. The Army because it is engaged in a struggle to bring to Spain the peace without which orderly and remunerative work is impossible. And religion because it has always been the refuge of the unfortunate and a determining factor in charity and social justice. If it is God's will that the National Army should triumph, the workers may rest assured that, having abandoned the handicap of a doctrine and tactics which are inherently destructive to the social order, they will finally find the way to achieve satisfaction of their just demands."

"It is difficult to understand how fanaticism and hypocrisy can deform the mind of a high dignitary of the Catholic Church," remarks Manolo Alba.

"He is not the only one," adds Antonio Ruíz. "There are many others, both high dignitaries and ordinary priests. You have the example of Navarra. One day, during a visit I received at the fort, I learned about some aspects of the ecclesiastical conspiracy in Pamplona. It seems there is a certain Benito Santiesteban, a tall, thin, bent individual, suffering from tuberculosis, who owns a tailor's shop not far from the Bishop's Palace in that city. His specialty is the tailoring of cassocks and the sale of all kinds of sacred vestments. The back room of his establishment, always filled with smoke and priests, was one of the most important meeting places of those who prepared the Movement in Pamplona. That monster was the organizer of more than 15,000 murders in the Province of Navarra, and he is proud of it and enjoys the satisfaction of having done his duty for the greater glory of God."

We political prisoners are still deprived of any legal trial. El Corbatas, on the other hand, is due for his very soon.

Together with other petty thieves, he raided a cigar store. His role in the crime appears to have been secondary and his sentence will probably be six months and a day. Since he has been in jail for half a year, his liberty depends on whether he maintains his defense or modifies it a little. In view of the sneak thief's friendship with prominent members of the C.N.T., the National Federation of Workers, and the personal enemies he has in the Falange Party, Alfonso Mato advises him to modify his testimony so as to receive a slightly extended sentence. He also points out two other solutions open to him: to enlist as cannon fodder, if they will accept him in the Army, or remain exposed to prey in the dangerous environment of the town.

It was too much to ask prudence and reflection of El Corbatas at the age of twenty, when women, wine, and liberty are in sight. During his imprisonment, as a result of his services to the political prisoners, he has managed to save some money, which he can't wait to spend. The trial is held three days after our conversation and, as Mato had predicted, he wins his freedom, but doesn't enjoy it for long. He

spent the first evening of freedom going from tavern to tavern, until
he finally ended up in a brothel down by the river, from which he
was violently ejected as a result of a brawl. At daybreak, he was
seen wandering through the streets of the red light district, wearing
the tie Jaime had given him as a parting present. Later, his corpse,
smeared with mud, and a bullet wound in the temple, was recovered
from one of the sewers that empty into the Ebro.

RELIGIOUS CONFERENCES
AND THE HOLY MASS

As ever, our main topic of conversation is the fighting in Madrid,
interspersed lately with much mention of the considerable increase
in the "sacas" from the Avenida jail—fifty five in two days. In the
long hours of our confinement we also discuss the lectures delivered
for our benefit by the Jesuits. Then, there is Guerrero to keep us
pondering about his madness. Guerrero is a middle-aged greying
gentleman of culture and princely manners, whose three-tone beard
frames his milky white complexion. Most of his family lives in
Calahorra, ancient Roman town and episcopal see, so rich in
produce that it alone regulates the tomato market in the whole of
Spain. Calahorra has suffered some of the worst cruelties of the rebellion in this province. Captain Benlló, the artillery officer who
has been made civil governor, hails from there, and he for one has
punished his home town with numerous death sentences, among
them that of his own childhood nurse. "He is not a man," Ruíz says
repeatedly. "He is a monster, and the woman would have done us
all a service if she had fed him poison instead of milk."

There are still some men left here from the batch that arrived
at the end of July, and they tell us Guerrero came in during the first
days of August, together with a group of eighteen prisoners brought
by truck from Calahorra. Five of them were executed the same night

and twelve got transferred to the dreaded fort of San Cristóbal, so Guerrero is the sole survivor of his group.

Shortly after his arrival he began showing a marked hostility to some of the prisoners, and he even had a fist fight with a prison official. (Fortunately, the official was kind-hearted and punished him only with solitary confinement.) But on the following Sunday, at the most solemn moment during mass, Guerrero suddenly stood up and attempted to give a sermon. Again he was locked up in a solitary cell, and this time he spent several days without touching food. A self-imposed penance, he said, for his sins. But his cries and lamentations so disturbed his neighboring mates that repeated protests reached the administration office. Some of the men believed he was feigning insanity in an effort to save his life. Finally the prison chief ordered him transferred to the insane asylum. For three months they kept him tied up, until, thinking him cured, they returned him to the prison. If his madness was feigned then, it now seems real. He is seized by a fierce religious fervor, and although he is not physically dangerous, he does annoy everyone with his eccentricities. As a result, the poor man spends many a day cut off in solitary.

This afternoon he walks into our cell with a basket of fruit he puts on the table, urging us to give him the pleasure of sharing with him this present from his relatives. "Gentlemen," he tells us, "I am an evil sinner, although not as bad as some who send many to their deaths when they forget their religion. My penance has brought me the peace of spirit I was lacking, so now that I follow the voice of God I am a happy man. I accept punishment with resignation because I believe it is justly due to God for my past trespasses. I am not mad and I was never mad before. My former violent behavior was an expression of desperation and the fear that my cowardly, impure soul might be exposed by one of the trials with which the Almighty tests men's courage."

Some of the men smile slyly, others listen with respect to this strange man whose fiery eyes are fixed on the ceiling. Undaunted he continues, raising his voice in elegant intonations.

"I used to live then in a forest where I was the god of a tree placed between two ponds. One of the ponds was small, almost empty, and inhabited by a great number of fish. The other one was large and pleasant, shaded by a thick spread of lotus blooms. It was a hot summer and the small pond was drying up. Meanwhile, the water in the large pond, protected by the lotus growth, was plentiful and cool. It happened that a crane flew over the ponds and stopped to reflect: 'Those fish down there would be a good catch. But fish are fast and they'll escape my beak if I try to grab them openly. I'd better use some cunning.' While the crane devised her strategy, a fish looked up and asked, 'What are you doing up there, venerable crane? You seem lost in profound meditation.'

'I am thinking about you and your sorry fate.'

'Our fate? What do you mean?'

'You suffer from lack of water. With this hot weather the water will evaporate. And . . . what will become of you?'

"Upon realizing the crane's warning, the fish became frightened. 'What can we do to save ourselves, venerable crane? Have you any suggestion?'

"The crane feigned another deep reflection. 'I think I've found a solution to your problem! Right next to you there is another pond, a large one whose abundant fresh water is protected from the summer drought by a thick growth of lotus. Go and live there instead! I'll take you in my beak.'

"The fish were about to accept the crane's proposal, when a wary crab exclaimed, 'I've never seen anything like it.'

'Like what?' asked the fish.

'Like this!' answered the crab. 'When has a crane shown the slightest interest in us, save to eat us up?'

'Miserable crab!' said the crane. 'How dare you suspect such a motive! I seek only your salvation. Put me through the test. Choose anyone you want and I will carry him to the good pond. Then see what you think of me when he returns and attests to my good faith.'

"Almost convinced, the colony chose for the test trip an old and wise fish. The crane took him safely to the other pond, and let him swim to his heart's content for a while. Just as safely, she returned him to his companions. When the other fish heard the traveler tell of the marvelous deportment of the crane, they begged, 'Take us, o crane, to swim under the lotuses!'

'I'll be glad to,' the crane said. And losing no time, she again

took the old wise fish in her beak, but this time not in the direction
of the pond. She ate him and left the bones at the foot of the tree
where I was god. Upon finishing her banquet, she returned to the
half-dried pond. 'Who is next? Who wants me to fly him to the
fresh cool lotus pond?' Impatiently, the fish stood in line and took
turns, only to be devoured, one by one. The crab, the last inhabitant
left in the small pond, was thinking suspiciously, 'I doubt that my
companions are swimming in the lotus pond. They've been the
victims of their good faith. But if I don't leave this slowly drying
puddle I will perish. I'll make this old crane take me with her, and
on the way, I'll avenge my friends.' Now the doubting crab asked
the crane, 'How will you carry me?'

'In my beak, as I did the others.'

'You can't, in my case. My shell is much too smooth and I may
fall. Let me hang on to your neck. I'll be careful not to hurt you.'

"The crane accepted the suggestion, and with the crab mounted
on its neck, flew away and again stopped at the tree.

'Why are you stopping here?' asked the crab. 'This is only half
way to the lotus pond. Are you tired already?'

"Finding herself at a loss for some excuse, the crane remained
silent, whereupon the crab began crushing its neck. 'Those fish-
bones at the foot of the tree prove your betrayal,' said the crab.
'You cannot fool me, fiendish crane. Maybe I'll die, but not before
I've killed you.'

"Feeling the crab's claws closing up around her neck, the crane
pleaded tearfully, 'Don't please! I promise I won't eat you.'

'Then, take me to the lotus pond,' ordered the crab. Obediently,
the crane flew to the lotus pond and extended her neck to let the
crab drop softly on the surface. But it was no use. The crab clamped
her claws tightly and serrated the crane's neck.

'Well done, crab,' said I, the god of the tree. As you can see, my
dear jailmates, cunning is not always the victor, and sooner or later
every treacherous crane meets its crab." And, bowing in a courtly
fashion to us, Guerrero walks out of our cell.

Is that man really crazy? Where did he pick up that story? According to the men, the crane is Franco; the crab is the Republic.

I've attended two of the series of religious meetings at the Industrial School. The priest is a small, bald, roundfaced man with very pale eyes. He resumes the lecture at the point where his colleague left off previously, and goes on to preach the catechism. He makes a derogatory mention of the group of intellectuals in the audience who may consider his words naïve. The more numerous uneducated among us, he states, alone justifies his lecture. His objective is this larger group, although he assures us that the learned too may well profit from his words. After all, wise sinners like Saint Augustine and Saint Paul one day confronted truth and found the way to glory. There are roads to Damascus where the most arrogant wise men can be touched by the grace of God. Now he mentions the responsibility of every man to his soul, and then launches into an attack on our ideas which, according to him have caused this bloody civil war. To reinforce his arguments he drops a few Latin quotations, perhaps in an effort to impress those he has called intellectuals. He draws a parallel between Christ and our sufferings and announces the envy he feels for such a remote analogy.

"Imagine you are climbing an immense ladder to heaven, and that with your sufferings you take a higher step each day. That and none other is the road traveled by the Lord's favorite souls," he says. Upon comparing the sufferings of the soul with those of the flesh, he attributes little value to the latter. The crucial issue is to save one's soul.

"And since it is no use deceiving yourselves, you know well why they knock at your cell at eleven every night, and how important it is to be prepared for that trip without return. Because, at the end, only those who know God will save themselves. If you repent your sins you will appear before Him pure and worthy."

Only Guerrero and a few others pay much attention, although fear of reprisals forces us to listen with a straight face. But here and there an eye winks and a lip twitches, especially at the end of the lecture, which lasts almost an hour. To everyone's relief the priest leaves us and goes on to repeat his well-memorized record to the female prisoners, and we are given the command to disperse.

"Goddam war!" exclaims Tinajas, a common prisoner. "Before, they didn't come around with their fucking sermons."

Rain and fog push us to the covered court. It's too crowded. Tired of elbowing our way through the human mass, we return to the cell.

We gather around the table and in a moment Celestino is among us. He is the short husky-voiced ex-policeman who never seems to manage a good shave. In his spare time he studies law. He claims to be half way through the courses and longs confidently for the day when he can change professions. He affects a tone of jest and underscores it now as he addresses Jaime. "What did you think of our illustrious prelate?"

"A pure cynic," Jaime answers. "What nerve! To say he envies us for being close to heaven. What kind of heaven can that be? It must be full of rich old ladies, and I bet the place reeks of incense and there is nothing there to eat except candlesticks."

"You can't deny that the passage about the ladder was a masterpiece," persists Celestino. "The trouble is that not everyone can appreciate such flights of literary grace."

"Get this crazy cop!" Jaime blurts. "Who does that priest think he's fooling? We, stepping up every day on that fucking ladder while everyone envies us! Why don't they change places with us? Aren't you fellows revolted by such crap?"

"Keep your shirt on," says Mato, the lawyer. "These militias of priests are part of a corporation and part of their business is proselytism. It's all the same to them to speak of ladders or wells. The majority of these poor peasants are simpletons. The idea is to terrorize them first with 'You know damn well what you're being called for at eleven.' The next step is to pity them, and the next to envy them. I'm sure they use those methods because they've found them successful time and time again. It doesn't matter to them if a small group like ours looks upon them with contempt."

Práxedes, who rarely takes part in discussions, intervenes. "This group is not as small as you think. It's not only us, it's also the workers, they are as revolted as we by this hypocritical nonsense. I wonder if the priests don't lose a soul for each one they save."

"You're wrong," Mato tells him. "You can't imagine how effective terror can be on certain individuals. And being cultured doesn't exempt anyone from fear. Take Guerrero and his followers, and Remigio the teacher."

"Guerrero and his pupils are insane, so they don't count. But what's the matter with Remigio?"

"He prays under his blanket. We didn't know it till a couple of

nights ago, when two of the men in his tier were taken in the 'saca.'
One of them, as he walked out, got tangled in Remigio's blanket and
pulled it off. And there he was, with a small rosary in his hands.
Arsenio, the one who sleeps next to him told us he does it every
night, the moment they put out the lights."

Celestino interrupts. "So what? Why shouldn't that happen occasionally among thousands of men? We are not classifying the
prisoners merely between workers and peasants. There are two
groups. One is large and easy to impress, and that's the one the priest
was talking to. The other is smaller and has strong beliefs. This one
doesn't interest the Jesuits. It's too hard to convince. Don't you
think so, Jaime?"

"Yes. But what is so great about dragging a bunch of frightened
men toward a belief?"

"To them it's an offering to Jehovah. The case of the teacher,
Remigio, is something else. I would call that mystical diarrhea,"
answers Celestino. "But, weren't you impressed by the eternal tortures and delights so well depicted by the reverend? The ones that,
according to the philosophers, cease to be tortures or delights by
the mere fact that they are eternal. Those beautiful passages deserved to be discussed at length some other time." And, blowing his
nose with a large dirty handkerchief, Celestino walks out, quite
satisfied with the wisdom of his words.

In a moment we return to the recurring theme, our obsession, the
fighting in Madrid. Our cell is like a laboratory where every note,
every word, every rumor is analyzed in an effort to reconstruct the
true situation of the war front. Because of our wishful thinking, the
consensus is that Madrid is impregnable. The enemy will exhaust its
resources in its efforts until the capital of Spain becomes the graveyard of fascism.

It is difficult but not impossible to receive newspapers, and in
one of those that reaches our hands we confirm our deductions regarding the situation in Madrid.

On November 5th of 1936 the columns of Lieutenant Colonels
Tella and Barrón reached the suburbs of Madrid: the first one, two
kilometers past Villaverde; the second, right into the Carabanchel
section. But they failed to cross the bridges over the Manzanares
River southwest of the capital. Two other columns commanded by

the military chiefs Asensio Cabanillas and Antonio Castejón, infiltrated the evergreen forest of El Pardo, trying to cross the river, north of the same line of attack. And there, too, the fascist efforts failed, with an impressive number of casualties. In the light of the defeats of the sixth and the seventh of November, nationalist General Mola—doubting that the capital would offer serious resistance —ordered a third attack on the tenth. That, too, was repelled.

Together with the radio news relayed to us by our visitors, that information was enough to fatten up many a night session of military strategy in our cell. Among the many fillers with which pro-Franco newspapers tried to camouflage fascist defeats, we read a communiqué that sparks much humorous comment among us:

During one of Franco's reviews to the troops stationed at the Pardo, the soldiers give vent to their delirious enthusiasm by spreading their capes in the path of their war genius, hoping he would bless them with his feet.

At that, Antonio Ruíz, the court clerk, bursts out singing *El Relicario,* a popular pasodoble whose lyrics tell of a bullfighter's plea to his lady on the way to the corrida:

Tread upon my silken cape, beautiful brunette,
So I will have a token of your divine step.

After singing Maestro Padilla's famous ditty, Ruíz adds, "I bet not all the rags thrown at the Caudillo's feet were regulation capes! There must have been some burnooses and turbans in the heap." Of course. The Moors are a part of Franco's fascist army.

Like a long-smoldering fire, the conversation dies out after a while. No more jokes. Dinner is coming. When it does, we eat in silence. Tonight the "saca" consists of four victims from the third gallery: two anarchists and two members of the CNT, the National Federation of Workers. Of this last team, one is a tall young fellow with muscular arms, pockmarked face and massive shoulders, always dressed in a blue mechanic's overall. When we talk about them in the morning, I can only remember the mechanic. I have seen him often at the courtyard, watching the ball game whenever he was not called upon to participate.

I have confirmed that the "sacas" are fewer in number and frequency here than in qualified jails. Also, life here is somewhat more independent. Our group is in touch with all the others, including the common prisoners. But close associations develop only among our own cellmates and some outside friends and acquaintances throughout the jail. Because there is a greater resonance in this prison building, the "saca" sounds reach us clearly, echoing through the corridors; the death truck, the raising of the portcullis and its clanging chain, the locks opening and closing. . . . In the quiet of our cell we follow the steps of the death march as our jailers approach or turn into other corridors at the "saca" hour. And accordingly, we shudder with fear or breathe with relief. Such is the human instinct for survival, and . . . we are only men. But the terror of the "saca" notwithstanding, there is less anguish, less tension, less suspension of life here than in other jails.

It is a rare joy to be visited by my wife and infant son. The bars that separate us fascinate the child, and all through the far too short meeting his small fingers play with them. I sink into a melancholy despair when I return to the cell. The cold afternoon is descending from the leaden winter sky. I see the rooftops through our little window, and I imagine the city enveloped in a cloud of blood rather than in the pewter-hued fog. To the left of my narrow field of vision I can see the trees, now bare and stripped. In summer their laden branches spread over the mint meadows bordering the river where I have spent many a happy hour. Deep in my thoughts I hardly notice how cold and dark our cell is turning with nightfall. But a rhythmic clanking startles me out of my reminiscences. It is the hour of the grille inspection. A prison officer walks past in front of every window, running an iron rod against the bars. By the sound alone can he detect a loose rung.

Next day after chow, we talk about the forthcoming holy mass. Mato leads the conversation, telling us that intelligent men should adjust to the inevitable circumstances forced upon them. We would gain nothing by a defiant attitude. Also—and this really impresses us—we must remember that the enemy, our jailer, looks upon our particular cell as a sort of Academy of Science and Letters. What may pass unnoticed in other cells is considered significant in this one, to be commented upon by guards and prison director and probably to reach the outside world.

Santolaya reinforces the argument, assuring us there is no moral cowardice entailed in our attending mass. "I don't know about you fellows," he tells us. "You are not children, but responsible men. But this is how I feel about it! If the price I must pay to see my family is that I attend mass, I'll gladly pay it. You know damn well that the least they'll do to punish us is to deny us visiting privileges."

It is a cold, but uneventful night. When Sunday comes around, the preparations for the mass begin at dawn. Before six, while still dark, the improvised altar is rigged up in the courtyard by carpenter jailmates. The priest arrives late, when the first grey rays of morning are seeping in through the transoms.

The ceremony is brief, and it is attended by almost every man. There is no sermon. Among those who take holy communion I see two fierce-looking Requetés from the platoon of gate guards, pistols dangling from their belts.

The most impressive detail of the moment is the arrival of the women prisoners through a back door. Slowly, solemnly, they walk into the courtyard in dead silence, while the men keep their eyes nailed to that door.

The older prison matrons lead them to the left of the court, to almost face a file of men. There are about thirty of them, all political prisoners. Their attire enhances the look of mourning of the entire group. Black headscarves, black dresses, dark eyes, dark shadows around them. What crime can those women have committed? The scant supply of water has precluded a mass washing of prisoners at that early hour. It is obvious in the dirty faces of the men and the wilted look of the women. Most of them are middle-aged. There are some beautiful faces among the younger ones, despite the miserable clothing, and it is on them that the men fix their devouring glances. I have never seen human eyes gleam with such desire. Some of them, standing on tiptoe with necks stretched, remain staring at them ecstatically all through mass.

"That small one," Arsenio whispers to me, "in the first line, to the right, is Mercedes, the one who throws notes wrapped in a stone over the wall. And the pale one next to her is the wife of Alfredo Martínez, the mayor of Casalareina."

A prison officer subdues Arsenio with a withering look. But in a few minutes he nudges me with his elbow and whispers again. "And that handsome tall one at the end of the first line is the fiancée of a falangist from Saragossa. What a gorgeous female! What I could do to her!"

Without a doubt, Arsenio is talking about the Venus of the lot. Her father has been executed, and one of her brothers is now at the provincial jail. I've been told how her public insults to her father's murderers forced the falangist authorities to arrest her. (Later, through her fiancé's influence in the Saragossa chapter of Falange, the girl is able to obtain her freedom. Her firm breasts and tiny waist have driven Celestino crazy, so he is far from happy when he learns of her departure from our jail. From then on he loses interest in attending mass. The ex-cop can no longer feast his eyes on "the goddess Atalanta leaning to pick up the golden apple," as he refers to the girl's kneeling during the ceremony, a gesture which in his exalted imagination she accompanies with significant secret looks which only he can detect.)

Among the young women prisoners there are two short dark ones who Arsenio—our specialist in keeping a census of our female jailmates—tells us are the daughters of Morga, the Socialist mayor of Nájera. At the outbreak of the Movement the situation in High Rioja was uncertain, despite the fact that Haro and Logroño fell immediately to the fascist rebels. But the city of Nájera and its suburbs were well under the command of Mayor Morga. His four hundred old shotguns and the well-disciplined resistance he had organized among his men were thorns in the side of the rebels. Thus the military chiefs in Logroño forced the Republican governor to help set a trap for Morga. The governor, seeking to save his own life, agreed to betray his friend the mayor. He telephoned Morga from Logroño and informed him that all was quiet, but that new developments were awaited momentarily. The mayor's presence was required in the provincial capital immediately in order to receive new instructions affecting the resistance of his men in Nájera. Believing the governor, Morga left for Logroño. His car was stopped at the entrance of the city, and the four passengers were executed that very night. Shortly after, the treacherous Republican governor himself was executed, confirming once again what Calderón de la Barca said in his play, *Life is a Dream:* 'The traitor is expendable once his treachery is performed.'

The potential resistance of Nájera disintegrated. Many of the men called 'Morga's riflemen' fell one by one, some assassinated in the mountains, others in jail.

In the calm that usually prevails in prison Monday mornings, we suddenly hear a burst of cries and screams. Out in the galleries and patios the men huddle in groups, wondering about the cause of the commotion. Some of the cleaning orderlies and kitchen help run to find out, and one of them returns to inform us that, while cleaning the office in the women's section, an orderly saw a security guard running out with a bundle in his arms. In a moment we learn the rest. The woman who is screaming is the wife of Alfredo Martínez, Mayor of Casalareina.

Alfredo is a veteran member of the provincial Socialist Party whose political struggles have often landed him in jail. Knowing the hatred he has bred among the reactionaries now in power, he did not wait long to go into hiding with an aide, the third day after the outbreak of the Movement. Enraged at the news of his successful escape, the falangist authorities ordered the police to search his house. For lack of anyone else, the police arrested his wife, who was in the last month of pregnancy. She was interned in the maternity ward, where next day she gave birth to a girl. In a few weeks, mother and daughter were transferred to the provincial jail. No one has bothered them here for weeks. Now, perhaps because it is against the rules to keep a child in prison, they sent two guards with orders to take the infant to the orphan asylum. In an effort to avert a scandal, the guards planned the abduction with the help of a matron. Señora Martínez was summoned to the office with the excuse that she had to sign some papers. And there, while the woman read the papers the matron offered to hold the baby, only to pass it quickly to one of the guards waiting at the door, while she and the other guard took care of the mother. But scandal has not been averted. The mother fought with the strength of a lioness. Upon hearing the commotion several prison officers ran to the women's section and together helped restrain the woman, who was left almost naked, her clothes torn, and without her baby.

When the news reaches the cells the women go on a hunger strike, and the men react accordingly, some with an accusing, stony silence, others shouting imprecations, most of them biting their fists to muffle their impotent rage. All games and promenading have stopped out in the courtyard, and in the silence that descends on the prison we hear the incessant cries and wailing of the woman. The prison officers look disconcerted, perhaps fighting a conflict between their personal feelings and their duty to comply with orders. This is the first day that I see León's kettles of stew left almost untouched. Also, right under the suddenly indifferent eyes of the guards, a shower of messages wrapped in pebbles and plaster clumps cross the wall that separate us from the women's wing.

"If they don't give her back her baby she's going to die," Santolaya says. For hours the wails and screams continue. It seems impossible that a human throat can have such endurance. The curious passersby who gather at the prison entrance are dispersed at rifle butt by the gate guards. But those who keep watch over the wall dividing us from the women express their sympathy by words and gesture.

After consulting with his subordinates, Pacheco the prison director, telephones the Civil Government and reports the growing unrest in the compound. At night, some new disposition allows the child to be returned to the mother. We never learn whether the change was due to fear of the city's indignant reaction to the incident, or if it were simply to rectify a mistake.

The women tend to child and mother with loving care, and León the cook provides for them plenty of milk and good food. To no avail. The baby dies in a few days.

PEOPLE AND EVENTS

El Señor Yarza was a Catalonian who lived in Madrid, a stout man who suffered from rheumatism. He worked in a state banking office where he was reputed to be a leading financial expert. Toward the middle of July 1936 he went to take his annual water treatment at the Arnedillo in Rioja.

When the "Movement" started, Yarza was caught up in the general atmosphere of terror and hardly left his hotel room. The bellboys told him that every night whole truckloads of men were disappearing. He spent a restless, anxious week. Perhaps because he didn't wear a red beret or attend mass, or simply because he was a stranger in town, he came under the suspicion of a local falangist chief. One dawn he was awakened suddenly, put in a truck with twenty other prisoners, and sent to Logroño.

"I saw places by the side of the highway where dozens of corpses were piled up," he tells us now. "I expected to be murdered at every kilometer we traveled on the way to this jail."

Yarza passed from the cells of the Civil Government to the collective cell here in the provincial prison. Guerrero is among his cellmates. The madman believed that Yarza was a spy, and for two consecutive nights he tried to strangle him. The first time the matter was kept quiet, thinks to the discretion of his mates. But the second time Yarza's cellmates were barely able to free him from the madman's hands, and Pacheco, the prison director, ordered Guerrero to be placed in solitary confinement.

The economist is very withdrawn and my cellmates are among the few people with whom he associates. More than a month after his arrest he comments bitterly:

"No one knows me in this region. You have relatives, friends, someone who can help you. I can't hope for anything and if they don't kill me, my bones will rot in this prison."

Two weeks after this conversation he is released with orders to go to Burgos, capital of the rebel zone.

When the matter is discussed the following day, some give Yarza up for dead while others think that with the scarcity of technical personnel in Burgos his transfer should not be surprising.

Prior to his transfer to the insane asylum, Guerrero becomes the butt of jokes and ridicule from his companions. I often see him washing and scrubbing for hours on end at the washtub in the courtyard, in bitter winter weather, too, his thin body and hands turning purple from the icy water. He says the Lord is testing his humility and charity. Since he feels that any remuneration for his work would be offensive, the most cynical prisoners take advantage of his services. Other times he prays, kneeling on the slippery stones covered with moss. With his eyes fixed ecstatically on the sky, he silently runs through his prayers, then resumes his work again with new zest.

One afternoon a group of us promenading in the courtyard see Guerrero as usual, scrubbing spoons and bowls with pieces of charcoal and other bits of discarded material. He removes black stains from metal utensils with potato and banana peels that he picks from the garbage cans, and someone asks him jokingly about it.

"We should use the things which nature provides," he replies. "That is God's will. Don't you see what insignificant materials birds use to build their nests?"

The next day, impressed by this conversation, Mato and I go to Guerrero's cell on the top floor, a very narrow rectangular room. On the left there is a tiny washbasin of rusty iron with a greenish brass faucet. A narrow pathway between the basin and the pallet on the tile floor leads to the rear of the cell and to a toilet under a window with more bars than openings. An old suitcase and a bench complete the furnishings. The walls are covered with crosses of every shape and material, of straw, old wood, and even toothpicks. Alfonso Mato counted forty two on one side alone.

Guerrero receives us courteously, although with some reserve. The conversation is brief since he is waiting for two proselytes his prayers among the prisoners have made, one of them a small young man who helps in the kitchen peeling potatoes.

Once a group of prisoners offended Guerrero in the courtyard for little reason, and the madman cursed them with the holy wrath of God. The next night two members of that group faced the firing squad, with the result that some men began to believe in Guerrero's clairvoyance and regard him with respect.

At our next meeting he gave us a new explanation of his previous animosity for the economist, Yarza. The real cause was the surprising resemblance between Yarza and a man who had wounded him seriously several years before.

Unfortunately, it becomes almost impossible to talk to Guerrero after they shoot the kitchen helper, his proselyte. We try to renew our talks with him several times, but we fail. Affected by the loss of his favorite disciple, he doesn't want to break his silence.

Almost every night we take out our map to evaluate the war news we receive during the day through various channels. The five of us in the cell, armed with pencils, engage in armchair strategy in which the pros and cons of every operation are thoroughly discussed. All of us, and especially Jaime, love the game, which we take very seriously.

"It's impossible for them to drive a wedge into Madrid with their forces without first cutting the Valencia highway," Jaime says one night. "The fascists were beaten off when they attacked the bridges over the Manzanares and now it looks as though they'll attack the Casa de Campo toward University City. Well, even supposing they do, it doesn't change the situation at all."

Alfonso Mato usually takes the other side in these debates.

"What do you mean, it doesn't change the situation at all? The fact is they've crossed the Manzanares River further to the north and have some positions almost touching the buildings in the Argüelles district."

"The Manzanares is a piddling little stream," replies Jaime. "And even if what you say is true, it's nothing but a change in position in respect to the point of the wedge. Just look at the map."

At the same time that he points with one hand, he places wooden spoons and forks on the map in the form of a V. He uses matches and sticks to show the location of the nearby towns and the hypothetical distribution of the attacking fascist forces. Carried away by his graphic illustration he continues:

"The main pressure of the counterattack should be against the legs of the V, on the north from the Escorial and on the south on the enemy's flank at Toledo. Or, even better, toward Talavera! Always at the places farthest from the point of the wedge, so that it will take the enemy some time to receive reinforcements. Under these conditions it will be impossible for them to advance if enough pressure is applied. On the other hand, if we could break the point of the wedge, all of their war matériel would fall into our hands and the Fascist shock troops, the Moors, the Foreign Legionnaires and the Italians, would be surrounded. But perhaps the Madrid government hasn't been able to organize mechanized units for such a large-scale operation."

Jaime looks a little uneasy as he expresses this last thought.

"All of that is unimportant," says Mato. "Without foreign intervention on the side of the fascists the Republic would win easily.

But I'm afraid the trains with the locomotives decorated with German and Italian flags that we saw from the window a few days ago are very eloquent. Those countries' recognition of Franco's rebel government means that they're prepared to go all the way. We all know how the forces from Africa crossed the Strait of Gibraltar. (General Franco took over command of the colonial army after flying to Morocco from the Canary Islands and rapidly overcoming the resistance of the few officers who had remained loyal to the Republic. Nevertheless, the failure of the military rebellion in the fleet made it impossible for these troops with the best officers and arms in the Spanish Army to cross the Strait of Gibraltar. In those decisive moments it was Hitler and Mussolini who saved the day, by sending the necessary air support. On July 24th, 25th, and 26th eleven Savoia 81 bombers, thirty Junker 52 transport planes, and six Henkel fighters landed at airfields in Spanish Morocco, all with their respective pilots and prepared for immediate action. Together with the few planes the rebels had in their possession they made it possible for the bulk of the colonial army to cross the Strait.) If they hadn't been escorted by Italian Savoia 81 bombers, all of those transport convoys would have been sunk by our fleet. Since then Germany and Italy have sent thousands and thousands of men, planes, and artillery, and now they've officially recognized the rebels in order to be able to help them even more. Gentlemen, we're not just fighting Franco alone, but Hitler and Mussolini as well, and that makes the matter a lot more serious than we can imagine."

Jaime points at the lawyer with a wooden spoon that has been a Republican attack division on his battle plan.

"Don't be ridiculous! Do you think that France and England are going to stand by doing nothing? They have vital interests involved in our struggle and they'll stop the fascist intervention for their own protection. This will become a European war and the fascists will finally have to eat the damn flags on those locomotives."

"England will only move when she thinks it is to her advantage," replies the lawyer. "Don't forget that the conservatives are in power there now. As for France, the people in the government don't have the guts to act. Only Russia is left, and she is so far away from us that her help will be insignificant."

"I don't trust the English, either," says Manolo Alba. "We'd have more of a chance if the Labor Party were in power."

"Miserable war!" exclaims Santolaya. "They're getting the help that we're waiting for and which may never come. The Republic can't fight against the military power of Germany and Italy! If we don't receive any international aid we're beaten for sure."

"Don't be so pessimistic," replies Alba. "Remember the proverb: Good can bear up under defeats, but evil can't."

"It's a shame Celestino can't hear that. It's worthy of Azaña," says Santolaya.

This turns the conversation to the comments we have read in the Franco press concerning the President of the Republic. The name of Manuel Azaña seems to attract all the hatred of the reactionaries, to judge by their continuous poisonous attacks on him in the press.

"I hear the gate opening," Mato warns suddenly. "They're coming to turn off the lights."

We hear the slow steps of the guard coming down the corridor. Jaime carefully folds the map and puts it in his mattress while the rest of us gather the eating utensils. Everything is in order when the guard looks through the peephole in the door before turning out the light. A little while later we hear the gate slam loudly. Before we turn the light on again we stuff dirty clothes and strips of paper around the holes and cracks in door and window. Even the smallest speck of light could be seen by the sentinel as he makes his rounds on the wall. Manolo Alba connects our secret wire to the switch and when the light is on again we renew our conversation and the game of strategy in low tones.

At the same time that the Jesuits gave their talks we began to receive visits from a Father Aspiazu, a member of the Order, a tall, slender man with the elegant manners of an Italian cardinal. We don't know why he visits our cell and we speculate about it a great deal. He is always friendly and brings us books selected for our individual tastes, messages from our families, and news from the town.

All of us are grateful to him except Jaime, who never hides his displeasure. Our library increases but the poor light makes it very tiring to read, and we have to get a more powerful bulb through the cook, León. That bulb is our treasure, and it is like a religious rite to take it out of its hiding place, place it in its socket, and later remove it.

In the cold, rainy weather we prolong the discussions after meals. Once, when we talk about people connected with the Civil War someone mentions Millán Astray, a general who, unable to assume an active command due to his age, has been used as a hero figure by the fascist propaganda apparatus. Stories abound in military circles about the old, picturesque general's fantastic charges against the Moors with the cry of "Long live the king"—the same Moors, traditional enemies of the Spanish military, who now are mercenary soldiers in the ranks of the so-called Holy Crusade.

In the Industrial School we heard confused rumors about Millán Astray's clash with Unamuno, the great rector of the University of Salamanca, on October 12th, 1936, during ceremonies commemorating the anniversary of the discovery of America, Columbus Day. Much later I learned that the general had challenged the rector with the cry of 'Long live death and down with intelligence' to which the philosopher replied calmly:

"You will conquer, but you will not convince."

The general, thin, one-armed, blind in one eye, looked like a caricature of Don Quixote. Perhaps the old romances of chivalry were also the cause of his madness. But since the general of the Foreign Legion lacked the genius of Cervantes, who had also been maimed—in his case at the battle of Lepanto—he regarded military victories as the judgment of God, and therefore didn't hesitate to use religion in his propaganda.

In the year 1920, the then Lieutenant Colonel Millán Astray was sent on a military mission to Algiers, where he visited the general headquarters of the French Foreign Legion. He was so excited by what he saw that when he returned to Spain he proposed the creation of a similar organization to the Viscount of Eza, then Spain's Minister of War. After the initial difficulties were overcome, a decree in the official gazette authorized the formation of a Spanish Foreign Legion.

The future chief of Spain "by the grace of God," Francisco Franco Bahamonde, was given command of the First Company of the Legion. The young officer who had been commanding a unit of Moorish regulars, had asked to be transferred to the newly created Legion.

Emulating Moses on Mount Sinai, Millán Astray drafted the code of the new military organization. Here are some articles:

Fourth commandment—The spirit of union and mutual aid: Wherever the cry of "To me the Legion!" is heard, everyone will respond and defend the legionnaire who is calling for aid, whether he is in the right or in the wrong.

Seventh commandment—The spirit of fire: Everyone, from one man alone to the whole Legion, will always go wherever they hear firing, by day or by night, even though they have no orders to do so.

Epilogue: All legionnaires are brave. Every nation is famous for bravery; but in this one it is necessary to demonstrate which is the bravest of all.

The rebels' general headquarters in the south was in Seville, under the command of Queipo de Llano, Captain General of Andalusia. Queipo, a traitor to both the king and the Republic, seized Seville when the revolt broke out. He was able to do so by means of mass executions, with the aid of Italian and Nazi technical advisors, the Fifth Company of the Legion—brought from Africa under the protection of Italian aviation—small groups of local reactionaries, and a radio propaganda which was as effective as it was crude. In the days following their coup the rebels received substantial reinforcements of Legionnaires, Moors, and Italian artillery and aviation, to be organized into the columns that were to advance on Madrid from the south. There were two possible routes for that offensive: the main highway through Andalusia to Madrid and the plains of Estremadura. They chose the second route due to the nature of the terrain and because one flank would be protected during their advance by the border of semi-fascist Portugal. This drive was vital, in order to join the colonial army with the forces that had rebelled in the north under Generals Mola and Saliquet. As a consequence of that campaign, Mérida was taken and the city of Badajoz fell on August 14th. The poorly armed Republican militiamen fled to the frontier for asylum, but the Portuguese border guards refused to admit them and turned them over to the conquerors. The culmination of the many crimes committed by the fascists in their advance from Seville was the slaughter in the Badajoz bullring, where sixteen hundred persons were machine gunned *en masse*. They say that some of them were tormented like bulls before they were shot. This bit of refined cruelty was nothing new, since the same thing was done to Manso, the Republican Member of Parliament from Salamanca. While they joked about his name, which means "tame," they stuck barbed banderillas in his back before they murdered him.

Shortly after accompanying the African troops on the first phase of their holy crusade, the Legion's tragic clown, Millán Astray, came to Logroño on a propaganda tour. He was received at the station with a band, and he reviewed a military parade followed by a banquet and speeches. By midafternoon he expressed a desire to visit the Provincial prison. This is how Manolo Alba described his visit:

When he arrived with his retinue he had the prisoners assembled in the outside courtyard and delivered the following speech:

"Comrade prisoners! I call you comrades because you who are listening to me are Spaniards. With this Movement of Christian hearts the hour of liberation has arrived in every corner of our motherland. The Lord, whose gaze is fixed this very moment on His beloved Spain, gives us the courage we need to carry our crusade to a triumphal end. I, who have always felt the deepest sympathy for the working class, have been forced to watch impotently how false prophets perverted your simple instincts and how the illusion of a Communist paradise was luring the best elements of the working class into its snares. I, who have never engaged in hypocrisy, I, who look men straight in the eye, I come with the Glorious Movement to bring you bread and forgiveness, because that Master of Masters, that good Rabbi also knew how to understand and forgive. Just as Christ forgave, we forgive, opening our arms to receive you with the pride of Spaniards who want a better Spain, free of the tyranny, despotism, and cruelty of the Reds.

"Men who were defiled with all kinds of crimes, who cut off the breasts of pregnant women, raped nuns, murdered old people and strangled children, have been punished by us with the necessary justice and harshness. Nevertheless, we are not butchers and our severity is tempered with the broadest sympathy for the poor man, for the worker and the soldier. How many more we could have shot! But on the contrary, we gave them the opportunity to enlist in the glorious ranks of the Legion. Their baptism of fire has redeemed their sins and made them into brothers. I could mention many names—I have a good memory—but their names would not mean anything to you. If there is some syndicalist, Socialist, or Communist here who is truly repentant and desires to purge his sins by fighting for an ideal, let him take one step forward. My arms will receive him as a friend and a gentleman, showing with this demonstration of affection that we bear no animosity and thus sealing our sacred word."

Of the five hundred men who were listening to him, one syndicalist who had either been moved by the harangue or was looking for a way out of our rat trap, stepped forward and fell into the general's open arms. The general, crying theatrically and with his voice breaking under the emotion, said, "You will be free and you will fight!"

During the long pause that followed he strolled before the prisoners who were standing at attention, while his look alternated between the men and the sky. Two falangists, one with a glass of water in his hand and the other bearing the general's white gloves, followed him like shadows.

"You're no worker," he said suddenly, looking at Manolo Alba. "You're strong, but you don't have callouses on your hands from manual labor. What are you?"

"An agricultural engineer."

"A good profession. What party do you belong to?"

"The Left Republicans."

"A bad party. How can you claim to reconcile your profession with ideas which, instead of sowing discipline in the lower ranks, give rise to discord and ambition? I see that there are many others like you, doctors, lawyers, and other professional men of whom the same thing could be said. Without discipline there can be no army, and without an army there can be no society."

Advancing toward the center of the front line, he shouted hoarsely:

"Look at me! Do you see this finger that I have raised? Do you see it? If I only let it fall, you will be dead. But I have not come here to do that, for I am a gentleman and I will die a gentleman."

In the midst of a dead silence he disappeared with his retinue through the courtyard door, while a prison official on guard duty gave the order: "Dismissed!"

We are given another religious sermon, during which the priest mentions the rule imposed by Saint Francis on the monks in his Order. "Disobey your superior if it is necessary to do so in order to comply more faithfully with the Rule, which is always above the minister. The oath of obedience was not made to the minister, but to the Rule." Since those words are off the subject of the sermon, we feel sure the speaker is attempting to justify the fact that the rebellious generals have broken their oath of allegiance to the Republic.

The execution of José Antonio Primo de Rivera in Alicante on November 19th, 1936, was followed by ferocious reprisals. The executions were intensified in all of the prisons, but especially in the qualified jails. It was several days before we knew the reason for that blood bath.

José Antonio, the spiritual leader of the rebellion, was given the title of "The Absent One" in the fascist press. I had met him in Madrid through some close friends who were relatives of his. He impressed me as being sincere, brave, and fanatical. In those days he had only an insignificant group of followers known later as the "old shirts." Most of the rightists did not share his ideals and preferred to follow the chief of the right-wing CEDA, Gil Robles, whose empty program of social reforms gave them a greater sense of security.

It was said that the government of the Republic had offered to exchange José Antonio for another prisoner but the offer had been refused by Franco. Other rumors had it that it was the head of the Republican government, Largo Caballero, who had rejected Franco's proposal in an exemplary gesture, since his own son was to be part of the proposed exchange.

When the rebellion began, one of the regiments garrisoned on the outskirts of Madrid received orders from the Republican government to march to the front in the mountains. On their way most of the officers rebelled and went over to the enemy with the whole regiment. The commanding officer, a colonel, committed suicide when there was nothing he could do to stop them. Socialist leader Largo Caballero's son was serving his military term in that regiment. He was arrested, kept as hostage, and later murdered.

Práxedes Toledo, a wealthy man, frequently visits our cell. He had been municipal treasurer for many years in Logroño. Many citizens are indebted to him, and their influence saved him when he was accused of political and personal affinity for the Left Republican delegate for Logroño province, a very serious matter at that time. Práxedes' only son, who was on my team during my last year as a soccer player, is a soldier at the front lines. This situation—a father in jail or executed while his son is at the front—is not uncommon in the fascist zone. After my uncle Matías was murdered, two of his sons were drafted into the fascist army, and the elder was sent to the Teruel front.

Another picturesque character in the prison is Melquiades, a small, nervous man who seems to be everywhere. On rainy days he goes from cell to cell talking about his release anticipated within a few days. As week after week goes by without his prediction being confirmed, Melquiades falls into a state of feverish impatience.

"If I let the cat out of the bag there's going to be an explosion," he keeps saying.

We all wait anxiously, he for his freedom and we for the cat to be let out of the bag. Apparently he knows some secret about a falangist chief, and from his veiled allusions to the matter, it seems that he has taken precautions so that whatever happens to him—if they dare do anything—the secret will become known.

Julio Pacheco, the prison chief, spends most of the time in his private quarters and we only see him on a few occasions, such as Sunday mass or when he accompanies important visitors, especially priests. The other prison officials treat us well and even do us small favors in some cases while keeping their distance. Don Fernando, Don Enrique, Don Salvador, and Very Well are the most friendly. The official who has been nicknamed Very Well by the prisoners is a tall, thin man with a sad face who studies English in his spare time. His method consists in going over lists of words written on long strips of paper he carries in his pockets.

One day Don Salvador received an official letter notifying him of the death of his eldest son on the Somosierra front. He and his wife were given a special pass to go to the front lines in that sector, where they placed a wreath of flowers and a wooden cross on the grave of their first born. He returned to Logroño to continue in his position as a prison guard. However, embittered by his misfortune, he now adopted a violent attitude toward the prisoners, whom he somehow considered responsible for the death of his son. After a few weeks he received a letter from France, in which relatives living in Madrid assured him in great detail that his son was alive in the San Carlos hospital. The funeral ceremony in the mountains of Somosierra had been held over the grave of an unknown soldier. The young man had been wounded during an attack and taken to Madrid. After his release from the hospital he was going to be interned as a prisoner of war.

Don Salvador again began to treat prisoners in his normal fashion and even held casual conversations with some of them. On one occasion he spoke enthusiastically about the price of meat. He knew the exact price per kilo for the different kinds of meat in comparison with pre-war prices. In his opinion this was the dawn of a new life, brought about by the "Glorious Movement." Everyone would be able to afford good meat in abundance in the future.

During the first months of operations on the northern front the fascist troops confiscated great quantities of cattle belonging to the villagers. The steers were sold behind the lines and slaughtered without restrictions, flooding the market and causing a sharp drop in prices. Don Salvador did not know that the boom would end very quickly as the country's supply of cattle became exhausted. As a consequence, his grandchildren would drink second or third-rate milk. Prevailing legislation provided for three different milk prices, depending on the amount of water it contained.

When the number of victims on the execution list reaches two or three times its normal level, we again wonder about our own uneasy future. The increase in the number of executions at the end of November continues into the following month and causes a curious incident.

One morning they free a young worker from the third gallery. Fearing he is going to be executed, he so adamantly refuses to leave the cell that the prison chief orders everyone confined to his own cell so that the guards can carry out their orders without witnesses. According to the kitchen staff, the eyewitnesses, the prisoner was dragged across the inside courtyard and handed over to the sentries at the entrance, who forced him out with kicks and rifle butts.

The high walls where the sentries make their rounds throw shadows over the courtyard, but there are a few spots warmed by the winter sun. I often go to one of those places beside the wall early in the morning in order to hear the laughter of the young women who play on the other side. According to the kitchen workers the old women knit while the young ones release their energy running and playing ball. Sometimes I can hear their fresh, clear laughter over the sound of the wind, and in contrast to the swearing, the coughs, and harsh voices of our world, it has a very soothing effect on my nerves.

One morning, when I return from that wall separating the men's courtyard from the women's, I find a group of prisoners criticizing the well-known private citizens who are seen on top of the wall performing voluntary guard duty. Santolaya, always moderate, tries to excuse them as just victims of the general wave of corruption and madness.

Jorge, a small, dark, thin individual with whom we talk sometimes in the courtyard, replies angrily:

"Victims? Executioners, you mean! Aren't they the same ones who have sent their sons to shoot at our people behind the front lines? Haven't they given their money to the fascists and don't they continue ignoring or even applauding their crimes? Come on, now. With all due respect for your age, you're living on the moon."

Jorge's excited attitude causes Santolaya to beat a hasty retreat. However, a few minutes later as we march toward our cell, Santolaya is still murmuring, "This is the rule of hatred."

Among the common criminals, some stand out by virtue of their strong personalities. There is the Brute, famous for his baths in the washtub when he finishes playing ball. He turns somersaults and performs all kinds of pirouettes with the skill of an acrobat as he sloshes in the water. Another of his feats is to climb up a corner of the smooth wall of the ball court through sheer coordination of his leg, arm, and shoulder muscles.

Tinajas, a great ball player, malicious and quarrelsome, can swear like a machine gun without stopping. The cheap, smelly cigars he smokes, spread such a penetrating odor that we always know exactly where he is in this building.

However, the one who enjoys the greatest prestige undoubtedly is Bartolo, a thin man with a rather cold personality. When the Movement began, he, together with the Brute and Tinajas, rejected the falangists' offer of freedom to all common criminals who would collaborate with their revolution. With the understanding that they would help hunt down and murder Republicans, the falangists freed common criminals, giving preference to the most hardened ones.

Bartolo's companions tell how he stood up to the renegades, calling them miserable toads. This strange, taciturn individual always shows great interest in the war news and several times provides us with recent newspapers. Out of sympathy for the Republican cause he abstains from playing ball and, on the days of large "sacas," he doesn't allow the other common criminals to use the courtyard, either. Two of his cousins are miners fighting on the Asturian front with the Socialist forces, and his Anarchist brother is in the Huesca sector fighting with the Catalonian 29th Division.

We have no doubt that if the falangists' offer of collaboration had been made by the Republicans instead, Bartolo would have accepted without hesitation.

EIZAGUIRRE'S ESCAPE

Eizaguirre, a man of our acquaintance, joins us at the provincial jail. To us he seems disguised or at least different, with long sideburns and a mustache, something new for him. Given his swarthy complexion he now looks like a gypsy. Also, he arrives at prison dressed in the bulky corduroy suit of a peasant. He has been affiliated with the Socialist Party, working as a close aide of the mayor of Casalareina, Alfredo Martínez.

There are those in the province who believe Eizaguirre was involved in the events of Vera, some years back, when the government of Primo de Rivera had attached undue importance to an isolated, feeble revolt in that frontier town. The police repression that followed sent Eizaguirre fleeing to the French border. From there he somehow embarked for Panama. Years later he returned to this region with some money.

At the outbreak of the fascist Movement, Eizaguirre was working for the Republican Government as a member of the provincial administrative board in charge of hospitals. He had already directed the changeover from religious to lay personnel in several hospitals, something which brought him harsh criticism from the rightists in Logroño. (Later, during my stint at the provincial hospital, I learn how effectively Eizaguirre struggled to raise the salaries of the hospital personnel, a measure promptly rescinded at the start of the civil war.)

Eizaguirre is no stranger in this jail where he has often been imprisoned. In fact, he has some friends among the prison officers.

The afternoon he walks into our cell to visit us, some of the men exclaim, "We thought you had escaped to the border with Alfredo!"

"I tried to, but I failed. Alfredo and I fled from Logroño at dawn on the twentieth. We walked all day through the fields, following the Ebro uphill but keeping away from the shore. We stopped at dusk and decided it was best to continue on separate ways. Alfredo was going to spend the night in Briones, with a trusted friend. I wanted to reach the Basque lines through Vitoria. So we embraced and parted, sure we would meet again soon. He advised me to change direction and go toward Laguardia. I did, and I slept a few hours in one of the mud huts in the vineyard. Next day, in order to avoid suspicion, I resumed walking in full morning rather than at dawn. I passed through town and took the high road to the pass of Peña Cerrada. It was almost noon when I reached the summit, unfortunately at the same time that a station wagon loaded with Requetés did the same from the other side. They were shouting like madmen, red berets held aloft on their rifles. A few of them jumped from the vehicle and stopped me. I answered their questions in a mixture of Portuguese and Castilian. Apparently not satisfied with the answers, the head man said, 'These suspicious characters are a menace to us and the best thing is to do away with them. This is no time to take chances.'

"I began to sweat. The blue sky was outlined by the motionless tree branches as I heard their laughter. They surrounded me and pushed me off the road, their rifles at my back. I thought my legs had turned to lead as they walked me toward a thick evergreen some forty meters off the road. Suddenly a truck also loaded with Carlists appeared on the road. Their chief stopped the platoon of Requetés behind me. Again I was asked dozens of questions which still didn't seem clearly answered to the fascists. When the first group had searched me they found some change and a one-hundred pesetas bill in my pockets. Had they torn the lining from my jacket they would have found a lot more, which alone would give me away as a fugitive. Now fearing a second and more thorough search, I began complaining. I knew nothing of wars and revolutions. What I sought was work, so I could save some money and return to my wife and children in Portugal, as I did every year. Perhaps my play-acting was more convincing this time, or maybe the second chief had a softer heart. His face was as red as the gold-tasseled beret on his head.

'This must be one of those migrant workers who cross over from Portugal every year to work in the harvest. Poor devil, leave him alone.' Turning to the chief of the first group, he added, 'It's good to be on our toes, but let's not overdo it.'

"In a few minutes both vehicles started toward Rioja and I found myself alone in the road, minus one hundred pesetas. I forgot to tell you fellows that I was dressed in corduroy clothes with an old greasy wide-brimmed hat and a shepherd's bag and a sickle on my shoulder. That's how I had left Logroño, and I think the costume helped a lot.

"I decided to walk only at night and try to reach Vitoria through familiar terrain. But I didn't know the northwest approach to the city was well patrolled. I spent a whole night trying to pass over to the Basque zone at the risk of being captured every minute. I turned north, thinking that the difficult, rolling ground would lessen my chances of being detected. But it was strange land to me and the stormy night made matters worse. Only by the flash of frequent lightning could I see the mountain crests I had studied during the day while resting by a rivulet. I was so excited and walked so fast, I was afraid that my loud heartbeats alone would give me away. I reached the front lines in a couple of hours. When I heard footsteps somewhere I jumped off the path. I saw five shadows come out of a cluster of brush. And in the distant flashes of lightning I saw the soldiers' capes, the river at the bottom of the ravine, and high brush above on the mountain side."

Eizaguirre's adventures so fascinate the men in this cell, that despite his prolonged pause everyone remains silent, all eyes expectantly on him.

"From the conversation I overheard it seemed that the patrol was looking for a deserter. But they were coming up the ravine and to avoid falling into their hands, I climbed ahead. I dragged myself on the wet earth until I reached the summit, and as I started down the mountain on the other side, I came face to face with a sentry. I was arrested and at dawn the sentry took me into a hut where a lieutenant questioned me. Maybe it was my luck, or maybe because I wasn't carrying a weapon. . . . For whatever reason, the officer believed I was a harmless tramp or a farmhand looking for work. He let me go, warning me not to be caught again roaming those hills. I didn't dare tempt fate again. Also, I thought this situation couldn't last more than a couple of months. I decided to retrace my steps and swim across the Ebro. I wound up in Fuenmayor, not far from the Montecillo farm."

Between the river and the road, there is a field of vineyards owned by a well-known winery.

"At last, in the morning, I had a chance to hang my clothes to dry and take a good look at the terrain. Near the ramparts of the high trees there were several small caves. I chose the biggest one and spent almost five months living there like a mole. Twice a week, before nightfall, I would shave with an old razor, leaving just enough of my sideburns and mustache to look a little different. I would bathe in the river and then start for Fuenmayor to buy bread and canned food. Always in small quantities, so as not to arouse suspicion. I found dry hay in an old barn and carried several armfuls to my cave to make a bed. At times I was able to steal food from the few fishermen who still went down to fish in the river. One day, as I crouched perched in a tree, I saw the astonished faces of two of them when they returned from the river and found their codfish stew gone from the kettle they had left by a fire smoldering in a ditch. But those were dangerous risks to take in broad daylight, and despite my craving for hot food I seldom took them.

"I had enough money, but most of it in large bills which were not easy to change without arousing curiosity. Then, too, there was the change of national currency. I had no recourse but to go to Logroño. There my wife gave me another blanket and new currency. It was a short visit, I don't think I was home more than a half hour. But some women saw me climb out a window in the patio and ran to tell the authorities. Now I learn that the police arrived only a few minutes after I had fled the house. I hid in Garrigosa's orchard waiting for nightfall to return to Montecillo. As the cold season got closer, nights became unbearable despite the two blankets and my heavy clothing. I'd wake up half frozen, with a cough that lasted all day. . . . But damn dogs! A so-called man's best friend—mine, till then—became my worst enemy one afternoon. Two men with a dog came within some thirty meters of my cave, walking on a little-known path. The dog began to bark furiously and ran toward me, followed by one of the hunters. When the man saw me he gave me a significant wink and then said loudly to his companion behind: 'He must have seen a snake or something. There's nothing here. Come on, Brandy! Let's go.'

"I began thinking. . . . Even that friendly wink was no guarantee of safety. I had better look for another lair, for if they came looking for me it would be the end. And crossing the Ebro just after the rains meant I would have to swim across a powerful, dangerous current. On the other hand, it seemed that the revengeful hounding of the first few months was subsiding. Those arrested were being tried now by military law, and General Mola guaranteed the life of anyone who had not taken up arms against the Movement. I had known jail, and the thought of being back there safely, eating hot food and sleeping under a roof, able to see my family, too, seemed like a heavenly solution.

"I had already thought of giving myself up, it was so lonely up in those mountains. . . . But, mulling over the situation, I did nothing. Two hours later the Civil Guard came and ordered me out of the cave at gunpoint. They bound my hands and took me to Fuenmayor, but they treated me well. They kept me for three days and then transferred me to this jail. Now I think of the birds singing at dawn, and the trees swaying in the wind, and the freedom I enjoyed in that solitude. . . . Man always longs for the things he cannot have."

Despite the interest of the falangist authorities in expediting his case, Eizaguirre spends four long months in this jail, often coming to our cell to get legal advice from Mato, and at times looking for our soft ball and rounding up partners for a game. He waits quietly and confidently for his trial, putting great stock in a letter he sent with a friend to the local press just before he fled from Logroño with Alfredo. The letter is commented on by all in this prison, and not always favorably. In it he praises the new governor and also expresses his protest, on humanitarian grounds, against the first bombings inflicted on the fascist zone by the Republican air force. Once, quite spontaneously, he tells us that in the letter he was trying to flatter fascist governor Benlló and clear himself as a safety measure, in case he was captured.

In summary cases it is compulsory for the accused to select his defense lawyer from a list of five, all members of Falange. Following Mato's advice, Eizaguirre chooses an attorney whose brilliant defense was nevertheless ineffective. In the climate of doom surrounding most cases, it is not easy for a lawyer to have the courage to comply with professional ethics to the end.

The military prosecutor used the famous letter mercilessly against the accused. "But they themselves recognize their inhuman cruelties!" he repeated in court, every time the defense attorney would mention the exhibit as an attenuating fact. At the suggestion of his lawyer, Eizaguirre applies for pardon, hoping it will help change the death sentence to a life term. Neither alternative seems to shake his aplomb. We rarely see him moody or depressed.

The only member of the Communist Party in this prison is a retired sergeant, always pale and nervous, whose family has been destroyed: mother and sisters put in jail, father, and only brother executed. Everything seems to justify this man's desperation. Free of the fear that grips other inmates, he thinks and talks out loud. To anyone who cares to listen he tells openly that he'll gladly give his life if he can take revenge on those criminals who wear white collars and carry rosary beads.

His defense lawyer also puts in a plea for commutation. His case and Eizaguirre's are similar and they take equally long to come to an end. A few days after I am transferred back to the Avenida prison, the answers to the pleas arrive. Negative in the case of Eizaguirre and favorable in the sergeant's. His commutation to a life term is the only one I know of during my years as a prisoner.

THE JUSTICE OF
DON PEDRO THE CRUEL

One damp and windy afternoon, Gilabert and Antonio Ruiz return
from the courtyard and enliven the dwindling conversation in our
cell. We recall some friends already executed, among them, Fermín
of Nájera. I tell them of Fermín's tale of ancient coins found in one
of his little plots of farmland in Nájera. Manolo Alba thinks their
value exaggerated, although he doesn't doubt that Fermín did find
the coins. With a hunter friend Alba has found old metal objects and
traces of human bones in the same area of Nájera. He too attributes
their presence there to the battle between Don Pedro the Cruel and
his bastard brother Enrique.

Ruiz tells how Enrique de Trastamara fled to France after fail-
ing in his first attempts to become king of Castile. There he sought
the support of the French forces commanded by Beltran Du Guesclin.
With the help of this Breton general and several Aragonese barons,
Enrique proclaimed himself king in Calahorra. Don Pedro fearing
disaster asked aid of the British. One of the gifts he surrendered in
his quest for help from the Black Prince and his Britishers was a
ruby the size of an egg which Don Pedro had stolen from the Red
King of Granada, Abu-Said. We see a parallel between those ancient
civil wars, with their foreign intervention, and our present one. Only
one of Ruiz's historical references is new to us, an ironical anecdote
depicting the exemplary justice of king Don Pedro the Cruel:

A priest had killed a shoemaker in Sevilla, apparently over a
woman. The victim's son, also a shoemaker, asked the church judge
for justice, and the priest was punished by being forbidden to say
mass during one year. A few days later Don Pedro arrived in Sevilla
and the shoemaker's son appealed to the king for justice.

"Would you be man enough to kill the culprit yourself?" Don
Pedro asked.

"Certainly," replied the youth.

"Then, do so."

The next day the town was celebrating Corpus Christi, and at the royal procession, as the culprit walked not far from the king, the youth slew him with his knife. He was captured immediately and brought before the king, who asked the youth the reason for the murder.

"Sire, that man murdered my father and justice was not done."

The church judge, who also was present, assured the king that justice had indeed been done as the clergyman had been forbidden the saying of mass for one year.

"Release the youth," said the king. "I sentence him to refrain from making shoes during one year."

A moment after Ruiz tells us that story we hear voices from the courtyard. Several prisoners run in front of our cell. We too run toward the center of the courtyard. A warden is trying to separate two men. It was a fight over a gambling debt. The aggressor is isolated and the other man goes to the kitchen to apply soaking towels to his bleeding nose. Just then the steaming kettles of chow are brought into the courtyard and at officer's command the crowd disappears.

Another episode that has left a great impression on the men occurred before I arrived at this jail; I hear them talk about it occasionally, and at last I learn the details. It concerns the killing of several men from Nájera, part of the group called "Morga's riflemen," followers of the mayor of Nájera. They were caught carrying their hunting rifles in the mountains, after a shepherd of the region alerted the authorities. Three of them had been treated with the customary cruelty that precedes being transferred to the provincial jail. The officer in charge of the guard had the eight of them placed in a collective cell, where they spent a week keeping much to themselves, hardly speaking to the other men. Finally, they were roped in a line with other prisoners and taken by night to be executed at the pond of La Granjera. On the way out of the cell, before passing the portcullis, one of them cut the rope of the next man in the file with a razor he had managed to hide. The next man did the same, and thus the razor passed from hand to hand and liberated almost

the entire string of men. When they reached the portcullis, the condemned men flung themselves upon the execution patrol. "If they're
going to kill us let's die fighting!" was their cry. It was a useless
attempt, justified only by the desperation of the victims. Not all the
men had managed to cut their bonds. Three of them, left behind
with hands tied, were promptly cut down by the guards' bullets. But
the guards couldn't shoot into the cluster of liberated prisoners for
fear of wounding one of their own. Soon the gate guards came to
the aid of the execution patrol and together they impaled the men
on their bayonets. Later they washed and whitewashed the blood-
stains off the wall, but not the indelible ones on the floor. They are
still there, marking the site of that miniature Sagunto battle, as we
are told by the kitchen personnel, the only ones allowed through the
arch of the portcullis. To avoid a repetition of the incident they
modified the "saca" procedure, and never again took men out in a
block from a collective cell.

Still, this suicidal riot had its repercussions. Caged men longing
for freedom have a special capacity for believing the most outlandish
dreams and also for forgetting all that logic and experience teaches
them. The commotion was heard in a nearby common cell and taken
for a sign of a rebellion. This may have been the result of recent
prison rumors about an uprising in the infantry forces stationed in
Logroño. The grapevine had spread "news" of the high number of
discontented troups in those barracks, all of them ready for "everything." Thus the occupants of that common cell, all spirited young
peasants, believed that the moment had come to fight for freedom
when they heard the shots and the uproar in the corridor. They tore
apart the few beds in their cell and with the iron bars tried to force
open the door, all to the tune of songs and cries and imprecations.
In due time, order was re-established, and the next night, four of
the credulous young rioters joined the thousands buried in the common pit of Lardero.

In several cases freedom has been obtained by some with actual
cash ransom; the most notorious case is that of Pedro Santos, a
wealthy wholesale grocer who has been city councilman several
times. He has spent two months in this jail, and there is still talk
of how successfully he competed with Tinajas, the common prisoner, in the art of swearing. Apparently he was unsure of the cause

of his arrest, because he would say often, "Who the hell can be the son of a bitch who got me in trouble?" According to the grapevine he paid over 300,000 pesetas for his freedom. While he was in jail his two sons were inducted into the army and sent to the front. I had struck up a cordial friendship with the younger during the time I lived in Logroño. The elder, an agricultural engineer, was among the promising young men whose lives were cut short by the civil war. He was sent to the protectorate of Morocco, where he died under bizarre circumstances. According to the official communiqué sent to his father, his pistol went off and killed him while he sat on the terrace of a café.

Jaime has been able to get paper, ruler, and colored pencils, but he never speaks of the price paid in money and effort for that modest drawing set, probably afraid of looking like a fool before the men. Every two or three days he completes a new and better drawing of the front lines. The fortifications are designed to defend Madrid, and so perfectly that the militia could sleep well nights in the complete assurance that their trenches would be there, intact, next morning. That's how well fortified they are on Jaime's drawings.

When the Madrid front is stabilized, our nervous tension of the past month lessens somewhat. We hear of certain favorable actions on the war front which prison optimism enlarges into decisive battles. Also, the star of governor Benlló seems to be declining. He has been losing the support of the most ferocious elements among the fascists and is even the object of criticism in some falangist centers. For the first time we hear rumors of his possible demotion, something once considered impossible.

The first snows! Standing on a crate in front of our narrow window, I watch the snowflakes falling slowly on the city. Soon the wind rages and whips a snowy maelstrom that swirls to the iron bars of our window. The sentries on the high wall kick their feet and shake their capes, trying to loosen the powdery white shower. There is a street fire burning at the main door. I can see the soldiers of the guard trying to warm their fingers while the sergeant pokes the bonfire.

Now, on the road near the railway, a tall, slender, black-clad figure is trying to protect his face from the wind under a wide-brimmed hat. It's Father Aspiazu. In a few minutes he'll reach the front door and show a white card to the guards who undoubtedly will greet him with a servile smile and escort him to our cell. His arrival is always accompanied by Jaime's grunts of disapproval, while Santolaya pleads for civility with a warning look. For his part, the priest couldn't be more courteous. With great tact he dismisses Jaime's grumpy welcome and proceeds to give us news of our families and of local events. Father Aspiazu concentrates his pride and vanity in the pulpit, where he holds his own famously as a preacher. When his talks with us become serious, his favorite subject is, of course, theology. And in that, only Mato and Gilabert—if they are among us— can fare well.

Most nights after those visits I lie awake reviewing the day's religious talks; the concepts of divine justice and mercy, the interpretation of God and other issues discussed by the priest. Seen from the reality of violence and cruelty surrounding us, those scholarly subtleties, those incursions into the realm of divinity, seem out of place. How can that priest expect a sincere response from us, here in this climate of brute force and coercion? And if all he seeks is some answer from us, however insincere . . . why that expression of sympathy we often detect on his face?

To the rumble of several men snoring in the cell, I wind up my speculations and fall asleep.

A SAD CHRISTMAS

Christmas is near, and with it increasing rumors of the possibility of freedom awaited by so many despite repeated disappointments. A chilly wind awaits us in the morning. It filters through every crack and door to continue hissing in the corridors. Well into midmorning, we learn that all visits have been suspended for the day, to be replaced by the last conference in the religious cycle, in preparation for general confession and communion the day before Christmas. Before going down to the courtyard with the others, I look out the window and get a glimpse of the last group of visitors being turned back at the jail door, all holding their privilege pass now rendered useless by the blessed religious conference. The disappointed faces, the sorrowful bent figures—some of them in mourning—turn around and cross the railway back to Logroño, buffeted by rain and wind.

In a few minutes we are gathered and suffering, with our usual straight faces, our last religious conference. Toward the end of the ceremony, there is an incident caused by a degenerate fascist militia who is serving time for making indecent advances to a female nurse at the provincial hospital. He suddenly shouts the patriotic falangist cries of "A Great Spain! One Spain! Spain Alone! Long Live Spain!" A half dozen voices echo him timidly, just enough to cover up the general silence of the others.

The afterdinner talk is endless today. The building is shaken by the icy wind and no one dares go out into the courtyard. Gilabert, the district attorney, tells incidents of his professional life, which vividly illustrate the double-faced justice applied so differently to the poor and to the rich. The leftist, too, is considered a fanatic and a dangerous individual, he tells us. But an about-face easily makes of him a law-abiding citizen. It's a system of weights and measures just as applicable to other professions. The district attorney's measured tone becomes violent when he speaks of anonymous accusations, which he considers the height of monstrosity in man. And to support his thesis he quotes from the letters of Emperor Trajan to his friend Pliny the Younger. Trajan approves the conduct of his friend as governor, including the persecution of Christians. But he calls his attention to one distinction: "Do not round them up *en masse*. Punish the stubborn, but not the others. And never pay heed to anonymous betrayals. That is a barbarous procedure that has no place in our times."

Now he tells us an anecdote of his early days as a jurist, in Burgos. The district attorney had to attend a banquet at which the auxiliary bishop invited him to sit between himself and a Lieutenant Colonel. "This is your place," the prelate said. "Between the sword and the cross." Listening to Gilabert, I often remember Adolfo Moreda, president of the Barcelona Supreme Court, my friend from the Avenida jail, assassinated at the Fort of San Cristóbal.

When the district attorney ends his stories, the conversation takes a new turn. Hilario de la Mata, director of Logroño's Central Bank, recently made some public statements condemning the cruelty of the falangist authorities, statements that naturally found no echo in the local press, or from the local henchmen. Several of the men now speak of de la Mata. They believe that despite his early enthusiasm for the military revolt, those statements voicing his change of heart place him among the group of persons who still have a sense of ethics. But according to Luís Vázquez, a veteran of the cell next to ours, the bank director is a habitual complainer, always discontented with any and all developments. And, like all aristocrats—Vázquez adds—a fierce enemy of the Republic.

"Don't you remember he donated one hundred thousand pesetas to the Movement on the first day of the rebellion? Have you forgotten that his son was one of the first to enlist as volunteer aide to Inerariti, the artillery commander?"

Luís Vázquez seldom visits our cell. But today he is in a talkative mood. Now he tells us a story that years ago was the talk of Logroño:

One afternoon, during the spring of 1910, Hilario de la Mata, his brother, the marquis of Vargas, and the family coachman were returning to Logroño after a ride. A road worker stopped the carriage, signaling the coachman to drive closer to the curb, since the center of the road was being repaired. Perhaps the worker's tone had seemed impertinent to the marquis, for his reaction was to grab the coachman's whip and slash the workman's face. When he felt the blood running down his face, the workman became furious and yanked the marquis from the coach and threw him on the ground. Hilario and the coachman ran to the defense, and after a brief struggle, they killed the workman, leaving the body by the side of the road.

After a long and complicated case, with some complacency on the part of the judges and a certain sum of money to seal the witnesses' lips, they were able to arrange for the coachman to take the blame for the murder.

"You've forgotten one detail," Manolo Alba says. "The workman tried to stab the marquis with his knife."

"You probably would have done the same in his place. After all, he had been whipped like a horse," Luís Vázquez replies.

"Perhaps, but that story has nothing to do with the way Hilario de la Mata is behaving now. All our enemies should be like him! Although I don't want to seem like a champion of the aristocrats, I remind you that their class has little political power now. The great tyrants who today represent the rightist reaction in the world are not a product of the aristocracy."

The cigarette smoke can be cut with a knife by this time. While Alba goes on taking up the defense of Hilario de la Mata, chow time arrives and at last silences us.

Andrés the contractor has been transferred here from the Industrial School. He arrives early one morning and is promptly assigned to a cell on the main floor. When he comes to see us he tells me that the old arithmetic classroom has had new inmates and five "sacas" in the past weeks.

At last, Governor Benlló is ousted and the news raises the entire prison's morale and optimism. The Civil Government remains under the Secretary while a new head is being sought. All matters pertaining to the prisoners—among them the most important to us, the "sacas"—are suspended. When we first hear the news about Benlló we remember a phrase used by Father Aspiazu, which now seems prophetic. Some weeks ago, when the inmates of this cell were discussing the subject of justice with the Father, Jaime had interrupted angrily, "What's all that boloney about justice? With this jewel of a governor I bet there isn't going to be one of us left alive to tell the tale!"

It was then that the priest, with his eternal little smile on his lips, answered, "Governors are not immortal."

We had forgotten that sentence, but now every man remembers it. We are convinced that it points to the high official sources of information available to the Jesuit.

The day before general confession and communion, there are heated discussions about the attitude we should adopt. There are rumors of forthcoming freedom for some, there is also fear of reprisals which undoubtedly would mean curtailment of visitors' permits and gift parcels. That, and the constant threat of death that hangs over us, succeed in breaking down our will to resist the religious farce. So, when time comes for confession, the entire prison population kneels in front of the priests, one by one, and . . . confesses. The only exception is a petty thief, Polish by nationality, a little blond man who speaks Spanish with a thick foreign accent. Next morning they repeat the mass ceremony, followed by general communion.

Our cook León presents us with an extraordinary Christmas stew redolent of sausage and generously dotted with meat chunks. Many men are allowed to remain with their visitors beyond the customary fifteen minutes, some as long as half an hour! Director Pacheco has relaxed the restrictions on gift parcels. Our cells, too, remain open much later that night. The privileges remind us all the more of the fact that we are spending the holiday separated from our loved ones.

After the night inspection, we connect our secret switch and Jaime attempts to carry on as usual and brings out his cherished map of Madrid to start the war discussion. But Mato cuts him off with this small speech:

"For us, the solution to this war is not in Madrid but in the Catalonian Pyrenees, or rather, in Port Bou. It is through there that we'll get arms from France, if we are getting them at all. In these next two or three days there's going to be no fighting on the fronts, not even small skirmishes." Then, glancing at our table laden with the Christmas delicacies brought to us by our friends and relatives, and recalling the student of the legendary "Diablo Cojuelo" he adds wistfully, "I'd like to be able to fly out the window now and over the open rooftops, to see the families sitting at their Christmas supper, watching the empty places of sons, brothers, and husbands, sisters, wives, and daughters who are absent, some forever. . . . I bet you that over the roast turkey I'd see a dark cloud of sorrow in every home. Even here, the brief joy we've seen today in all faces is a lie. Listen. . . . You hear the sentries singing Christmas carols? As soon as they lose the glow from all the wine they've had, they too will start thinking. They too have homes."

We hear the sentries singing:

> 'We the shepherds come from far
> To pay homage to the Child.'

And down at the gate, the soldiers answer:

> 'Glory to God in heaven, and
> Peace on earth to men of good will.'

"What a joke," exclaims Jaime. "What a goddam joke those carols sound like now," he repeats as he throws the blanket over his face.

Christmas does not bring the freedom expected by some of the men, but the year begins at Hotel Fontanillas without the usual nightly fear of the "sacas." The new governor, Francisco Jordán de Urries, takes over. There is a general order from Burgos which applies to all the provinces held by the rebels. The "butcher" governors, most of them military professionals, are replaced by civilians who are ordered to review the summary cases and give them a semblance of legality. The change may be good for us and we talk of nothing else. Undoubtedly, looking back at the lawless bloodshed that has prevailed for the past five and a half months, we can only feel hopeful at these new developments.

At the end of the first week of January they start reviewing our proceedings. To many of us this is the first legal inquiry into their cases since their arrest. We are called to the glass cabin in the center of the courtyard in groups of threes and fours. Secret agents examine us at length, often with insidious or stupid questions. They accumulate reams of statements which we suspect are destined for burial in the basement of the Civil Government building.

The cases examined are divided into two groups: those with the backing of influential persons who seek the freedom of a friend or a relative; and those the authorities are determined to prosecute in order to execute the greatest possible number of men by classifying them as 'dangerous.' The first group turns out to be insignificant, and the second small in comparison to the number of those already brazenly executed. The rest of the thousands of hopeful men are no better and no worse after the lengthy written examinations.

We are graced by the arrival of a famous pickpocket, famous for his extraordinary feats as well as for having escaped from no less than three jails. His last escape was from this very prison, while the guard called Don Antonio was in service. Now, by coincidence, Don Antonio is in charge of receiving the notorious prodigal, and this time he is determined to avoid a repetition of the escape that nearly cost him his job. He takes every precaution, although he makes an effort to prevent the slightest physical damage to his prisoner. He places him in a cell facing the courtyard and orders a large red cross painted under his window as a warning. Word is sent all over the jail informing the inmates that the sentries on the wall have orders to shoot on sight anyone who gets closer than two yards to the place marked by the painted cross.

But somehow all the precautions are violated by the heads of the committee of common prisoners: The Brute, Tinajas, and Bartolo. They manage to send their isolated friend notes and cigarettes through some complicated mechanism involving rope and chunks of plaster. It is a little more difficult to send him food. But they manage that too with the aid of a broom attached to a rod long enough to lift small bundles to the very window bars. Their solidarity is impressive. Any of them caught in the act will be shot at sight.

Andrés the contractor is very confident that his village priest can use influence on his behalf, especially now that there is a new governor. The panel truck he used in his building contracting firm has been requisitioned by City Hall and his eldest son drafted as its chauffeur. That enables the son to get close enough to the falangist authorities to reinforce the efforts being taken by the village priest to help obtain his father's freedom.

One visit a week and the inevitable holy mass are our only contact with the outside world. During our afterdinner discussions León the cook often comes in with coffee. He exchanges a few pleasant words with us and leaves, to return much later for the coffee pot. Whatever the subject, when a conversation turns into a heated discussion Celestino the ex-cop joins it ipso facto. Wheat is one of Jaime's favorite topics because of his business. Tonight he reminds us of the farcical wheat deals that prevailed in Castile during the Bienio Negro—The Black Biennial, the repressive period 1934 to 1936 when the Republic was dominated by reactionary forces which conspired to overthrow it. The law had fixed the wheat price at 78 pesetas the *fanega* (1.60 bushel). But when the farmer came to sell, the official agents would offer him 68 pesetas, alleging that "Spain was flooded with wheat and it was impossible to meet the fixed price. The offer was a special favor granted the peasant, in exchange for a receipt acknowledging the 78 pesetas demanded by the law." Jaime adds that the five years of the Republic was the only period in one hundred years when Spain did not have to import wheat.

"Have you read the news in the *Aragón Herald?*" Celestino asks him. "Wheat sowing in the Republican zone is going to be done with modern Russian machinery."

"There must be some venomous interpretation to that news," Jaime replies. "Who the hell believes those falangist newspapers?"

"The news doesn't sound much like Franco propaganda," Celestino tells him. "In fact, there are some veiled praises for the Madrid government. It's no use hiding it, my friend. The time has come for the Spanish peasant to end his backwardness and realize he's in the twentieth century. He'll never have a better opportunity."

Santolaya joins the discussion. "That's absurd. I am a planter myself, and I tell you, to hell with machinery in this case. You don't need machinery for little parcels no bigger than a bed sheet. And, anyway, the peasants don't know how to handle machines. They are an underdeveloped class and it's no use hoping. That news must be the dream of some idealist, or perhaps of some opportunist."

"You are a kulak!" exclaims Celestino.

"I am nothing of the kind! At six in the morning, when you are still snoring, I am out in the fields, often guiding the plow. See my hands? Where do you think I got those cal999es? The trouble is that in the country as in the cities there are too many lazy good-for-nothings."

"Olé for the wealthy landowner! We're not just talking about work, my friend, but also about the rightful hopes of the peasants. They have every right to demand land. I've got a friend down in the courtyard who tells me how the landowners in his town left the lands untilled when the Republic was proclaimed, while many families didn't have enough bread to make soup with. If the Republic had not been so damned lenient those landowners wouldn't have been allowed to let the country go to pot."

Antonio Ruíz can't keep quiet any longer. "Listen, the Republic has been just, lenient, and respectful to all alike. It's the reactionaries who sabotaged the agrarian reform. And the delay in implementing the law can be blamed on traitors like Alejandro Lerroux. I remind you that the chief of the so-called Radical party joined the rightists to help Gil Robles get in power. And we all know what that brought about in the Republic: the well-named 'Two Black Years' of '34 and '35. At any rate, we're only playing their game when we place men in fixed classifications like cave-dweller, the center, the extreme left. Nothing is that black and white in life and politics. There are many half-tones in the picture and the liberal mind can be conservative on certain issues and revolutionary on others. Freedom of thought itself breeds that flexibility, man! The true liberal is not a doctrinaire about anything, including the agrarian reform."

Manolo Alba joins in. "The agrarian reform was more talk than anything else. Judging by the protests and screaming of the landowners you'd think the land expropriations took everything from them, when actually things were quite different. Two years after the Republic was proclaimed fifty thousand owners still held half of Spain's 45 million hectares of arable land. And the next group, the small owners, still held another 14 million hectares. Figure it out and tell me what the hell was left then for the millions of peasants!"

But Antonio Ruíz is not going to be stopped. "We democrats don't intend to favor lazy good-for-nothings or dispossess owners from what legally belongs to them. What we seek is a just distribution of the wealth derived from toil and talent. This whole thing is like a race where the team of peasants has been handicapped by a chain and ball. There is no political system that could eradicate injustices completely and create a state of total prosperity for all. But to place all teams under the same rules and let them compete equally in the race is as close to a clean game as one could get."

Santolaya is annoyed and declares himself not against the game, but against having the ball and chain merely change from the feet of one team to those of another. He pierces Celestino with a look and adds, "You with your sympathies for Russia. . . . Don't tell me that's not exactly what is happening there."

"I can't deny or confirm anything because the information we get from Russia is scant and damned confused. We do know that in the field of education the only qualification there is brains. And we do know that education in Russia is free and that no one gets a ball and chain clamped on his feet before he's sent to race anyone.

The trouble is that the reactionary mind cannot survey Russian reality because to him it's something unspeakable and that alone prevents him from even thinking about it."

Just then, Léon the cook comes in looking for his coffee pot and as usual, Mato ends the discussion with one of his blithe and often wise comments. "All right, compañeros. That's enough talk about wheat, whether from Russia or from Manitoba. We have enough to worry about. Let's talk about whores, for instance. That's a lot more entertaining subject, and a less dangerous one."

Despite our ferocious differences of opinion there is a true brotherhood among us. León picks up his coffee pot and gives us a sly wink of complicity as he departs.

Now it's time for Manolo Alba to perch himself on a crate by our window and throw breadcrumbs through the bars toward the adjacent roof. A flock of faithful pigeons are already awaiting the never-failing shower. Behind Manolo, we watch the birds clean up the crumbs in competition with the hundreds of mice that nest in the crumbling crags of the roof.

MÁLAGA

Homosexuality rears its head the day Luís is brought into our prison. He is a young petty thief who sways around the men provocatively with a definite feminine gait. Quickly he is nicknamed Luisita, and soon has some of the common prisoners competing for his favors. Visits to his cell—originally intended for one and now occupied by three inmates—are carefully arranged by his male paramours who draw lots to see who will share his quarters for the night.

This kind of activity can not go undetected indefinitely, no matter how skillfully those involved fool the guards. So one day Pacheco the Director finds out and Luisita is placed in solitary prior to being transferred to the Valladolid jail.

There are nights when Santolaya's earthshaking snore competes with Jaime's, and then trying to sleep becomes an exercise in futility.

If one falls asleep before the "concert" starts there is a chance of spending a restful night, otherwise there is nothing to do but hope for a lull, or as I often do, go to the corridor, look out the window, and gaze at the sky. One of those evenings, while I look at the stars, Alfonso Mato comes quietly and does the same. I do not notice him until he muses:

"When one looks at the sky on a night like this, one's soul grows larger and one's miseries become smaller."

Through the bars of the window, the moonless night is twinkling with stars. The silence surrounding the prison is broken by the barking of far away hounds. We keep our lighted cigarettes below the window frame so their glow won't be detected by the guards walking the ramparts of the prison wall. Mato tells me how, after becoming a lawyer, he established a friendship with a mathematics professor who was an ardent amateur astronomer and had himself become greatly interested in astronomy.

"I'd read any book on the subject I could lay my hands on," he says. "You'd be surprised how my new knowledge of astronomy would help me at times in arguing my cases in court. I think I'd have chosen astronomy instead of law if I had been bitten earlier by the bug."

The chat had no other purpose than to while away our insomnia. We talked for some time about the latest astronomy book lent to him by Father Aspiazu. Mato also believes in astrology and thinks the stars influence our lives. He sees this connection in the terminology used by the *Movimiento*. For instance, when a falangist dies, they say "he went on watch duty among the stars" (taken from the falangist newspapers).

The snoring has subsided, and we go back to bed. Stretched on my bunk, Jaime's remarks about the strange falangist phraseology comes to my mind. "If we ever get out of this alive we'll have to go back to school to learn the new language, their 'Upward with the triple load,' 'Journeys of preferred courage,' 'Surfaces with preferred depth,' 'Military emotion,' and all the jargon of that renegade Villena." He was referring to a young local newsman who, resentful at not getting the job he wanted went from the extreme Left to the extreme Fascist Right, putting on the Falange Blue-Shirt.

Jaime had also said in derision: "Of course all that gibberish about stars comes from the litanies. Those who die in the morning go to the morning star, and the ones that get bumped off in the afternoon land on the evening star. What a bunch of idiots! Going to do watch duty on the stars in their blue nightgowns with their arrows embroidered on the chests!"

We have contact with only a few of the common-crimes prisoners. There is a communications barrier between us and the rest, through no fault of the political prisoners. The fact that we share the same prison is sufficient for us to consider them companions in misfortune, but they think we belong to another world and keep a polite but distant attitude.

On afternoon at the end of January, Eduardo Andrés has a visitor and comes running with important news. General Queipo de Llano, supported by thousands of Italian troops and dozens of Italian airplanes, has just launched an offensive against Málaga. The Republican Government has dispatched the army of Levante and the entire navy from the Cartagena base, to defend the city. Another piece of news is that local contingents are leaving for the Madrid front. The wives and mothers of Logroño answered with silence to the "Vivas!" and "Arribas!" heard at the railway station when the troops were about to depart.

"They have their rendezvous with death," says Manolo Alba. (The reference is a quote from the Spanish Foreign Legion Song, which says, "I am the fiancé of Death!")

"What do you mean 'they'?" Celestino exclaims. "What about us? Haven't you noticed that nobody is spared at the summary trials?"

Manolo cuts him short saying, "It's too early to jump to conclusions. Our condition has improved since they fired Benlló, and now we can sleep peacefully. Sure, there are death sentences, but, mind you, many escape with only 30 years, and that, my friend, is sweet cake in comparison."

Jaime butts in to say that we are going through the in-between period, that this is just a stand-by, that Sergeant Sánchez—the man in charge of the executions, whose name spells terror in the prisons— has said so at the Espolón bar. "The second act is approaching," he declared.

"I'm not defending Sergeant Sánchez," says Celestino, "but some take the blame and others the dough." Then he adds, as if privy to a secret: "I, as an ex-policeman, know certain things. . . ."

"This goddamn cop!" exclaims Jaime, "always mysterious."

"Sergeant Sánchez might be a son of a bitch, but he's only a cog in the whole machinery of terror," says Antonio Ruíz. "I have a relative who is also a sergeant and he is a decent man. Two times he commanded an execution squad in Soria, and the third time he refused. And he wasn't sacked or executed because his company captain saved him by sending him to the front."

"I also know," puts in Santolaya, "about soldiers that got sick from having to fire against relatives and friends, but they did it anyway. During the first days of executions many in the squads, trusting that their buddies would do their job, shot above prisoners' heads. Their compassion, though, many times resulted in terrible agonies among those hit, because in the confusion they forgot to give them the *coup de grace*."

"That's a lot of bullshit," cries Celestino. "That might have happened a couple of times; but remember that the execution squads were all falangists, blue-breasted birds, yes sir, with their red berets, who did their job as if they were playing a game of checkers."

Celestino browses around our little library trying to find a book to read. He picks one out, but Manolo Alba suggests an essay by Dr. Gregorio Marañón instead. The erstwhile policeman rejects it, quipping about "empty pages." (The quip refers to a five-hundred-page "book" a man from Madrid with means and a sense of humor had had published, entitled "Dr. Marañón's Record During the Sessions of the Constituent Assembly.") The "book" contained only two words, "yes" and "no" interspersed among the hundreds of blank pages, thus ridiculing the disappointing performance in Congress of the great scholar who had done so much to bring about the birth of the Republic in 1931.

Celestino's witticism is picked up by Antonio Ruíz, who goes on to say:

"And they are really exploiting him now as well as other turn-coats 'who have seen the light.' Damn it, and we never hear about it when one of them sees *our* light! What is it? Lack of confidence on our side? Is our propaganda set-up so dumb?"

"It is that blasted inferiority complex that has always been a trademark among the politicians of the Left in Spain," says the district attorney, with sententious finality.

At the end of January, Jaime is released from prison but confined to the limits of a small town near Vitoria until further orders. His initial joy is somewhat dampened when he learns he won't be allowed to operate his flour mill. Jaime's brother-in-law, a higher-up in the Civil Guard, after much paperwork and the payment of a moderate fine, has finally gotten him released. Next morning, Eduardo Andrés and ex-District Attorney Gilabert, are also set free. A wave of exhilaration runs through the prison. As events would later prove, it was false hope.

The improvements in the Spanish penal system implemented by Victoria Kent, the Chief Commissioner of Prisons during the first years of the Republic, are evident in our jail. Regulations in force are far better here than in other prisons, especially regarding visitors, food, and books.

News from Málaga is bad. On February 5th, the Italian forces broke the front at several points. The cruisers *Baleares, Canarias,* and *Almirante Cervera* (in rebel hands since the start of the Movement), in conjunction with Italian air units have subjected the northern and southern exits from the city to intense bombardment to impede escape and retreat. On the sixth and the seventh of February effective organized resistance ceased. It was every man for himself. On the eighth the Italians entered Málaga singing "Giovinezza."

The Legion and the Moors followed. Then came the falangists to do the killings. Moderate estimates put at 4,000 those executed during the first two weeks.

The news is celebrated in our town with the pealing of churchbells, which we can hear in the distance, the prison being outside the city. Dinner is silent, and the afterdinner conversation like a funeral. Once all the explanations about treason, incompetence, foreign military intervention, etc., are given for the fall of Málaga, the conversation turns to the subject of law.

"I don't know where I read that a lawyer is 'a conscience for hire,' " says Mato, the lawyer, slyly.

"That's a wisecrack," says Celestino, "I don't believe you hold your own profession so low. An architect, an engineer, and a doctor do likewise, but it is one thing to sell one's talent and another to hire one's conscience. Anyway, you're just trying to be funny."

"Yes, I was kidding; nobody spits on his own profession," he admits. "But in a certain way we all cultivate our brain to sell a portion of it. Although there must be a limit. In our professional life some times we must handle distasteful cases, though an honest lawyer can refuse. The summit of professional ethics would be to reject a client intent on perverting justice. Better still, for a client not to seek the counsel of a lawyer who thinks his claim is unjust. In such a world, wolves and sheep would live peacefully together, men would be angels and lawyers would outlive their usefulness."

That is the last peroration of the evening and Mato's last visit with our group. Next day, in the morning, he is released from jail. We expected something like that after noticing that several influential people had come to visit him.

The absence of Jaime and Mato creates a vacuum among us, specially at dinner time. We miss them.

Two days later we are ordered to get ready next day to move *en masse* to the Avenida prison. We are to leave behind Celestino, the policeman, together with Antonio Ruíz, Eizaguirre, Jorge, Guerrero, Práxedes Toledo, and another half dozen political prisoners. In the wee hours of the morning, a detail of Assault Guards gets us in their trucks with their automatic weapons at the ready, leading us to the Avenida jail. We cross the empty streets, the town still asleep.

RETURN TO THE CIRCLE

I find myself back where I started the day of my arrest on July 22nd, last year. There are fewer old familiar faces. Macario has been set free. Poli, Emilio the student, and Salvado the veterinarian have been transferred to other prisons. Santiago, Don José's nephew, and the little old man who told Carlist tales, Martín, together with many others, have been executed in the last few months. Angel, the Protestant pastor has disappeared without anybody knowing how or when. New inmates have taken the place of those gone. Used as I am to the air and sun in the courtyard of the provincial prison, I feel depressed in this unhealthy dungeon. It is as crammed with prisoners—perhaps more so—as when I first came here.

A large batch of prisoners is brought over from the Industrial School jail. Since it's impossible to pack so many people in the ball court, they make temporary arrangements in the former movie-house. Some are sent to different provincial prisons. For a couple of days there is frantic activity while they ship people away and make room for the torrent of prisoners from the Industrial School.

The first friends I meet again are Rafael, Pereda, Adolfo Alvarez, and the worker from the Ortigosa Dam. Several peasants in the arithmetic classroom have been shot, whereas the number of those expected to be released by the new governor, has been disappointingly low, no more than a handful at both the Industrial and the provincial jails.

Don Pedro, the warden, runs the prison as harshly as ever, they tell me. One of the interns, the one who helped me with my injections, was among those executed. He was the mayor of Lardero.

At the beginning of the second week, Dr. Rodrigo Varo, a physician and provincial inspector of sanitation, is brought in. He was taken into custody at the outbreak of the Movement and suspended from his job, but he managed to make a deal with the Rebels with the help of influential friends, and then enlisted in the medical corps serving at the Madrid front. There he remained until someone denounced him. They arrested him and brought him to the Logroño jail.

Varo is reserved and timid but he has an agreeable disposition. In the performance of his duties he has picked up information unknown to us. Pessimistically, he believes the Italians, with all the matériel they have assembled, could take Madrid by assault against all Loyalist opposition, no matter from which sector they chose to attack.

After several frustrated attempts to cut off the Madrid-Valencia highway—the only lifeline left open to the Spanish capital—the

Fascist Command decide on a two-pronged attack that would en-
circle Madrid and force the city to surrender. One arm of the pincer
would break through the Jarama River and the other through
Guadalajara.

The Italians, flushed by their easy victory at Málaga, demand that
Franco allow them to proceed alone, save for the Soria Division
under General Moscardó, and that only for appearance's sake. It
must be said that Moscardó's "Division" was a division only in
name, and so undermanned that it could hardly qualify as a brigade.
This division was to cover a flank of the Italian advance, taking the
Jadraque passes and to march on along the main Guadalajara road
in step with the Italian onslaught. The Italian attack force comprised
Divisions I, II, III, and the Littorio Division, under Generals Rossi,
Coppi, Nuvolari, and Bergonzoli. The opposing Republican Army
had two divisions, Mora's and Líster's; four international brigades,
and the battalions of Modesto and El Campesino.

The fascist offensive broke out on March 8th. Moscardó over-
whelmed the Jadraque passes and continued his advance. The
Italians, operating along the Zaragoza-Madrid highway, pushed
forward to a point 45 kilometers from their starting point without en-
countering any resistance. In the early morning hours of the 12th,
the Republican troops launched a counteroffensive that was to
transform the easy Italian "walk" into a dismal rout. They had concentrated so much mechanized equipment in such a small area that,
in their retreat, in heavy rains and cold weather, they got themselves
choked in a bottle-neck, and had to abandon much of their equipment and leave behind large numbers of prisoners. The counteroffensive ended on March 22nd. It proved that the legal government
had an organized and disciplined army.

The news of the Republican victory, confusing at first and then
reported in detail, has a magic effect on the inmates. Discipline
relaxes somewhat; the guards and prison officials indulge in certain
courtesies to the prisoners and at times even smile at us. Dr. Varo
changes his mood to one of boundless optimism.

"I've seen their armament," he exclaims, "and if with all that
they haven't won, then there is no doubt about the outcome. The
Republic will win!"

There were adverse factors in the situation—such as cowardice

or egoism on the part of the democracies, audacity on the part of
the dictatorships and the international conspiracy of the big banks—
that would have weakened Rodrigo Varo's conclusion, but since
he and the rest of us didn't know about them, his logic made sense.
By this time there could not be the least doubt in the European
foreign offices about the shameless intervention of Hitler and
Mussolini in the Spanish Civil War.

The Guadalajara defeat and the mocking comments on the doubtful courage of the Italian Army, enraged Mussolini who determined
on revenge. He poured more men and matériel into the Spanish
war, soon reaching a total of 60,000 together with complementary
services. Hitler also increased the number of his technicians, fliers,
and armament, sending up to 25,000 men. Such a torrent of troops
and matériel could hardly be counterbalanced with the 16,000
volunteers of the international brigades and the often defective
Russian equipment paid for by us in gold.

A month after staying in this dungeon I catch a bad cold and
have to go for treatment to the infirmary on the first floor. I am given
a double dose of cathartic and iodine-glycerin. Being the last patient
in the line I miss the others going back to the ball court. I descend
the stairs alone. There is an open window, and the sun and the soft
spring air are coming through. I can't resist the temptation to enjoy
them after five weeks locked up in the stuffy ball court. I let the sun
soak my skin and close my eyes in delight. A sharp pain puts a sudden end to my rapture. A guard has dropped the stock of his rifle
on my foot.

"What are you doing here?" he barks.

"Clearing my head," I answer holding back any sign of pain.

"I'll clear it good for you if you don't get moving to the ball court.
Feel lucky I don't go squeal to the Corporal about this."

He seemed surprised that I had given no indication of pain. I
heard that he later commented on it.

This makeshift jail is under a professional warden of the Prison
Corps, a tall, slender man, about fifty years old. Once in a while
you could see in Don Enrique's jovial face a certain sympathy for
the prisoners; he even shows kindness and understanding without

losing any of his authority. With fewer facilities at hand than his colleague Don Pedro, the Industrial School prison warden, he manages to have all services running in the best possible way.

During my absence in other prisons, he has installed an additional toilet and a washbasin, so one waits less in line, though the char men do their job much less well than Macario and his helpers did when I was first here. The rat population has increased fabulously. Every day, two sack fulls of dead ones are carted away. Yet, nobody seems to be much disturbed by the fact. I, like most people, had always felt queasy on seeing them, but after getting used to them here, I watch them scurry along my blanket with indifference and finally with something approaching affection.

Among the new prisoners a few catch my attention. Bengoa, a good-looking twenty-eight-year-old, is the most interesting. He soon has Don Enrique's confidence and is assigned many functions in the prison. He has free access to all parts of the building and is not afraid to intercede in favor of his fellow prisoners, something that wins him great popularity among the inmates. Everybody accepts his favorable situation without criticism because he has earned it through ability and his *simpático* disposition, with no traces of apple polishing in his conduct. He has an astonishing capacity for remembering names and knowing the most insignificant details relating to the internal life of the prison.

In spite of Bengoa's competent help, Don Enrique is always swamped with problems about services, security, transfers, and consultations with the Civil Government. Important business suffers delays no matter how hard he works, mostly on account of his inevitable absences. He requests from the Civil Governor permission to accommodate his family in the prison premises in order to cope both with his official and domestic duties. Soon the family quarters are ready on the first tier of boxes of the cinema hall. Among his numerous children Don Enrique has several pretty daughters; the eldest ones waste no time in being kind to Bengoa, a fact that provokes jesting remarks among the prisoners, not all of them in the best of taste.

Another interesting character is Tuno, a little fellow who talks fast and makes quick gestures. He is a cobbler by profession and an amateur musician by vocation. He played the trumpet and the violin in the orchestras that made the rounds of the town fairs in the area of his native village of La Rioja, called by the fine Biblical name of Galilea. According to prison talk, he "made America," working for a construction company in Buenos Aires for a couple of years. Upon his return to his home town, the military insurrection broke out, and, afraid of getting killed, built himself a brick cubicle with his wife's help in the backyard of the house. There he hid for several months hoping for better times.

Tuno's wife would frequently go around the streets wailing and weeping:

"Oh, my poor little husband! He ran away to the mountains. Oh, he must be dead by now."

In this way she hoped to protect her husband by making his disappearance believable to the local authorities. She did it so well in fact, that the mayor and the falangists truly believed her man to be dead, and found the noisy mourning most natural.

Tuno also tells us that the cubicle communicated with the chimney of the house, and that at night he'd climb a rope to the roof to catch a breath of fresh air and stretch his legs. He would have continued that way indefinitely had it not been for one member of the household who didn't understand the situation: his hunting dog, who kept sniffing and howling around his hiding place. His wife punished the hound, but the animal loved and missed his master. The dog's protests made some neighbors suspicious, the authorities were alerted, and Tuno was discovered, arrested, and sent to the Logroño jail. At least he avoided, for five and a half months, the initial terror of the Civil War.

Twice Tuno asks Don Enrique's permission to get his cobbler's tools and try to make some money with his work. When the authorization comes, he makes Don Enrique a pair of shoes that are a masterpiece, as a gesture of gratitude. Tuno is also given the job of distributing the milk in the infirmary, a new service in the prison. He takes advantage of it by drinking big swigs from the milk jars. He justifies his pilfering by blaming it on the small rations and the tiring climbing up and down stairs he has to do in the performance of his duty.

Besides Tuno and Bengoa, there is another prisoner who enjoys great popularity. His name is Felipe, a shoeshiner, chubby, with white wavy hair, and of undetermined age. When assigned to the cleaning detail, he amuses us dancing the rhumba with his broom, shaking wildly, and making funny gestures. He has lived in Havana for some time where he picked up his Cuban slang and accent. At times he complains of rheumatic pains in his legs and spends two or three days on a wooden bunk in the infirmary wrapped up in a blanket, "keeping my warmth," as he says. When he recovers he comes back with new, outrageously tropical lyrics for his repertoire of rhumbas and *danzones* which he sings while dancing, to everybody's merriment. If the conversation ever turns to war or politics, he avoids the subject saying:

"After all we've gone through, this is a picnic."

Some times the security detail is composed of falangist volunteers among whom we see friends and acquaintances. Their strange salutes behind the Corporal's back point to their fear. The Security Guard works as an independent body, acting as liaison with the Civil Government, watching over visitors, inspecting packages and performing other minor functions. The detail more often assigned to our prison is composed of Fernando, the Wild Wolf, Juaguín, Tagarnina, Davalillos, and another young man who always makes a twosome with the latter. Davalillos is a man of great physical strength and was seriously wounded a long time ago during a labor strike. Together with the memory of his wound he nurses a deep grudge against prisoners affiliated with the C.N.T. (Confederación Nacional del Trabajo).

For several weeks we anxiously await the favorable results of the Republican victory at Guadalajara on the course of the Civil War and our future. Disappointment never produces long-lasting despondency, and the most excitable ones are the first to forget.

My health had improved noticeably at the provincial jail. There my back pains had become less severe and frequent. But the unhealthy Avenida jail and a bout with intestinal flu set me back. I get permanently transferred to the infirmary.

With the approach of Easter, they announce the second "voluntary" mass communion to be taken by the inmates. The day before, in the afternoon, when the priests arrive, they order everybody to stand in line. Queues are formed leading to each priest sitting at the end of the court, where the prisoners in turn make their confession kneeling down on the filthy floor.

In order to know how many holy hosts will be needed for next day's communion, the priests kept count of those who confessed by dropping beans from their pockets into a handkerchief.

Fear among the prisoners has diminished since the nightly "sacas" were discontinued, so, more than half of them refuse to go to confession. In many cases their refusal is prompted by their being forced to do it, rather than by a lack of religious feeling. Next morning, with a temporary altar set up and in the presence of officials, the ceremony takes place. Among those present are the Chief of Police, the Governor's secretary, and several officials in charge of criminal files. Word of reprisals against those not taking communion passes among the inmates through gestures and whispers. Fear, as in the provincial jail, spreads among all of us, so when the time comes for communion, almost all the inmates go to the rail, making the bean count a failure. There is a short intermission while they bring more holy hosts from a nearby church. From my sick bed against the bannister of the theatre boxes, I have a bird's-eye view of the spectacle. When the priest finishes giving communion below, he comes to the infirmary to offer it to those ill in their beds. When my turn comes I remain paralyzed with his hand before my mouth. My first impulse is to tell him that I have not gone to confession, that I have eaten food past midnight—all true and enough to make a sacrilege of communion. But I fear that my explanation will be taken as an act of defiance, that it will bring me reprisals. I don't utter a word. Later I am ashamed of myself.

The ceremony and its attendant incidents supply enough material for commentaries during the rest of the morning. I hear one from a sick man, by the name of Abundio, so thin he almost looks transparent:

"Miserable black toads that drag their skirts on the floor and pretend to cover infamy with a cloak of hypocrisy full of holes.

What a false love for their fellow men! They could have done so much, and did nothing! They think they can do anything as long as they keep up appearances."

"It wasn't that bad," says Adolfo Alvarez. "Besides, the truly responsible ones are those high up in the hierarchy, and not all of them. The lower clergy, only obey their orders."

"Lower clergy, high clergy, my foot!" retorts Abundio. "They all know they force us to be insincere and even blasphemous. If they entered the clergy full of love for God and their fellow men, time has wiped it out. They can't hide behind their make-up of old prostitutes; you'll find their true ugly faces underneath."

"In the last instance," insists Adolfo, "the moral responsibility would rest on the military for creating this environment of terror and cowardice that envelops us all, because neither you nor I had the courage to say 'no,' and we've taken communion like many of our prison mates."

"But they are priests," replies Abundio, "and their acts are therefore more repugnant. We have no pacts or vows with God!"

Adolfo takes issue again. "Priests are made of bones and flesh like any of us and their vows give them no immunity to fear. Some have protested courageously, risking derision and threats. There you have Bishops Vidal and Barraqué, Múgica, the Bishop of Vitoria, almost the entire Basque clergy, and many more. Who among the civilian sector has done the same?"

Dr. Varo tells us that during his short period of freedom at the front, a colleague had shown him a French newspaper reporting notable members of the French clergy who condemned the Movement and their murders, among them the Bishops of Lyon and Toulouse. (His reference was to an illustrious group of high French clergymen who later on took the same stand against the killings of Jews by the Nazis.)

Abundio, his eyes sparkling with anger, answers back:

"Don't you tickle my balls with your stories! Many would have done the same under the protection of the frock. This is Spain, not France. I don't roast devil-dodgers and I believe in God. Also, I admit that the Republic, generous with all, was not so with them. But let's not pull wool over our own eyes either. You talk about a small minority. But what about the immense majority of them? Fascist bastards, that's what they are!"

He can't continue. Violent coughing overtakes this sick man who died a few months later in another prison.

Next day we read an item published in the local press:

"The inmates of the Avenida prison yesterday took the holy Easter communion with a religious fervor that shows the beginning of a sincere repentance for their crimes."

Between the recently finished quarters for Don Enrique and his family and the stairway, there is a large room used for storage and as sleeping room for the guards' relief during the night. In the mornings, the straw mats and blankets are stacked in a corner to make cleaning easier by the prisoners' char force. It's easy to get in and out of this room from the infirmary. It takes a long time for some of us to discover that those doing the cleaning exchange the guards' blankets for those with contagious diseases in the infirmary! "Bacteriological warfare," they call it to justify their deed. The trick is easily done because the texture and color of the blankets are the same. We never know whether the blanket switch has the desired effect. In any case, neither the rest of the prisoners nor the penal authorities ever find out.

One afternoon I am told what had happened to a relative of mine, Eduardo Andrés, the road contractor, since his release from the provincial jail.

Once set free, Andrés returned to Islallana, his hometown, where he lived practically like a hermit without daring to venture beyond the front porch of his house. One morning a police detail came to pick him up in a truck and take him to Logroño to make some deposition by order of the Civil Government. After a few hours of detention and interrogation, either on account of his convincing answers or because of the weak grounds of the accusation, he was set free by nightfall.

There was no bus connection with his town until next morning, so he decided to spend the night at his son's house. It must have been about two o'clock in the morning when a falangist patrol under a captain gave "the knock on the door," ordered him to get dressed, and took him away. They took him as far as a couple of streets down, around the corner, and there the three-man patrol jumped on him and gave him a beating. A few neighbors, hearing the commotion, opened their windows and closed them again. Bleeding and unconscious they left him at the curb. A few minutes after regaining consciousness, Andrés dragged himself back to his son's house. He made himself heard by the tenants on the first floor, unable to pull himself up and ring the bell. They called his son who took him to his floor, where he lay in bandages with two broken ribs for a couple of weeks. I never got to see that relative of mine again.

The above account, given by a prisoner, inspires comments on the cowardice of the falangist patrols. It also makes me remember that one day I was riding on a streetcar up Preciados Street in Madrid when I saw a strange platoon of young men in blue shirts marching to the rhythm of slogans. They seemed like a mixture of students and workers and some tough-looking gunslingers who even then were mixed up with Falange. The streets leading to the Puerta del Sol, Madrid's very own square, were packed with people, among them many members of the workers' political parties. The falangists were looking for trouble. Next day I read in the papers that the clash that ensued left several dozen wounded. Maybe those provocations were part of a plan to create the propitious atmosphere for a civil war. Maybe they were not stupid simply as they appeared to be at first sight. All the combined falange forces in Madrid engaged in that kind of open challenge were no more than 3,000 or 4,000 strong. They were the future "Camisas Viejas" (literally, Old Shirts—the charter members of Falange, not to be confused with the New Shirts, or newcomers that swelled the ranks during, and mostly after, the Civil War), whose display of arrogant violence was not without certain sincerity in accordance with their own ideals.

They have started work to improve landing facilities at the Recajo airfield. The military are short of manpower. They draw it mainly from the prisons and the fronts. In order to entice the prisoners they offer several material advantages to those who sign up as volunteers.

The quota of one hundred able bodies is immediately filled at our prison. The desire to breathe fresh air and see the sun is probably the strongest incentive. For about a week things proceed normally. Afterwards the volunteers begin deserting. It was hard work; vigilance was extremely tight and food did not turn out to be what had been promised. Enrollment shrinks progressively until there are no more than a couple of dozen names to be counted on. Finally, when the project is well under way, they cancel the voluntary enlistments. From then on, as far as public works is concerned, all pretenses are cast aside and the voluntary enrollment becomes just plain forced labor.

One who had signed up is Manolo Alba. As an engineer he knows about surveying and topography. He was made a foreman in charge of a twenty-man gang. On account of a wrong reading on the transit theodolite made by a sergeant he got chewed out by a captain, without a chance to open his mouth. Next day he scratched himself off the voluntary list.

Dr. Varo and Adolfo Alvarez are devotees of the game of *mus* (a game played with Spanish cards). Among the prisoners that come daily to the infirmary for treatment there is one from the town of Lodosa, called Facundo, whose loquacity is not in the least inhibited by his numerous boils. He looks over our shoulders to see our game and gives us the latest news from the ball court below. One morning he tells us they are preparing new rounds of religious rallies, particularly for female prisoners. Dora has gone to see the Bishop of Calahorra to get his backing for the lectures that a group of pious ladies intend to give in the women's prisons. Dora, or Dorita, is a well-known churchgoer, who in the opinion of many cellmates is the Bishop's mistress. This gossipy accusation would be believable if the Bishop had horrendous taste, but His Lordship is not particularly known for that. Among the pietist group to which Dora belongs, the favorite slogan during the initial terror was, "He who has not wronged has nothing to fear" . . . a phrase that inflames the fury of many prisoners.

Tuno and Bengoa have the run of the place; both gather plenty of war news that they immediately communicate to us. At times they are able to get hold of newspapers, but their main source of news is the radio set in Don Enrique's office, on when they go into his office or turned on during his frequent absences.

THE FLIGHT OF THE
REAL ESTATE INSPECTOR

One day during my previous imprisonment at the Avenida jail, we got news of an extraordinary escape. Although there was no clear information as to name or town, no one doubted the reality of the event. It concerned a man who had fled from the place of execution, leaving part of a finger on the barbed wire. With his mutilated hand bandaged by a Republican doctor, the man managed to cross the French border through Navarra. Sergeant Sánchez, head of the execution squad, had received a letter from Bayonne in which the fugitive asked Sánchez to do him the goddamned favor of saving him his finger, for he would soon return to pick it up. This episode, whether true or false, was very much celebrated among those then imprisoned in the Avenida jail.

The news which arrived this afternoon is more concrete. The local real estate inspector and Marín, an aviation officer on active duty, had escaped together in a military car from the Recajo Airport. In this case too, a letter later arrives from France in which the inspector predicts an early return to assume his job once more and cleanse the city of the criminal garbage which infects the streets. The letter is addressed to the civil governor.

In general, the comments on this escape are to the effect that, if people like the inspector and Marín—who are bound to the city by family ties—have taken that step, it means they have no doubt as to the eventual triumph of the Republican cause.

Nine years later I learned the details of that escape when I met Marín in New York.

Among the family groups in the Avenida jail are the Carcamos. Two brothers and three cousins make up the clan, all of them arrested simultaneously at the beginning of the Movement in their home town of Briones, where they owned a small flour mill. The younger brother because of his friendship with a guard at the main entrance, is able to receive food packages. The elder brother Jaime is a man of thirty five, very strong and heavily built. About this time he begins to suffer from intense headaches and to behave in a strange manner. His talk gets incoherent, making obvious his lack of co-ordination. He swallows dozens of aspirins without results. The combined pressure of his family and the prison's chief land him, against his will, in the small prison infirmary. I met him there unaware that a few weeks later and under depressing circumstances we will meet again. Sometimes he feels good and eats with tremendous appetite and talks normally; when under pain, he wraps a big scarf around his head. Carcamo looks like a dying sultan immobile and silent but for some harsh sounds like those of a wounded bull.

All the medical services were under the direction of Dr. Salinas, the Chief Surgeon. Other doctors from town help him, sharing the abundant and hardly remunerative work.

Several prisoners, using their influence or a variety of tricks, remain permanently in the infirmary, even after being cured. Not many of them, but just enough to give rise to jokes and malicious rumors in the penitentiary. These stories are encouraged by the security guards on duty, who amend and embroider them, and at the end of their shifts bring them to the civil authorities.

When the criticism is widespread, the Governor intervenes. Fearful of incurring suspicion of partiality, the prison chief decides to clear the infirmary of all patients. Sick and healed alike are thrown out into the court.

Four days later those who have tuberculosis and other serious illnesses are readmitted to the infirmary. Perhaps due to my foolish pride, I don't request to be added to this group.

The offensive on the Basque front begins. With General Mola pushing from Vitoria, and the Italians along the coast of the Bay of Biscay, a joint assault is launched against the "iron belt," the name given to the system of fortifications defending Bilbao. On the afternoon of June 4th we learn of Mola's death in an airplane crash as he flew from Vitoria to Burgos. The distance between these two cities is so short that it can be covered in a few minutes' flight. Heavy fog prevented the plane from finding the landing strip, and it crashed on a hill near the Castile de Peones, a small town in the province of Burgos. This accident is considered a setback to the assault on Bilbao, and consequently is greeted with joy in the jail court. The scantiness of the fog around Castile in early June and the belief that the pilot had survived—a belief later proven wrong—gives rise to a number of interpretations. Some people attribute the accident to sabotage by the Germans because of reported friction between Mola and the German High Command. To others, the whole thing is a plan by Franco to get rid of one of his most prestigious rivals in the rebel camp. The only basis for this speculation is the absolute belief among the prisoners in the unlimited ambition and criminal nature of the Caudillo.

During Primo de Rivera's dictatorship, Mola was Chief of Security, and in the performance of his duty distinguished himself by his harsh methods in dealing with striking students. The enormous influence of the Carlists in the Province of Navarra had made it easy for Mola, as Captain General, to lead the region in armed uprising against the legal Republican Government. And so the inventor of the phrase "fifth column" disappeared, covered by the dirty laurels he won struggling against his own people. Despite the mass slaughters which he ordered in Navarra, there was in Mola's fanaticism a certain frankness which placed him in a less hateful light than his comrades, the generals who betrayed the Republic, like Queipo de Llano, Cabanillas, Goded, and others.

Mola's death did not alter the course of the campaign in the North. The days which follow bring news discouraging to our cause. One after another, the Basque towns fall into fascist hands, and on June 19th the Basque Front is destroyed.

When the fascist attack on Bilbao began, the maps of the then famous fortifications of the "iron belt" fell into rebel hands. They were brought to the headquarters of General Mola in Vitoria by a military engineer called Goicochea. Goicochea's defection, with his command of highly classified data on fortifications, greatly facilitated the success and speed of the fascist assault on Bilbao.

I can't follow the developments of the struggle with the same passion as before because of the rapid deterioration of my health.

Sharp and continuous back pains accompanied by intense pangs in my stomach make eating impossible. I become so weak that I spend most of the time lying on my pallet. Within a few days I am unable to move, and in lieu of the latrine I use a tin can, a gift from one of the maintenance orderlies. During the sweeping chores, four comrades voluntarily remove me from my corner, bedding and all, until it is swept, and then they place me back on the same spot. My diet is reduced to a few spoonfuls of some medicine which my stomach doesn't always tolerate. I see myself slowly dying amidst flies, noise, and dust.

At that point, gathering strength I didn't think I possessed, I sit up on the quilt and vilely insult the guard stationed on the first row of benches, without forgetting to add a kind word for the Caudillo's mother. At the conclusion of this bold and useless act of defiance, I sink back onto the bed, completely exhausted.

This scene is repeated the following day. Unconsciously I seek a bullet to free myself from so much suffering. The mixture of indifference and resignation into which I fall induces in me a feeling of timelessness. I don't look at my watch even once, and my jailmates appear to me as shadows. The reaction of the men in the court is a prolonged silence. One more death meant nothing, but my slow agony and resignation seem to impress them strongly. The conversations they carry on at my side are in hushed tones, like those of relatives who surround the bed of their dying kin. I only vaguely remember what thoughts I had then. Of the many faces approaching my bed only one draws me to something out of the past. For the present, its identity eludes me.

When news of my condition leaks out, it creates a small problem for the jail authorities, who then begin to take an interest in avoiding having me die here. But ultimately the final decision falls within the jurisdiction of the Chief Surgeon. Doctor Salinas is another one of those good-natured men whom fear has made cold and indifferent. On his last visit I see his lips tremble as he takes my pulse. Much later I learned that, alarmed by my extreme weakness and fearful of a sudden death, with all the resulting criticisms, he decided to consult with the Civil Government.

Salinas had sufficient authority to make his own decisions with respect to sick prisoners, and he had done so before; however, this seemed to be a special case, and he didn't dare to resolve it without having the complete backing of the civil governor.

Late in the afternoon a stretcher from the provincial hospital arrives. The stretcher bearers place me on it. At the last moment, just as I am leaving the court, Alba snatches the cigarette stuck to my lips and says: "Courage, Pedro. You are going to the hospital and you must get well."

The stretcher bearers close the canvas coverings which form a canopy over the portable bed and begin to walk.

Before I got married, I had traveled to Logroño to see my future wife in all kinds of vehicles: motorcycles, cars, trains, and even fruit trucks returning from the markets of Madrid. Now I experience a new form of transportation. The smoothness with which the two men carry me in less than a half hour astonishes me.

Shortly before arriving at the hospital, they stop. One of them sticks his head inside the canvas.

"We're almost there. We've stopped to light a cigarette," he tells me.

Before renewing the journey I hear childlike voices mention the word "prisoner" and I want to look at the faces of the children, but upon separating the canvas I see nothing. Perhaps fear or some gesture of the stretcher bearers has made them scurry along.

✑ **Part IV**

Provincial Hospital, Confinement,
and Deportment from Spain

There is a mystical happiness in accepting existence without under-standing it.

George Santayana

THE HOSPITAL

It is almost nightfall when we arrive at the hospital. They carry me up an old stone staircase. My first impression of the ward is vague; I can see only a few patients, their beds lined up against the wall. The stretcher bearers lift me onto my bed. A few minutes later I get up. With a great deal of effort I reach the latrine, which is located in a corner of the room on the other side of a thin partition. On the way back, all my strength leaves me. I try to climb back into the high bed, but my hands slip on the bed's iron bars and I drop to the floor. Two sick prisoners help me back into bed. A nun on a tour of inspection comes in and seems to offer me some food, which I refuse.

It's a long night, and I sleep little. In the morning, when sunlight fills the ward, a doctor and his assistant come to examine me. I am given a shot and forced to drink a spoonful of a sweet, black liquid. Later, around noon, Teresa comes in. She pretends she is very happy with the diagnosis the doctor had just made: my back pains are caused by nerves—nothing is wrong. With rest and light but frequent meals, I'll soon recover. Normally, I would doubt such a quick diagnosis, but given my state of mind, I readily accept it.

Teresa doesn't have a visitor's pass and can only stay for a few minutes. She comes back later in the afternoon, carrying a thermos bottle, from which she makes me drink. She keeps me company for a long time, trying to cheer me up. After dinner a nun closes the windows and turns off the lights, except for one small bulb above the entrance door.

Wrapped in this oppressive silence, I spend the night prostrated in bed in the prisoners' ward, the worst in the hospital. My mind dwells on the past. It's senseless to think of the future, I have no influence over it. Besides, I am afraid of remaining disabled for the rest of my life, if I ever manage to get out of this place. I try to recall the face which I so often saw at my bedside in the Avenida jail, without ever being able to recognize it. . . .

. . . It was a warm afternoon in early summer. The tracks left by pushcarts on their way to the fields covered the dusty road. We had our arms around each other and walked without touching the ground, almost floating. The fields had the charm of an early summer afternoon, when the warm soil still retains the spring greenery that soon will be parched by the strong Castilian sun. The peasants sang as they gathered their tools. Their deep voices, tempered by the distance, lent a singular beauty to their chant.

To one side of the road there was a narrow path which crossed some planted fields, ending in a thick grove by the riverside. Three men bearing spearlike canes and big baskets crossed the path. The last one had a swarthy complexion and a badly shaven beard sprinkled with grey hairs. As he went by he raised his head slowly and greeted us. (It is when I recall this scene that I remember the face of that prisoner who came to my bedside in the Avenida jail.)

We sat down amidst the cheerful sound of birds twittering in the trees. The sun was sinking below the horizon, and toads and frogs began their nightly serenade. They were joined by crickets, who drowned out all other sounds. The wind caressed Teresa's hair and through the foliage we could smell a deep perfume of mint. . . . But where I am now, there are neither trees nor a mint aroma; only a strong smell of bandages and carbolic acid which permeates the room, a guard who, armed to the teeth, keeps watch over the dying, the dirty beds next to the dilapidated walls, and a pile of cotton balls steeped in pus which one of the interns has left on the room's center table. Suddenly men, beds, and walls disappear and again dearest memories of love cross my mind.

The man in the bed facing mine has his eyes wide open. The other patients in the room at least move. But not he! He only stares. Yes, it is inevitable that those searching eyes should see and know everything. But I am better off not pursuing that thought. . . .

. . . It was a cold November morning and we were on our way to Copenhagen. When we crossed the grey waters of the North Sea a strong gale left us battered and exhausted. The last time we changed ferries three of us got stranded. Part of the soccer team had arrived in the city a few hours ahead of schedule, and when the rest of us got off the train, we were met with the welcoming ceremonies meant for the whole team. Reporters and the coaches of the opposing team stared at us in disbelief when they saw our disheveled appearance. I heard Juanito Carcer, our trainer, say: "These guys think that we of the Real Madrid team are a bunch of dirty bums."

The scene changes to a train station in Hamburg. A blonde seductive prostitute beckoned me with her eyes.

The curtain of memory goes up again. A bar in Lille, bottles and glasses crashing to the floor, as some terrible, painted women looked fearfully at us. My mind wanders on and on—the memories seem endless. . . .

Heavy footsteps are coming; it's the guards in the hall. Dawn is beginning to shed a faint light in the spacious room. I fall into a deep sleep.

After three days of being forced to rest and eat, I feel somewhat better and I begin to get curious about the layout of the place and those in it. Ward Eleven is at the end of a wing of the old building, built almost at the edge of the Ebro. Two rows of seven beds each line the long sides of the rectangular room, and at one end there is the latrine and a washbasin. At the opposite end is a small lobby where the guards usually sit.

The large windows allow plenty of sunlight and air to come in whenever they are open. A large marble table in the middle of the room is surrounded by stools, to be used at mealtimes, the same table I often see covered with used cotton balls. During the past few days two prisoners who had been cured were returned to their

respective jails, and two tuberculars have been transferred to Ward
Twelve, across the lobby from the guards. The other patients are:
Pizarro, a peasant with a ruddy face; El Jarrero, a dark boy in his
twenties; and Astudillo, who worked as a carpenter in the cigar
factory.

Three nuns attend this room, one of them we don't see often because she also serves in Ward Twelve. The other two, Sister
Joaquina and Sister Asunción are very formal and cold toward us.
The only one they seem to like is El Jarrero. Sister Joaquina, a
middle-aged nun whose face still shows traces of past beauty, seems
to have a frustrated maternal instinct. This is most evident in the
attention she lavishes upon a seven-year-old, almost paralytic gypsy
boy in a nearby ward. I can't imagine where she manages to find
the candy and chocolates she brings him, her face beaming with
happiness. The child responds to the nun's affection and often comes
into our room looking for her.

Of all the male nurses in the hospital, Valentín is the most
tolerable. His colleague Antonio has such an imposing physique
that he seems capable of shattering stones with his bare fists, but
actually his strength has been undermined by liquor and he probably
couldn't kill a fly.

Another male nurse who helps Valentín in our room is perhaps
the biggest freak in the hospital. He suffers from a strange illness
which blinds him temporarily. Once, he comes into the room carrying a food tray and all of a sudden I see him nailed to the floor, his
eyes blinking weirdly. I think he is trying to play a joke, but later,
when I learn the reason for this strange behavior, I become accustomed to seeing him repeat his act without paying much attention.

Every week a barber comes around, a skinny, short, wrinkled
fellow who hardly has any teeth left. His skill is as bad as his razors,
which he keeps in a worn out velvet case. Both the razors and the
case could have easily belonged to a barber in the service of medieval
kings. El Jarrero says that it's too bad the barber doesn't bring his
cat, so he could throw him the slices of flesh!

Astudillo, a carpenter, who has a heart condition, occupies a bed
opposite mine. He weighs no more than 100 pounds, and he seems
to be slowly drifting into death. He can't breathe freely when lying
down, so he is forced to sit up in bed. I never see him budge from

this position. To alleviate his weariness and suffering, he bends forward and leans his bony arms on a bunch of pillows. He inspires sadness and compassion throughout the room. The agony of this man is more than I can take. It's the only thing I can't get used to in this hospital. At night, every time I open my eyes I see his crooked body and glaring eyes fixed on me.

The battle of Brunete begins on July 6th, 1937. The attack, started by the Republican arm, is one of the bloodiest in the Civil War. The battle spread from Brunete to the towns along the Guadarrama River. I had become acquainted with the terrain as a student, when I used to roam through the towns around Madrid. Since I have recovered considerably, I give the male nurses a tip and get hold of the newspapers, which are banned. Once again I follow with excitement the course of the battle. The attack came a little too late to save the North Front, but it made it easier to evacuate a small number of troops from Asturias and Santander. As was often the case, the Republican Army had been on the verge of a great victory. But, again, Franco's troops were rescued at the last minute by fresh foreign reinforcements, and the battle was a stalemate.

One of my sisters-in-law begins to bring me some books, on which there are fewer restrictions than on newspapers. As long as the battle of Brunete lasts, I pay little attention to novels. When my hopes die down, I immerse myself in Thomas Mann's "The Magic Mountain." By now I am up almost the whole day, attuned to the hours and habits of my roommates.

Most of the guards never address us; fear or stupidity oblige them to keep up the pretense of a hate which they don't feel. Two of them, however, ignore the mutterings of their companions and act friendly toward us. One is Abad, a textile merchant, who had a shop on the best commercial street of Logroño, and the other is the owner of a well-known restaurant. The latter, who is in a difficult financial situation at this time, is the most dedicated of the guards. In addition to his own shift, he covers those of other wealthy men of the city, including that of a well-known industrialist of Logroño, who pays him fifteen pesetas for the service. Both militia men violate the hospital rules and often speak with the prisoners. One afternoon Abad allows me to cross the lobby and look inside the tuberculars' room. The overcrowding of patients in there is appalling, since all the hospital facilities are designated for those wounded in war and those transferred from the new Falange hospital, itself insufficient to care for the growing number of wounded soldiers. Through Pepe, who has been transferred there from Ward Eleven, I learn that there are five very sick prisoners in that crowd, three of whom will die soon.

When I return to Ward Eleven I see large rain clouds over the nearby Navarra mountains. Lightning flashing between the mountains of Cantabria and El Corbo warn of an impending thunderstorm. It isn't long before large drops become a torrential rain. The blackness of night slowly engulfs the hospital and all its sadness.

One evening, at the end of my third week here, Carcamo arrives from the Avenida jail, on the same stretcher and undoubtedly carried down the same road as I was. As one of the stretcher bearers leaves the room, he says to one of our guards:

"You know, rather than bringing these skeletons here, it would be better if they ordered us to toss them in a trash can."

Slowly and with great effort, Carcamo walks toward a bed, aided by Pizarro the peasant. Gone is the kind nature of my old companion in the Avenida jail. One can see by the folds of skin hanging on his neck how much weight he has lost. The almost stupid expression on his face, and the enormous rings circling his bulging eyes catch my attention. Without bothering to look at anyone, or to remove his clothing or shoes, he instantly falls asleep and spends the whole night snoring. The following morning, in a rare moment of lucidity, he tells me some scanty details about our old inmates in the Avenida prison. The infirmary has readmitted most of the patients that the warden had thrown out into the court. This change indicates that the hail of criticism no longer exists, and that the warden's relations with the civil governor are more solid. Carcamo has no news about the war, nor does he seem interested in any. Two doctors examine him, indicating by their gestures that his condition is very serious.

Sometimes when spoken to, he cringes like a frightened dog. Other times he becomes very aggressive, letting loose a flurry of curses. Once El Jarrero drinks the last few drops of water in the room's jug, and Carcamo attacks him violently. Pizarro and I try to calm him down, while the frightened Jarrero runs to the opposite end of the room. After the incident, the boy approaches me and, still shaking, says:

"Don't you think, Don Pedro, that this guy should be in an insane asylum? He's like a wild animal. I'm afraid of him. I'm going to ask Sister Joaquina to move me to another bed. I don't want to be next to him."

Near the hospital there is a natural spring with very cold running water with which they fill the jugs for the room and for the guards. Carcamo is never satisfied with our supply of water. With Valentín's help he buys a larger jug, which he keeps under his bed like a miser. He empties jug after jug in no time, and he gives money to the male nurses to replenish his supply of water. What he doesn't drink he pours over his head. He says that the shower cools the fire in his "nut." As a result of drinking so much liquid, he urinates like a dog, when and where he pleases. Sometimes during his night walks through the room he pisses on the bars of my bed. Perhaps because we've been together in the Avenida jail infirmary, I am the only one here who has any influence over him, and in his moments of lucidity he comes over to speak to me. One afternoon I am leaning on a windowsill when he comes near and says:

"If I leave here tomorrow at dawn and walk all day, I can reach my town. My family is expecting me and I should go. I've been away from home a long time. These guards are weak, they're made of jelly, and I have to teach them to carry two-hundred-pound sacks; nobody knows how to do it like Carcamo. What cute girls there were in my town some years ago! Now they are all ugly. Why is that? In the winter they wear so many petticoats that one can look at them calmly, but when the good weather comes, the festivals, the Feast of St. John . . . well, men's affairs, you understand. My brother always had better luck with them. I'm very awkward and he is more refined . . . a kind of señorito."

During this confidential monologue, I see a tiny gold medal hanging on his neck. This casual glance elicits another confidence from him.

"I don't believe in priests, but I do in medals. My mother gave me this one when I was a child and I've worn it ever since; I wouldn't feel right without it, as if I were undressed."

The doctors find that Carcamo has an incurable brain tumor.

Toward the end of the month he spends in our ward, his speech becomes a childlike babbling, of which the only intelligible word is "shit." One of the interns notifies him one day of his impending release, and he receives the news with no sign of joy; his brain is already too far gone. That very afternoon an ambulance takes him to his village. Three days later we in Ward Eleven learn that Carcamo died the previous morning in Briones.

Almost four weeks elapse before the doctor on duty in the room decides, after consulting with Dr. Salinas, on a plan of treatment for me: light exercise every day combined with heat therapy three times a week. This plus rest and sufficient food will make me well in a month. However, the back pains will take longer to go away, since they have to do with my nerves. The doctor's words raise my spirits.

The heat therapy room is on the ground floor. I am taken down the winding staircase and as I am about to enter the room I find several soldiers undergoing the same treatment. The stretcher bearers leave me outside in the corridor next to a big window which opens onto the garden, allowing the sun to come in. I have to wait long. I sit up a little and pull off a leaf from a small branch near the window. I feel a maddening urge to leap outside and press my face against the green grass.

Nuns, doctors wrapped in their white uniforms, soldiers, and patients, all pass by gazing curiously at me. They then go on about their business, disappearing amidst the glaring beams of light which pierce the darkness of the corridor.

It is now my turn, and I enter a narrow room where they keep the hospital's only heat treatment machine. The session lasts twenty minutes.

The following day Astudillo's long agony begins. His brothers-in-law and the deputy fascist mayor Amelibia are very interested in having him die in his own house, but their appeals are unsuccessful. When he starts to breathe his last, the nuns and the chaplain try to gain his consent for confession. The man refuses with all the strength left in him. As soon as he is left alone he signals with his hand—he no longer can speak. We realize he wants to write something. We give him a pencil and he scribbles on a piece of newspaper the words "I don't want to." The pencil falls out of his hand and he lays there staring at me with his glassy eyes.

An hour later there is a second attempt to have him confess, with the same results, whereupon I voice my indignation as loudly as possible. I can't stand this indecent comedy, taking advantage of a powerless patient against his conscience right at the point of death. From then on, the nuns lose whatever interest they had for me and treat me with indifference and neglect. With a cavernous gasp, Astudillo the carpenter gives up his soul amidst the gloomy silence of the chamber, as the sun sinks below the horizon.

The news is relayed to the guards and a doctor comes in to confirm his death. Valentín places a canvas over Astudillo and a half hour later some men put him on a stretcher and take him to the morgue in the basement. When the guards change shifts, we learn that the burial will take place the following morning at ten. A little after ten Valentín, El Jarrero, Pizarro the peasant, and myself begin to keep watch from one of the side windows. Twenty minutes pass, and when we begin to doubt that we had been told the correct hour for the burial, a simple pine casket is carried out through a back door. Walking behind it are a priest, the two brothers-in-law of the deceased man, and Amelibia the alderman, whose presence there indicates a close friendship with Astudillo's family.

They place the coffin on a small cart pulled by a donkey, and the sad procession vanishes from sight over the stone bridge, on its way to the cemetery.

By dawn I am already awake, listening to the song of the lark in the trees nearest my window. Listening, too, for the trumpet of reveille from the artillery barracks. The light is deep lavender, until Sister Asunción opens that window and lets in the morning.

I no longer am faced with the fixed eyes of Astudillo. Instead there is a squalid figure, half naked, twisting and turning in a bundle of soiled bedding. Just before Astudillo died we got that new patient in Ward Eleven. When they brought him in and uncovered the canvas topping of his stretcher, he stood up enveloped in the ragged remnants of a mixture of civilian and military garb, a tall bony figure of a man. It's El Gudari, a Basque warrior made prisoner in the Asturian front. At first we were surprised to see him here, so far from Asturias. We soon find out why. He has a case of typhus. Our new patient spent several days fighting his ailment, no better and no worse. When we learn it's nature, Teresa goes to complain. He is a contagious patient

and should be put in an isolated ward. The answer to her complaint
is simply to stop visitors and incoming packages and isolate Ward
Eleven from any contact with the outside world. Teresa then appeals to a distant relative, a director at the Health Department, and
at last they take El Gudari from the middle of the ward and put him
in a corner instead, isolating him from us with a mere canvas screen.
When they again allow us to have visitors, Teresa tells me that the
Health Department director told her he was sorry, but . . . there is
no other place for the man at present.

Of the two nuns who attend this ward, Sister Asunción is assigned
the care of El Gudari. When time comes for her to give him an
enema she is so overcome by shame that she turns around and does
the job with her back to the patient! During one of her visits Teresa
sees the cumbersome maneuver and is astounded at the unprofes-
sional squeamishness of the nun. They try to keep the windows
open, but the fetid smell of that poor patient spreads all over the
ward. That, in turn, attracts flies, and soon Gudari's mouth becomes
a black ring from the persistent swarm. For some reason—perhaps
because it's in the nun's way—the screen disappears and El Gudari
lies there in front of everyone. Teresa brings him lemons, which she
slices and places in his mouth. He sucks them avidly. At times, the
fever makes him delirious and he is seized with memories of the
recent battles he has fought. Aviation seems to be his main obsession. "Here they come!" he screams, wrapping his arms tightly
around his head. Other times he mutters something about his town's
priest who, apparently sided with the Republicans. "Josechu," he
cries in his Basque dialect, "great wish I have to take off cassock
and shoot fascists!"

El Jarrero makes every possible effort to keep away from that
bed. "He makes me very sad," he says. I think he's trying to avoid
contracting the dreaded typhus.

Soon the Basque warrior sinks into a coma. Despite the scapular
hanging from a string on his hairy chest—which depicts his religious
fervor—El Gudari is not subjected to pressures to confess, as was
Astudillo the carpenter. They leave him completely alone to die in
peace. After the doctor's last visit, a priest comes around and
mumbles the last rites. And half an hour later, El Gudari dies.

One can't blame the nuns for their detached, seemingly cold

attitude in the face of one more death. They've seen so much misery and illness! Actually, all of us are relieved to see the infected body rolled out of the ward, for El Jarrero was not the only one afraid of being contaminated. Next morning we again see the simple funeral departure from our window: a rough, unfinished coffin in a cart, pulled by a melancholy mule led by a man wearing a black blouse. Those scenes leave us for days lost in sadness and depression.

I haven't seen my fascist cousin since the day she came to bid me what she thought was farewell forever and hung a scapular around my neck. This mid-August afternoon she appears at the ward's door. Straight as a broomstick, she comes to a halt and raises her arm in the fascist salute. "Arriba España!" she pronounces loud and clear before she proceeds to my bed. I think coming to see me is a very affectionate gesture on her part, so that alone compels me to keep my mouth shut. It's no use trying to talk to her or convince her of our differences. I merely suffer the fifteen-minute visit as best I can. She leaves a pack of cigarettes on my table, and after repeating the Roman salute at the door, she departs as martially as she arrived.

"That lady is crazy!" El Jarrero exclaims when she leaves. Someone informs him quietly that the woman is my cousin, and embarrassed, the boy comes over to apologize.

"Forgive me, Don Pedro. I meant no offense. But . . . don't you think that lady is a little . . . ?" and here he omits the word and makes instead the traditional eloquent gesture, signifying insanity.

"I agree with you, Jarrero," I tell him. Relieved, he beams a frank, sincere smile.

Pizarro the peasant is a small landowner. He dresses well and wears a thick gold ring. He has a natural intelligence and in all his comments about war and politics sings the praises of the Castilian campesino.

"We gave them their first weapons," he says. "Who is responsible for making Mola Captain General of Navarra? And without Navarra there wouldn't be a civil war."

Pizarro has cancer of the throat, although he doesn't seem to suffer from it. But the state of his illness is so advanced that he is allowed to smoke and drink wine and eat whatever he can purchase.

We've been told not to speak of it to him, he doesn't know how sick he is. But the well-guarded secret is revealed one day quite openly by a brutal military medical aide, who walks into our ward one morning and shouts, "The guy with throat cancer! Come over for your examination."

No one moves, of course. We are all astounded. In a moment, Pizarro realizes he's been called, and he starts for the door. When he returns to us we try to make him think that we've attached no importance to the incident. To no avail. From then on he begins losing weight and he sinks into a depression. He also gargles frequently. Soon he has to be transferred to the lower floor. We never see him again, but months later I hear of his death.

Two new nuns arrive at Ward Eleven one afternoon. Valentín, the nurse, tells us they got into the fascist zone through the Sigüenza front in one of the rare exchanges of people during the Civil War. The youngest one has a beautiful and kind face, and she makes the round of beds smiling and inquiring about each of us. When she leaves, we tell each other we hope she'll be assigned to us permanently. But both new arrivals are destined for some other part of the hospital. Word reaches us of how the little nuns praise the courtesy and attention they received from the Republican escort that accompanied them to the fascist zone. We also hear they have been reprimanded and told to refrain from mentioning the incident. Of course. Their experience contradicts the fascist propaganda about "Red" cruelties toward the church.

Valentín the nurse has been transferred to another floor now that new arrivals of war wounded fill every ward. He is no longer here to help take me down to the therapy room in the stretcher. The alcoholic nurse takes his place. But not for long. In his drunken stupor he can hardly carry his side of the stretcher, and as we go up or down the narrow stairs he bumps me and the stretcher violently against the walls, causing me unbearable back pain. I make such a row about it one day, refusing to be carried if he is part of the team, that they have to send another stretcher bearer from then on.

During August and September we are subjected to several air

attacks. Planes of the Republican government—probably from the Catalonian front—drop their bombs most often near the river. That can only mean one of two things, we think: either a military objective—the bridges—or orders to keep the bombs as far from the civilian population as possible.

Anti-aircraft defenses didn't exist in Logroño at the start of the Civil War. There was only one anti-aircraft gun in the whole province. Italy and Germany soon took care of that, bringing in plenty of artillery and sufficient personnel to man it.

According to Valentín, the worst result of the bombings is the panic and the ricocheting empty shells, for they had chosen the tallest building and the churches as anti-aircraft emplacements, all handled by Italians. The first attack I experienced in this hospital created havoc. The guards on duty in our ward ran in panic to take cover in the basement, leaving even their rifles behind. The sound of the approaching planes and the burst of the first bomb came almost simultaneously. El Gudari was still with us then. He didn't move. The only bombings that impressed him were those relived while delirious from fever. I saw a patient near me protect himself by throwing the mattress over his head and instinctively I did the same. The explosions broke the window glass and the ward was littered with the debris. An uneasy silence followed the commotion. I saw Sister Asunción struggling with the impedimenta of her wimple and habit, trying to crawl under a bed for cover. The confusion was so great that a couple of patients seized the chance to leave the hospital for a few minutes. Much of that was remedied next time we were bombed. The guards, properly instructed, simply locked the ward and took to the basement, leaving us free to protect ourselves as best we could. A bomb fragment left a hole two-yards wide in the wall of the nearest bathroom, but no one bothered to test the soundness of the wall later.

One of the patients who was able to walk out the front door in the first bombing is from this ward, a bricklayer called Emeterio. He was interned with an anthrax infection contracted at the Industrial School prison. He's a good-looking chap with dark eyes and curly hair, patient and courageous as hell. I've seen him being treated without batting an eyelash as yards of drainage were pulled out of his wound. There is a girl nurse on the main floor who apparently has been Emeterio's girlfriend and the affair doesn't seem to be over. She has been working in this hospital for years and knows the habits and schedule of the place well enough to allow her to get to see Emeterio with or without permission and bring him cigarettes and small gifts. When the nuns detect this romance they put all kinds of obstructions in her way. El Jarrero helps at times, keeping watch for the lovers at the door of the ward and coughing madly when a nun or a guard approaches. In a few days Emeterio is fully cured and returns to the Industrial School prison.

After the last bombing the officer in charge of the hospital guard comes around to examine our ward's doors and windows. He takes note of the damage in a little notebook. After he finishes the inspection he turns to us defiantly. "When *we* bomb we do a job of it. We hit hard and leave dozens of buildings wrecked and hundreds of dead. For this piddling rumpus your Republican friends might just as well have stayed home."

I have been following the doctor's instructions faithfully. Every morning I stand in front of the window and slowly do my exercises. The pain only increases with the treatment, to the point that I fall exhausted in bed afterwards. Also, the bump I've been noticing in my spine is getting bigger. . . .

The doctors pay little attention to these symptoms, and although I've been here all this time, they haven't taken X rays or kept a fever chart. One morning during one of my exercises I feel something snap in my spine, and immediately after an unbearable pain. From then on I leave my bed only to go to the latrine, and then I have to lean and support myself with hands on knees. The infection in my spine has affected three vertebrae. (Later, at the first X rays, the ailment is diagnosed as Pott's disease.)

My only friend in that ward was El Jarrero, whose appendectomy was postponed several times due as much to the lack of medical personnel and the preference given to the war wounded as to a bit of intrigue on the part of Sister Joaquina. The nun had taken such a liking to Jarrero that the only way she could think of to avoid his being returned to jail was to delay his operation. But El Jarrero had a relative in his town town who was intriguing a lot more effectively than Sister Joaquina, trying to get him released after his operation with the proviso that the boy would enlist as a volunteer to fight against his own.

In all my stays in the miserable places I had to live during those years, I always found a ray of hope and joy and color in some brother-in-misfortune. And El Jarrero provided all of that at the Provincial Hospital. He would sit near my bed and tell me stories of his hunting trips with his uncle in the sierras of Urbión and San Lorenzo. He was experienced and inventive in setting traps to catch rabbits and hare and he showed me his ingenious methods by knotting his shoelaces in lieu of rope. He also spoke of his amorous life, which consisted almost exclusively of a half dozen visits to the bordellos of Logroño. But he did mention an impossible platonic love for a girl of his home town, one too high above his station to be accessible. He was very musical and he often sang, albeit with more style than voice.

One morning they took him down to surgery. They brought him back at noon. Sister Joaquina told me the operation had lasted almost two hours. He was not to drink at all for two days. I heard him from my bed wailing, "Mother . . . water. . . ." Sister Joaquina was in and out the ward dozens of times a day, just to watch over him. Soon he recovered and began eating voraciously. In less than two weeks he was well and talking of nothing but a great wish to be out for the yearly festival of San Mateo. The morning he was set free he was beside himself with joy.

"If I could only take you out of here with me, Don Pedro," he said wistfully. "Everyone here speaks so well of you. I'm sure you'll soon be leaving too, all cured and well again."

Simple as they were, those words moved me. As he packed his possessions he sang his last copla:

> When I money lend
> I fear to lose a friend
> And gain an enemy
> At the cost of my money.

With a handshake he says good-by to me. Without turning his head and accompanied by Sister Joaquina, he leaves Ward Eleven.

Two weeks later I learned he was fighting in the Aragón front.

Pain and solitude have taken over. My only refuge is reading every book I can lay hands on. I speak only with my visitors, and the words I must exchange with nuns and doctors. Valentín comes to see me always complaining of the excessive work they've assigned to him down on the main floor. Father Merino comes to visit me. He was my arithmetic teacher in primary school, something I had forgotten. He speaks of nothing but religion and a few hazy incidents of my childhood. Upon parting he says, "Pedrito, every day I pray to the Holy Virgin for you."

When my cousin Milagros stops coming to see me, I begin to get visits from Elena, her sister. She's an excellent woman, a dressmaker, always hard at work at her sewing machine. Her husband, a schoolteacher, has been fired and sent to a small town. I notice her fear, thus her visits are all the more appreciated.

As I lay prostrate on my bed, I am unaware of certain events which soon will have a bearing upon my future.

After the defeat suffered by the Italians in Guadalajara, the most active war front moved to the north. Being centrally located between the Basque and the Aragonese fronts, Logroño was chosen as a strategic point from which orders and supplies could be dispatched most expediently to the northern fronts. The battle of Guadalajara was a great disappointment to Mussolini. There was much sarcastic comment in the European press about the dubious capabilities of the Italian Army. The fascist dictator reacted by sending many reinforcements and ordering a total change of commands. In one of his first new directives, General Gustavo Gambara was named supreme chief of the Italian expeditionary forces in Spain.

The Italian High Command took up residence in Santa Isabel, a suburban villa just outside of Logroño owned by relatives of my wife who had been absent in Argentina for some time. A vast park and orchard surrounded the well-appointed house. The estate was supervised by my mother-in-law. Thus it did not take long for my wife and her family to establish friendly contact with the Italian officers, the highest of whom, General Gambara, became interested in my case.

Also, two of Logroño's best doctors began giving me the attention I could not expect from the hospital personnel. Armed with fever charts, X rays, and with the help of the hospital director, the physicians put in a petition to be signed by the Civil Governor, asking the authorities for my transfer to some seaside area. The result was a provisional commutation from jail to confinement in a small town on the Bay of Biscay.

I became aware of those negotiations only two days before they took effect. One morning in the middle of November I left Ward Eleven. My departing stretcher met an incoming one at the door. A new prisoner enters the room that would otherwise be empty.

PEDERNALES

My stretcher is carried down the tortuous stairs for the last time and we proceed to the ambulance waiting at the entrance. Just outside town, we crash into a passing car and I am knocked out of the stretcher onto the floor. We emerge with only a crushed fender and a broken light; the orderly adjusts straps around me for the rest of our journey. Four hours later we reach the town of Pedernales, 160 kilometers from Logroño.

I didn't get much chance to look out the ambulance's narrow windows, but the highway from Guernica to Bermeo on which we were driving is edged with charming little towns rising from the foothills, a kind of postcard landscape typical of the Basque provinces. Pedernales is between the towns of Busturia and Mundaca. Most of its two hundred inhabitants at that time lived in houses stacked upon a hillock to the right of the main road. It was a popular resort in summer, when tourists from Bilbao came seeking the healthy climate of its shore and mountains. The rest of the year it was just a quiet, placid little pueblo with the feature of a small Biblical town. One heard the train arriving and departing at the station, an occasional motorcar, and at night, the fish trucks from Bermeo. The rest of the time the silence was broken only by the creaking of the oxen carts whose primitive wooden wheels rolled by as they have done since ancient times.

We arrive at our destination in midafternoon, with the sun shin-

ing as if it were a spring day. The owners of the house I am confined
to also are relatives of my wife, an aunt and uncle who live in Bilbao.
It is an almost empty six-story building. The owners rent it only in
summer, always reserving the main floor, orchard, and gardens for
themselves. The orchard extends down to the sea. It stops at a large
wall edging the water, broken at one point to form a little pier which
we call the embarcadero.

There is no doctor in Pedernales. The sick are under the care of
a physician who comes from the nearest town, Busturia. His name is
Dr. Mendieta, a tall husky Basque whose excellent character and
professional competence have won him the respect and esteem of
the entire district. His first visit takes place on my second day in
Pedernales. He leaves me convinced that I am in the hands of both
a good physician and an honorable man, one who is not contaminated by the cowardice that has become widespread among civilians
since the outbreak of the Civil War. The war has taken its toll of
dead from the surrounding houses and I am told about the most
notorious execution to date: that of Ramona's husband. Ramona
owns a tavern not far from this house, and until we become settled
and organized, she takes care of our meals. While the Basque government was in charge of the situation during the first year of the
war, the only deaths in this town were those killed fighting at the
front and the usual ones from illness and old age.

Among the first people I meet in Pedernales is an old mariner, a
retired merchant captain. They call him Pedro Plasta, and since
plasta means mess in vernacular Spanish, I am amused and interested enough to inquire about the origin of his name. It dates back
to his adventures at sea during the first world war when he was
torpedoed by a German submarine off the English coast in the
channel of St. George. With his ship almost split in two, Captain
Pedro tried desperately to cut through a thick fog and reach port,
only to collide with another merchant vessel and sink totally. Upon
being rescued he of course cabled the news to the ship's owners in
Bilbao. With typical Basque economy—which legendarily applies to
words as well as money—he composed a succinct message giving
an account of the disaster: "TORPEDOED STOP SPLIT STOP SUNK
STOP MESS." From then on he was called Pedro Plasta, Pedro Mess.

I also make the acquaintance of a fine woman called Amelia

whose husband has escaped to France. She has seven children, the eldest a boy of fourteen. Her sister Concha helps her tend to her large clan. The family used to live comfortably. Now they barely manage, huddled in an apartment atop Ramona's tavern.

And I meet Betanzos, a barber who is also a sexton, farmer, and woodcutter. His brother has been hiding in the hills since the fascists took over Pedernales. That fugitive is a source of much concern in town, for he was a Basque miliciano and thus a coveted target of the fascists, who often organize hunts and go into the hills searching for him. So far they've been unsuccessful, to the general rejoicing of the citizens. Everyone in town breathes with relief when a search party returns emptyhanded.

I am confined to the main floor of the building which is flanked by two terraces, one facing the road, the other facing north toward the orchard. A local smith has fashioned a wheel-bed for me. Thus, for eighteen months I live on my back, traveling from room to terraces. Sunlight and fresh air are the first requisites of the treatment so far prescribed for me.

One sunny morning, on Dr. Mendieta's third visit, the farmers who tend the orchard wheel me down to the garden. While Teresa is busy in the house with our child, the physician talks to me.

"I've been studying your X rays and your reports. I think you're going to be all right. Mind you, I am only a general practitioner and have been for most of my life. Many times, when I've been called on an emergency, I've climbed these hills on horse, not knowing whether what awaited me was childbirth, an infection, a fracture, a wound. . . . I've had to operate by candlelight rather than risk losing a life. I tell you all this because I'm not a specialist and perhaps my diagnosis won't carry much weight."

His massive figure is outlined against the branches of an apple tree. The orchard is quiet, gilded with sunlight. . . . After living among the shadows in miserable prisons and the hospital, this seems like an enchanted garden.

"As I see it," the doctor goes on, "we can try two different methods in order to get you well. One is to graft a piece of your tibia to the three vertebrae affected by the infection. That would be the most efficient, but the operation will have to be performed by an orthopedic surgeon, extremely difficult to find nowadays and quite expensive. The second method requires patience, total quiet, and plenty of nourishment. You'd have to eat as much as possible, even forcing yourself until you're stuffed. I assure you that if you have the will power and can make the effort I'll do the rest. Aside from the infection, there is nothing organically wrong with you. Your body functions perfectly, and that's enough of a foundation for a start. My esteem for you goes beyond my professional concern, and unless I'm wrong, I think you feel the same way toward me."

Beyond the wall edging the orchard there is the isle of Chacharra-mendi in the distance, its trees surging like an oasis from the sea. There is a hotel on the island, almost empty now, but I know that another patient awaits Dr. Mendieta there. I ask the physician about the curious dot of land linked to the mainland only by a narrow wooden bridge. He tells me the isle used to belong to the town of Pedernales until the Municipality sold it to a succession of promoters. It finally fell into the hands of a well-known family of Bilbao. "A fast and simple transaction, much like the sale of Manhattan by the Indians. When I first heard about Peter Minuit buying Manhattan for twenty four dollars' worth of glass beads, I laughed. Later I realized the wisdom of the Indians. Had they not acceded to the negotiations, they would have lost both their island and the beads."

The doctor says farewell, and after announcing he will start giving me calcium shots on his next visit, he disappears from the orchard. In a few minutes I see his lonely figure towering on the bridge, moving steadily toward the isle and his other patient.

It becomes cold, damp, and rainy just before Christmas. Our small son contracts a cold which soon develops into a serious case of pleurisy. Because of the lack of facilities and the continuing bad weather, Teresa decides to take the child back to Logroño. She puts in a call, and next morning one of her sisters comes in her car. They wrap the child in a blanket and I see them depart from the terrace. Thus I spend Christmas alone and anxious. The vision of the child's pale face and lifeless eyes as his mother and aunt drove him away is persistently in my mind. There's been a temporary interruption in communication and a tightening of censorship because of developments on the Teruel front. News and letters reach me with considerable delay.

Dr. Mendieta's visits are a welcome relief to my loneliness. In the cold winter afternoons we chat if he has time. He tells me of his friendship with Indalecio Prieto, the Socialist leader who happened to be in Pedernales at the time that the assassination of Calvo Sotelo triggered the actual outbreak of the Civil War. Prieto had to leave for Madrid immediately, and upon saying farewell to the physician, he had told him, "This can only mean war, my friend."

Another of Mendieta's confidences concerns his own arrest when the fascist troops entered Busturia. He was imprisoned for two months in the jail of the city of Vitoria. He had served with other physicians of this district in La Colonia, a modern hospital for poor children of Bilbao which at the start of the Civil War had to be converted to a war hospital. All during the time this district was under Republican Basque administration, Mendieta won the esteem and respect of the nuns who ran the institution. So, when he was arrested, they pooled their efforts and influences and finally succeeded in obtaining his release.

It takes me less than two hours to go through the newspapers and I get nothing else to read. I have plenty of time on my hands. Why don't I start reconstructing the notes I lost in my transfer from jail, now, while memories are still fresh in my mind?

Ramona's tavern is only some forty yards away across the road. On his way home from there, Captain Pedro Plasta often stops to visit me. At first he talks guardedly, but once he trusts me, he reveals that he has two nieces imprisoned in the town of Saturdarán, near Pedernales. The girls were taken with the first truckload of prisoners rounded up by the fascists when their troops entered Pedernales. Saturdarán's jail is serviced by nuns under the direction of the Penal Corps. Every two weeks Captain Pedro and María Jesusa, his sister, mother of the unfortunate girls, take the public bus, carrying bundles of food and clean linen for the two prisoners.

Before the war, María Jesusa and her two daughters used to manage a tavern and an adjoining tearoom which was very popular in summer. Only the bar is open now. Pedro's sister curtails his drinking, thus forcing him to go down the road to Ramona's tavern. I wish he would stop to see me on his way there rather than on his way back. His drinks, together with his Basque dialect, make conversation almost impossible.

News from the Teruel front spreads tension over the whole district. Dr. Juan Negrín has become president of the Council of Ministers. Prieto is now Minister of War. General Vicente Rojo has been appointed Chief of the Armed Forces. The previous government fell because of the reverses suffered by the Republic in the war and the communists' animosity for Largo Caballero. The new Minister of War, a distinguished Socialist leader and member of parliament for the province of Bilbao, is known to be a capable, honorable, and courageous politician. Everyone in the Basque provinces expects much from him.

Franco's army, reinforced by Moors, Italians, Germans, and Portuguese, now consists of over 650,000 well-equipped troops. The Republic has some 500,000 soldiers; inferior equipment, commanders, and organization; and far fewer planes. The front is 1,800 kilometers long, some 1,200 miles. Because of the irregularity of the terrain in certain sectors, there are some points at the front lines so weak that any surprise attack is sure to be successful.

On the 15th of November, Franco was ready to launch a new attack on Madrid through the Guadalajara front. Prieto deterred him by ordering an offensive at Teruel which forced the fascists to change their minds about Madrid. Two Republican columns assaulted Teruel under the command of Líster and Heredia. They advanced from the north and from the south, in a pincer operation which soon surrounded the city. Most of the advance defense positions fell in the first thrust. The remainder of the fascist forces retreated to the center of the city, some seven thousand troops surrounded by the attackers. After fighting in the streets of the old city, the principal military and civilian fascist elements barricaded themselves in public buildings, to resist the siege until the 6th or the 7th of January.

On December 29th, 1937, the fascists launched their counterattack to regain the city and save their entrenched garrison. Two army corps took part in the operation, those of Galicia and Castile, commanded by Generals Aranda and Varela and supported by all the available artillery and aviation of the Germans and the Italians.

The forces commanded by General Varela advanced as close as Teruel's outskirts. But those under General Aranda were stopped in the town of Concud, with considerable loss of men and equipment.

A tremendous snowstorm on New Year's Eve paralyzed all operations for several days.

1938

With her sister Concha as well as Ramona, Amelia has spent the last hours of 1937 glued to the radio. Next morning she comes to me with the latest news. General Queipo del Llano has made a speech from Seville in his picturesque, coarse language. He assured the radio audience that Teruel is not in the hands of Republican forces. It's only a matter of two or three days before the last buildings being held there by the "Reds" will be taken over. He extolled the virtues of the commander of the besieged troops. "I know Commander Rey D'Harcourt! Let them put plenty of 'Reds' in his path. He will never surrender!" were Queipo's last words.

The contradictory dispatches and propaganda have confused the people, and Amelia wants to know my opinion about the situation. I give it to her, and since it coincides with her wishes, she beams a joyous smile.

The march of the Republican forces into Teruel was characterized by a general effort to safeguard the city's art treasures and historical heritage. By dispatching several expeditions beyond the front lines they were able to save more than 100 art objects and over 500 ancient documents which belonged to the cathedral's archives. This attitude contrasted markedly with that of the rebels' throughout the Civil War. After the rebels bombed the Prado Museum in Madrid on November 16th, 1936, the then President of the Republic, Don Manuel Azaña, made an appeal to both sides to protect the nation's art wealth.

"It is more in our interest to save art treasures than to save the Republic itself," he said. "For, if we lose the Republic we can recover it eventually. But who could recreate Spain's art treasures if they are destroyed?"

In a rescue operation then unique in history and equaled only by France during World War II, more than 2,000 cases of art treasures were shipped to Geneva, to remain in the custody of the League of Nations to be returned to Spain at the end of the Civil War.

Through the underground Amelia has received a very optimistic letter from her husband. The Basque refugees in southern France are full of hope over the capture of Teruel, which can only mean that the exiles will soon be able to return victoriously to their cherished Basque land!

On January 7th the rebels' resistance collapses and Teruel is taken over by the Republican government. The surrender is openly admitted by Franco's official communiqué. Newspapers print veiled barbs directed at the commander of the besieged garrison, Rey D'Harcourt. Amelia rushes over with fresh comments from Seville made again by Queipo de Llano, who apparently has forgotten his New Year's praise and now describes Rey D'Harcourt as a pig.

German and Italian aerial bombings from their bases in Mallorca have been resumed. Progressively they increase in frequency and intensity.

Teresa returns from Logroño and tells me of our son's recent operation. He is out of danger, in the care of his grandmother in Logroño.

Rain and bad weather continue. It is very cold in this seaside region and the house is not equipped with central heating. Soldiers from the Teruel front crowd La Colonia hospital with cases of severely frozen feet. Pedro Plasta keeps track of the numbers which he promptly passes on to me. During the whole of January and part of February a fierce battle rages in the snowy mountains of Teruel. The second phase of the battle is favorable to the fascist army. The Franco press keeps totally silent as to the thousands of prisoners that were taken by the Republican forces upon their initial success. Only the unconfirmed execution of the Bishop is vaguely mentioned. One year later, at the collapse of the Catalonian front and the chaos of the Republican avalanche of exiles escaping to the French frontier, the Bishop of Teruel, Aurelio Polaco, was executed by the

Loyalists and not killed by fascist air bombardments of Barcelona, as was rumored in the village of Pedernales. Unfortunately, during the course of the Civil War, six or seven bishops and many priests were assassinated, their ideological belligerence being considered sufficient grounds to justify their execution. Ideological belligerence was also used to justify the shooting of twenty five Basque priests by the fascists.

Mendieta my doctor recalls the slaughter of hundreds of faithful who were caught in the churches of Durango and Guernica by Nazi airplanes. He repeats the words told to the Bishop in Victor Hugo's *Les Miserables:* "If we are going to weep, dear Bishop, let us weep for all."

The doctor talks further about Guernica, where he lost dozens of friends and patients in the German bombing.

"Within twenty miles around the city there isn't a hamlet that's not in mourning. They chose the day and hour well for the massacre. It was market day and the crowd at its height, too, when the first wave of planes appeared. They turned the city of Guernica into a pile of smoky ruins. And there were no troops there, no military objective of any kind to justify the attack. Their only purpose was to spread terror behind the lines. When the city was completely destroyed, the German planes came back, flying very low this time, to machine gun the hordes of campesinos, mostly women and children, who were fleeing terrified along all roads leading out of town."

Not far from this house, across the road, there is a stone quarry in operation. The explosions usually take place at midmorning. A foreman blows a trumpet as a warning, while two workmen with red flags wave all traffic to a stop. This morning I am on the terrace and see Captain Pedro Plasta pass by on his way to Ramona's tavern. The trumpet signals him to halt. After the blast, he approaches and tells me he and his sister went yesterday to the Saturdarán jail to visit the girls; today his mood wavers between sorrow for his nieces' plight and rage against their captors. A new explosion at the quarry stops our conversation, and when the noise subsides and traffic is resumed, my friend Peter Mess bids me farewell.

"A blast like that I'd like to put up the Caudillo's ass," he tells me, half in Basque, as he departs.

A few hours later he returns pushing a wheelbarrow. In our conversations I have complained of my lack of books and he's told me that his deceased brother, also a merchant captain, left quite a library which is now stored in the basement of his house. He reads very little, he said; the books are at my disposal. And this morning the old seawolf keeps his promise, wheeling a respectable mound of books onto the terrace, dumping them next to my bed. He leans the wheelbarrow against a wall and tells me he'll pick it up on his return from the tavern.

The books are printed in large, clear type. They are mostly old editions, many with beautiful engravings. The selection includes works of Virgil, Ovid, tales of mythology, histories of revolutions and tyrannies . . . all covered with spiders' webs woven during years of neglect in the old basement. Captain Pedro returns at nightfall with a red nose, the beret cocked on his head, and a cigarette dangling rakishly from his lips. He doesn't seem to have wasted much time at Ramona's well-stocked establishment. Picking up the wheelbarrow, he gives me a wink of farewell.

"So long, pal," he says, again in half Basque. "Bastards they are, but screw them we will."

I watch him disappear around the bend of the road, slow of step and weaving a crooked path.

The 6th of March a Republican torpedo boat sank the Francoist cruiser Baleares off Cartagena. The optimism produced by that naval action vanished two days later with the ferocious bombardment of Barcelona by Italian and German planes, with a total of twelve hundred dead and several thousand wounded among the civilian population. Meanwhile, in the European panorama, Hitler invaded Austria on the 11th of March, 1938, following the dismissal of the Austrian Chancellor, Kurt Schuschnigg. Two days later, the new Chancellor, Seyss-Inquart, proclaimed the union of Austria and Germany.

During the month of March important actions took place on the Aragón front. The attacks of the fascists in the Teruel sector put their lines along the Alfambra River and brought them into advantageous positions for an advance to the Mediterranean coast.

Toward the end of the same month, in the face of a large fascist offensive along the Huesca front, the Catalan Divisions 28 and 29, whose positions had been entrenched at the city of Huesca, had to retreat back to Lérida, a town that fell into the hands of the rebels a few weeks later. When these advances were consolidated, the main activity of the fascist army shifted into lower Aragón. The new operation had two objectives: first, to advance along the Ebro to the coast in order to cut the Loyalist zone in two; second, to take over the blast furnaces at Sagunto. The first objective was successfully achieved, and on the 15th of April, Italian troops reached Gandesa on the shores of the Mediterranean.

With all the factories devoted to supplying the front lines, and with the enormous destruction caused by almost two years of war, all kinds of foodstuffs become scarce. With money and great long walks through the surrounding villages, my wife is able to solve the food problem. This is our most severe problem at this time. With the approach of spring, Teresa goes to Logroño and returns with our son, completely recovered from his illness.

Amelia's daughters and her niece come by many afternoons to keep me company. All of them are hardly more than children, and when the weather is not right for their games they listen enchanted to my long stories. Writing my memoirs about my life in jails and reading takes up the rest of my time. Dr. Mendieta has made a small incision in my back from which the infection drains, ridding me almost completely of pain.

During the summer of 1938, I receive visits from several friends, old companions from my professional or soccer days, on their way to the nearby beaches. Among them is an industrial engineer, recently escaped from Madrid. I listen as he tells about his detention and imprisonment for several hours in the Fine Arts building, which he calls the "Fine Arts Cheka." During our past student days, both of us frequently went to the soccer field of a sports club in Madrid, where we played mornings in the company of a group of fans and players.

One of the most diligent members of the club was a post office official whom my engineer friend had the good luck to bump into upon his entrance into the Fine Arts building. That man, who filled a post there of secondary importance, vouched for the engineer before the tribunal, thus securing his freedom. Fearing he would be picked up again, my friend sought refuge in an embassy, from which he passed into Franco territory. He is surprised when, upon hearing his references to the Fine Arts Cheka, I assure him that similar Chekas exist in this region, with the difference that I don't know anybody who has been set free because he was vouched for by a friend.

Through the words of my friend I am able to get a glimpse of the condition of the terror prevailing in government territory. His saddening narrative, including many well-known names now disappeared, lasts a long time.

The most important visit for me that summer is that of Carmelo Goyenechea. In 1924 we had gone together to the Olympic Games in Paris, and many times we had played on opposite sides of the middle line during our active life in soccer. Our cordial relations of former times are transformed into a close and hearty friendship.

Toward the middle of the summer, Luz Montero arrives at the hotel of the nearby Chacharramendi island to spend her vacation. She is the daughter of the doctor whose place I took in the provincial jail at Logroño shortly after his attempted suicide and his later execution.

This young lady is tall, dark, beautiful, and had made friends with a German civilian, a summer resident in the same hotel. Hans is a man with bright eyes, of medium height, whose suits made of ersatz materials synthesized by German industry very much impress the town. Among his many skills, he is a radio operator and an excellent photographer. Perhaps in memory of the beginning of their romance, they have returned to the hotel on Chacharramendi as newlyweds, prior to their departure for Germany.

That Nazi civil servant speaks Spanish very well and hates the clergy of whatever denomination. I hear a curious incident from him about his companions in the Condor Legion. It happened during the recent campaign in the north.

In the territory dominated by Franco, the clergy has decreed that bathing suits worn by men and women can only expose a few inches of skin.

The Germans, indoctrinated in the pagan Nazi spirit, have no respect for the severe regulations imposed in the matter. Their bathing suits are the reverse of those designed by Father Laburu, to whom the invention of the modest style is attributed.

One day when they were bathing on the beach of Santoña, a group of German aviators were approached by a prison chaplain. The priest, scandalized by the exhibition of so much fair flesh, went toward the edge of the sea and delivered a beautiful speech on morals and modesty, insisting on the example that they, more than anybody else, should show in public.

With malicious winks, the aviators made a circle and to the rhythm of a Germanic song began to push the poor priest around. A few seconds later he was plunged into the water, hat and cape and all. Notwithstanding the indignation caused by that episode, the young Germans came out of the adventure with nothing more than a reprimand from one of their commanders. Had this act been committed by civilians it would have had other consequences.

The fascist authorities of Logroño seem to have forgotten my existence. For seven months nobody has bothered me. One morning toward the end of July, while I am sunning myself on the terrace, two armed Civil Guards come in the house. One of them tells me that they have been sent by the first sergeant of the military post at Bermeo. They are here on a mission of surveillance with orders not to lose sight of me.

With natural surprise I reply that if that is all they've come for, in the next room they will find chairs which they are welcome to place and use wherever they want. My wife, very much alarmed, starts a conversation with them. The distrust of the soldiers is great, and they have no more words with me.

They pass the night in a room next to mine, showing themselves occasionally at the door between us, which remains open. The next day another team comes to relieve them, and thus the changing of the guard is repeated for several months. After four days, the first team returns. They are more communicative now, and I find out that the orders from the Civil Government of Logroño have been received via Bilbao by the commandant of the Civil Guard in Bermeo.

"Custody and surveillance of a dangerous prisoner who might try to escape," is the order, according to one of the soldiers.

I smile and indicate the open wound in my back.

"But even if I wanted to, with these legs, atrophied by so many months of immobility, I would be unable to move."

"Don Pedro, we are only carrying out our orders."

I don't pursue the subject, but for the first time I consider the possibility of fleeing! Even without their surveillance that adventure would be a foolish dream. But that is what their presence suggests to me.

Little by little the distrust of the men in charge of watching me is disappearing. The treatments given me by Dr. Mendieta, sometimes in their presence, together with the continuous personal contact, end up by dissipating the little doubts that they could have had. Teresa assigns them beds and blankets, and each night those men sleep unconcerned about the surveillance until morning, when they greet me after which they walk back and forth on the terrace waiting to be relieved, sometimes confused and ill at ease. "It's a shame, so many rifles to guard an invalid," people say. Those comments come to their attention and they don't find them very agreeable.

In sunny weather I spend most of the day on the terrace. People passing along the road on the way to Mundaca or toward the station look with surprise at the bed and the armed Civil Guards talking with me!

My fame, as "the dangerous sick man," spreads throughout the surrounding region. In my powerless condition it is some satisfaction to think that people don't believe me to be an inert heap of molecules, but a man capable of escaping. Later on all this contributes to my being considered by the peasants—generally reluctant to speak with strangers—as one of themselves. Of the many whom I come to know, ninety percent are enemies of the Franco regime, and among them many have relatives who fled to France, or have been imprisoned, or who are hidden in the mountains. The bombing of Guernica is an obsession with them, and in any lengthy conversation they bring up the disaster.

The surveillance to which I am subjected has its influence on my visitors who, although they don't stop coming to see me, usually stay a shorter time. That situation lasts until the end of summer. The First Sergeant of the barracks of the Civil Guard in Bermeo receives numerous complaints from his subordinates. At times, after leaving their tour of duty guarding me, they have to go on special missions into the mountains to search for escaped prisoners, or to investigate other such matters, which doubles their hours of work. As a result of the complaints, the First Sergeant presents a petition directed to the Civil Government of Bilbao, explaining the facts and insisting that to waste half his force in the surveillance of an invalid is senseless and represents an obstacle to the performance of other, more important duties. When the petition is considered, the counterorder comes quickly, and the Civil Guards stop coming. Just when I was becoming friends with several of them.

The Quincoces sisters stop by to visit us. They are two women already a little removed from their youth, dark and short, on whose faces are still sharply engraved the marks left by the execution of their brothers. Since at that time relations with the Civil Guards guarding me are excellent, they try to keep as far away as they can during my visits, and I am absolutely free to talk. I want to avoid allusions that might revive dark memories, but the obsession of both sisters with their bereavement brings them to the very theme I want to avoid.

Regarding their younger brother, Felipe Quincoces, the news secured through friends in the military service was so evasive that nothing was really known except that he had been arrested and immediately executed in Seville. The shooting of Felipe Quincoces occurred during the first days of warfare and a few hours after he had landed at Tablada—the airport for Seville—in order to refuel for his flight from Morocco to Madrid. Of the other brother, José Quincoces, and of his father-in-law, the civil governor of León, Emilio Francés, the story is told about negotiations to save their lives.

For many years the father Quincoces was colonel of the artillery regiment stationed in Logroño. The colonel's friendships among military men had been numerous and influential, for they considered him the best man who had ever occupied his post. Many of the acquaintances and friendships of Colonel Quincoces were kept up by his family following his death, which had occurred quite some time before. It was relatively easy for the daughters to get an interview with the Military Junta of Burgos. On the appointed date both sisters made the trip to petition for clemency.

A colonel, an old friend of the family, had arranged the interview. The extensive proceedings ended this way:

"What office did he hold?" General Cabanellas asked.

"Civil governor of León."

"In the future, Colonel, we would be grateful to you if you would refrain from participating in activities concerning insignificant matters, for they distract us from duties that are necessary and vital for everybody at this time."

In my relations with the owner of the house, Don Ricardo, my patience is strained all summer long. Given my resentments and his fanatic temperament, our conversations always come to the boiling point. Aunt Fabia, his wife, behaves quite differently toward me. The good woman is convinced that a change in my ideas will bring with it, *ipso facto,* health, freedom, and good fortune. Aside from her intense proselytizing, she shows interest and concern for me. My memories of that eccentric old lady are fond, but I can't say the same of her intelligent and ill-willed husband. Don Ricardo shows a special interest in coming to a corner of the garden, right under the place where I habitually lay in the sun. There, with some friend he would discuss the news of the war.

"Don't you worry! Madrid will fall like a ripe pear, and no crime will go unpunished," he would say.

The splitting of the government territory in two by the wedge introduced by the Italians along the Ebro brought our morale to its lowest level since the beginning of the Civil War. On the other hand, the enthusiasm of the fascists rose considerably. They were convinced that the struggle was practically concluded in their favor. The battle of the Ebro started in the middle of that climate of Francoist optimism. During the night of the 24th to the 25th of July, 1938, the Republican army of the Catalan front, separated from the rebels' positions by the Ebro and protected by the moonless night, crossed the river at different points between Mequinenza and Amposta. The secret preparations for the attack contributed to the initial success of that operation, planned and directed by Republican General Vicente Rojo.

According to the information of a retired captain, a friend of Pedro Plasta, the pontoon builders of the Republican army, in preparation for the attack, had constructed several temporary bridges over the Ebro. Some of them, submerged about two feet under the river and covered by the muddy waters, escaped observation by the German and Italian reconnaissance planes. Others were constructed out of flat pontoons bound together side by side, making up a distance equal to the width of the stream at each crossing point. Bridges of this type were hidden by trees that grow densely along the river bank, with the end pontoons tied to sturdy posts driven into the ground. From that position, upon receiving the order to attack, the shoreward pontoon was loosed from its mooring and the bridges turned like stiff boards into the current, to come into a position on the opposite bank. When the ninety-degree turn had been completed the end pontoon was again anchored to another post, and the way was open for the crossing of artillery, tanks, troop trucks, and the rest of the military equipment. The enthusiasm of the soldiers was tremendous, and to the rhythm of songs that later would be known the world over, the Republican army of Catalonia crossed the Ebro.

The news, as always, reached the rear with the usual distortion from both sides. The Republican side asserted that the retreat of all the soldiers of the Moroccan army had been cut off, with more than ten thousand prisoners taken in one day. The decisive battle was the greatest victory in the entire course of the Civil War. The news from Burgos denied any importance to the attack. "Only at the first moment, and under the favorable circumstances created by the element of surprise, had the Republican forces, 'the Reds,' achieved a few small gains. The sluice gates of the dams of upper Aragón had been opened; the tremendous torrent inundated great stretches of land and carried away all the temporary bridges. Thousands of soldiers had drowned. The communications and the supply lines of the attacking army were all severed," they said.

For several days, from my observation post on the terrace, I saw the faces of most of the people beam with satisfaction. The international press and the broadcasts of French radio stations—as surprised as the fascists by the unexpected Republican victory—constantly praised the masterful operation and renewed their comments about the possibility of a Republican triumph.

In order to maintain the advance and secure its success, the Republican army counted on the delivery of great quantities of armaments that had been semiofficially promised by France. In the face of the impossibility of carrying out these deliveries, the French prime

minister, Léon Blum, shed tears while embracing the emissaries of
the Spanish Socialist Party sent to France by the Republican government. The grief of the prominent socialist was of no practical value
in those decisive moments.

French reactionary elements—especially important in the army
at that time—and the political attitude of the British and the Ameri-
cans were most likely the difficulties that tied France's hands.

All available troops of the fascist reserve were rallied immediately
in order to hold back the avalanche, trying, after a bitter struggle, to
stabilize the front and launch the counterattack. With the Republican troops firmly entrenched along the conquered banks of the Ebro,
the bloody battle went on for over ten weeks. In spite of their heroic
struggle, because of their crushing inferiority in armaments, the army
of the Catalan front was forced to recross the Ebro.

The European political situation took on a somber aspect. In the
face of Hitler's claims on the Sudeten region of Czechoslovakia, war
in Europe seemed imminent. Among its probable consequences, at
least then, was the impossibility of a fascist triumph in Spain. On
the 15th of September of that year, Chamberlain's direct negotiations with Hitler began. Finally, on the 30th of the same month,
the four men who at that time directed European politics, Hitler,
Mussolini, Chamberlain, and Daladier concluded the shameful Munich Pact. The democracies abandoned their principles and delivered
Czechoslovakia to the mercy of the German dictator. Chamberlain
returned to London with the pact signed by Hitler and Mussolini,
which was, according to the unerring estimate of Pedro Plasta, the
old swindle.

One September day an old tramp makes his appearance in Pedernales. He has a beautiful face, abundant white hair, and very dark
eyes. Several times we give him food at our house. He sleeps in the
storeroom at the small railroad station and by day earns some money
cutting firewood in nearby villages.

One afternoon, when he finishes filling his earthen pot in the
kitchen, he sits down in a corner of the terrace. After devouring his
ration slowly and silently, he comes over and talks to me. Right after
Asturias fell to the fascists he was imprisoned for nine months, and
now set free, is going toward San Sebastián with the hope of finding work.

After looking around to make sure we are alone, he adds:

"Spain will be soaked with blood once more, and bad men will be killed with their wives and children, so that this country will not have to suffer again. I am old and I will not see it. My brothers are buried beside the mines, my house was destroyed, and I, like so many thousands, am unable to find work. These are evil people, unworthy of pity the day things change. When we were masters of Asturias for more than two weeks in 1934, we did not kill anybody; those who fell were killed in battle. Only cowardly assassins kill defenseless men, and it is a duty to exterminate those people at the root, now that we know what they are like."

Since my former days in jail, I haven't heard anyone express himself with such an intense hatred. The following morning he continues his journey on foot toward the border, which he will try to cross without documents in case he doesn't find work in the capital of Guipúzcoa.

The last of the summer people to leave the town, already into October, is a woman with two children, married to a rich industrialist from Bilbao named Echevarría. This lady was the daughter of the Austrian consul in Bilbao, who, convicted of espionage for Franco, was executed on the orders of the Basque government. Throughout the whole summer I had listened to remarks about her caustic language against anybody who has the slightest Republican sympathies. One afternoon I am on the terrace with Doctor Mendieta when she passes by on the road.

"This woman," remarks the doctor, "would bathe herself in blood every day if she could. But her rancor can be explained. On the other hand, the feelings of other summer people who parade by here is inexplicable. And among the people I refer to there are no fascists. The middle-class people who support the military revolution are on the side of Alfonso XIII, at least in this area, and particularly the women."

I remember the young Madrid monarchists at the time of the proclamation of the Republic. Seated at the bars of café Pidoux and café Chicote, they exhibited their bracelets enameled with little monarchist flags and sang:

> One month of the Republic
> Another one of anarchy
> And after that, the monarchy.

This was the ditty they made fashionable among themselves at that time. Some of those enthusiastic monarchists would have been petrified had they known that Alfonso XIII would die years later alone in a hotel in Rome, calling Franco "the usurper" and leaving orders in his will not to be buried in Spain as long as the Caudillo usurped power.

At the end of October my old companion of the Avenida prison, Salvado the veterinarian, passes through Pedernales. Confined for thirteen months in a town of the province of Valencia, he had been investigated to their satisfaction by one of the military tribunals and was able to return to his profession. The post they offered him for the time being was in the town of Guipúzcoa, and finding out about my presence in Pedernales he has made a detour of a few hours in order to see me. We recall our days of captivity and talk about our fellow prisoners.

Manolo Alba had been transferred to the jail at Alfaro. In his capacity of prison engineer he directed some public works done with the forced labor of the prisoners detained there. His training gave him certain advantages, and he seemed to be as resigned as possible under the circumstances.

A board of trustees offering prisoners the completion of their sentences through work was organized. The idea of the Jesuit priest, Pérez del Pulgar, had found a favorable echo among the falangist authorities. Later on this idea was extended to all the provinces, but the cuts and modifications made to the original plan turned it into something wretched and cruel, beneficial to the Franco regime and its supporters.

The Valley of the Fallen, near the Escorial, initiated as a Pharaonic monument to eternal hatred among Spaniards, was later constructed by prisoners included in the aforementioned plan.

Some newspaper articles relating to the shipping business which Salvado and I had read bring our conversation to the bizarre figure of Juan March. The pirate of the Mediterranean, as March was called, played an important role in the preparation of the military coup. He was a decisive element in the financing of arms at the beginning of the Civil War. March's birthplace was Mallorca, which he abandoned as a youth following a family scrap. The first thing he did upon disembarking at Barcelona was to get new clothes for himself. Making up a package of his old outfit, he sent everything back to his family, with a note to his father, saying:

"In order not to owe you anything, I have decided to begin my life naked, just the way my mother brought me into the world."

During the Republic, the shady business deals of this man reduced the income of the government, causing the then Minister of Finance, Señor Carner, to say in parliament, words that achieved great popularity in Madrid:

"Either the Republic will put an end to March or March will put an end to the Republic."

Following a parliamentary debate March was arrested and taken to the prison of Alcalá de Henares, from which he escaped by bribing a guard.

The story was known to me, with the exception of the episode about March's arrival in Barcelona. The swift career of the distinguished smuggler was also well known in Madrid and had brought about the publication of a book describing the history of his immense fortune. The path of that fortune appeared to be sown with the corpses of customs guards. Later the business deals became more lucrative and less dangerous. Among them was the delivery of fuel to the German submarines operating in the Mediterranean during the First World War. At the end of that phase, March's fortune was the largest or the next to largest in Europe.

Salvado, with allusions to the power of money, takes the theme further:

"An enormous amount of money places the unscrupulous man beyond good and evil; it allows him to enjoy absolute impunity; to kill, to rob, and to invest his fortune as he pleases, many times in violation of the law. I know on the basis of a reliable source that last winter, aided by one of his English agents, March took jewels, money, and even a very valuable collection of works of art out of Madrid."

The state of my health surprises him; undoubtedly Salvado recalls the emaciated figure of the Avenida jail. Immobility and overfeeding have brought my weight up over two hundred pounds. He hears the whistle of the train that leaves in a few minutes, just in time for him to get to the nearby station. With a warm embrace, and wishing me a quick recovery, my old prison companion says good-by. I am submerged in memories until in a short while Pedro Plasta arrives. Upon hearing about my visitor, he remarks:

"The world small it is." These Basques!

On these balmy autumn afternoons, I like to look at the sea. The orchard workers roll my movable bed and take me to the small pier built against the wall circling the orchard. I didn't know about oranges growing in the Basque country and I am quite surprised to see here, for the first time, several rows of orange trees whose fruit, not yet ripe, has already been turned to a reddish yellow by the sea breeze. The tide is very high and, when it rises, it covers a great expanse of golden sand. The spectacle, in addition to being a distraction, brings me tranquility.

One afternoon on the solitary terrace I meet a young man named Pablo who works on the railroad line between Amorabieta and Pedernales, its final station. That boy is twenty four years old and has a handsome masculine face. He is a great soccer fan. After a few successive visits I begin to trust him. I ask the reason why he is not in military service like other people of his age. With a serious and thoughtful expression, he confides in me.

"I too was drafted for a couple of months. I was taken prisoner at Mondragón with a large group. Some were shot, others sent to different prisons, and a few of us set free. Because I belonged to the regular army and not to the Basque militia, I was set free."

"You've been lucky," I tell him.

"You are right. In addition, I'm a railroad worker, and in the railway service just as in many other occupations, there is a shortage of workers. I am an enemy of the Falange just like everybody else in this country, but even if I had the opportunity to fight again I would not accept. I lost my father many years ago, and my mother and my younger brother need my help. But aside from these responsibilities, what could we do? With the Basque army I had to retreat from San Sebastián. For every airplane we had they had fifty; for every cannon and every machine gun they had hundreds. The struggle is useless. I have seen the Gudaris (the Basque Republicans) fight like lions and wind up always yielding ground. Many of them, half bleeding to death, kept on shooting to their last breath. But wars are not won with enthusiasm and without arms. For nothing in the world would I want to spend those days in jail again. Every night except Sundays they would shoot a few prisoners, even priests who always are respected in this country where all are good Catholics. The night of the 24th of October they executed three priests of the Mondragón parish, Leonardo, José, and Joaquín Arim. A fellow prisoner named José Ignacio told me that during the same month they had murdered two priests, Martín Lecuona and Gervasio de Albizu, from his town. A few nights later José Ignacio was shot. As the guards began to tie up those on the "saca" list, I heard him say, 'It is sad to die, but if God has arranged it this way, I resign myself and you don't need to tie me up.' The guards let him say a short prayer, and with his hands tied, he said good-by to me. 'This is like being run over by a train. So long, compañero.' I saw him go toward the execution patio smiling. In the end, the best thing is to forget until better times come, and in the meantime see, hear, and be quiet. . . ."

I continue to see Pablo for the rest of the autumn, whenever his work and the weather permit. At the beginning of the new year, he changed his job, and I never saw him again.

With the numerous punctures of the calcium injections and with the sunbaths, my skin becomes as hard as leather, and Dr. Mendieta sometimes has trouble with the hypodermic needle. One afternoon while he is replacing the broken needle, I ask him about the executions of priests, remembering the confidences of Pablo.

Slowly the doctor says: "Upon entering Tolosa the Franco people shot three whose names I don't remember (later identified as Fathers Adarraga, Aristimuño and the organist F. Oñanindia). Another of those executed in Elgoibar was the priest Celestino Olaverría. Here in Vizcaya they followed the same method with members of the clergy considered to be opposed to the Franco regime. Among them were three whom I knew: the director of Amborabieta school, Father Román, José Sagarra of the parish of Berriatua, and José Peñagaricano of Marquina."

"How do you explain the silence of the Catholic hierarchy?" I ask as he pauses to give me the shot.

"With the leadership of the Spanish church in the hands of fanatical bishops, archbishops, and cardinals like Segura, Gomá, and others who bless the fascist cannons, there is nothing surprising about it. What surprises me is the silence of Rome. The venom of the Civil War has penetrated all levels of society. A few months ago I was told about an old priest in a small town close to Bilbao who was arrested on the denunciation of another priest. Because of his advanced age, seventy nine years, several people tried to free him on the basis of a simple retraction of his political ideas. His refusal resulted in a thirty-year sentence which the priest received thanking the tribunal for conceding him so long a life. There have been several similar cases in Guipúzcoa, and as far as I know none in Castile. The Basque clergy is closer to the heart of the people; perhaps for that reason they are respected and loved."

The doctor quickly puts his instruments away in his case and says good-by. A light epidemic of typhus in several villages keeps him so busy that I don't see him for several days.

During the early hours of the afternoon, whenever the sun is shining, groups of priests walk back and forth along the road. With slow, majestic steps, they almost cover the road. Pedro the captain, upon seeing them, says: "Here comes the English fleet!" To his seaman's mind those words symbolize maximum power. Among those who pass by, there is a thin, middle-aged priest—known as the most fanatic in the neighborhood. I am told that he belongs to one of the churches of Mundaca. They also tell me that once, when somebody brought to his attention the executions of priests committed by the Francoists in this territory, he responded, "All the collaborators with the forces of evil are well dead." When the same person pointed out to him the contradiction between his words and the commandments of the Law of God, the priest replied, "Let us leave the Commandments in peace. What is important now is to win the war. When we have won it there will be time to concern ourselves with all that."

One afternoon I try to verify that story with Mendieta.

"I too heard it told some time ago, and although I am unable to assert anything definite, it wouldn't surprise me in the least if it were true. People here are not inclined to invent stories, least of all about priests, for whom they feel a great respect. At the beginning of the fascist offensive in the north, we began to receive news about the shooting of priests, which many didn't believe. Later on, those crimes were attributed to the Moors and the Legionnaires in the fascist assault forces. Finally the evidence came. Those murders were committed on the orders of the authorities exactly like all the other shootings. Rarely a week went by without the arrival of information about those slaughters; two in Hernani, another in Elgoibar, and four were found in Vera's cemetery, with only the cassocks on in order to discourage identification. It was one night two years ago that I heard about the execution of Fr. Iturralde Castillo in Tolosa. One of his relatives gave us the complete story. More than five hundred priests of the province of Guipúzcoa fled to France before the fascist troops entered their respective towns. Some day the world will know these facts about the so-called religious crusade."

The barber, his head encased in an enormous beret, comes on alternate days to shave me. His brother-in-law is in hiding, and I am convinced that the barber knows where.

My conversations with him generally are about simple things: fishing, happenings in the town, his firewood, and his two cows which provide us with milk. That saintly man causes me to modify the poor opinion I've had till now of the trade of sexton.

From the 16th of November, when the Republican forces retreated from the Ebro, until the 23rd of December, all activity ceased on the Catalan front. An immense accumulation of men and matériel took place during that interval, as preparation for the final attack upon the lines of combat defending Barcelona.

In a Chilean newspaper that fell into my hands, I read:

"During the last few days Franco has concentrated his forces in order to open the battle over Igualada: six Francoist divisions and three Italian, around fifteen hundred artillery pieces, and at least fifteen squadrons of pursuit planes and as many bombing squadrons. According to observers attached to the Republican army, the Loyalists have enough troops, but they are very weak in matériel and outnumbered in airplanes by a ratio of eight to one."

The news reaching us from the French radio and press reflected the same situation of inferiority. That reality was confirmed by the speech of Anthony Eden in Coventry:

"Franco is conquering Catalonia because of air and military power more formidable than anything so far seen or known in this war. Where does this power of armaments come from? The world knows very well who has delivered the arms and who continues to ship them in open violation of agreements and pacts. Meanwhile the air forces, all of them foreign, continue to bomb Spain, the foreign artillery goes on shooting, and the foreign infantry keeps on marching over Spanish soil."

On the morning of the 23rd of December of 1938, the attack began. The initial shock was received by the XI and XII Corps of the Republican army; the first, with a great number of casualties, maintained their positions, but the second, along with two brigades of the 56th Division, after giving way before the violent attack, retreated in disorder. When Líster arrived with reinforcements to close the gap, he was thrown back by the Italian troops of General Gambara. The campaign continued throughout the Christmas season, with the towns falling one by one into the hands of Franco.

Pedro the seaman continues to see me every day. He is profoundly affected by the collapse of the front and, as always when things go bad, he prefers to keep quiet or to talk about something else. One night I hear him tell about one of his voyages as captain of a large sailing vessel. It was a crossing from Madagascar to Ceylon. A gust of wind broke one of the masts and knocked down a member of the crew splitting his head.

"No thread we had but what was used to sew the sails. I sewed him up, and cured he was, in a week." I'm getting to understand him well, by now.

For the first time since my arrest I spend the Christmas season with my family. The dinners are quiet and simple, a condition which scarcities impose. The traditional joy is present only in a few houses and among the soldiers of La Colonia hospital. The convalescent soldiers, provided with special passes, food, and drink, make a racket in the lonely streets of the town between their stops at different taverns.

At midnight a group of Carlist soldiers gathers in the road in front of the house singing the hymn of Oriamendi:

> For God, Country, and King
> Our fathers fought.
> For God, Country, and King
> We fight too.

THE INDICTMENT
AND END OF THE REPUBLIC

It's cold, this January of 1939. Rainy, too, so I don't get a chance to be wheeled out to the orchard. Only a few times can I venture to stay on the terrace.

Late in the month two men come to see me, the judge from the town of Busturia and his secretary. The latter carries a thick folder containing all charges and documents pertaining to my case. The Logroño court sent the indictment to Bilbao and from there it was forwarded to Busturia, judicial site of the village of Pedernales. The military courts are racing to expedite pending indictments in anticipation of hundreds of thousands expected from the captured cities, they explain. (I can only suppose they mean Madrid and Barcelona, which certainly will yield an avalanche of cases.)

The judge informs me that, like everyone else in the district, he was aware of my condition and thus he has already secured a certificate from Dr. Mendieta attesting to my inability to present myself at the courthouse.

"We want to comply with our mission and we look forward to your cooperation," the secretary says as he opens the bulging briefcase.

I assure him I am quite disposed to help, and then I ask why civilian officials are taking over the handling of a case which is under military jurisdiction.

"Nothing is unusual in these abnormal times," the judge answers affably. I begin answering my way through a maze of infamies and false accusations emerging from that briefcase; the interrogation by the police chief the day I was arrested; the one which followed with Captain Conde; the statements I made to the investigators in the glass cabin at the provincial jail, early in 1937. . . . All this is mixed in with statements and depositions made by other people, most of whom are unknown to me.

The first accusation is "Active collaboration in the rebellion against the regime." I give them an account of all my moves since leaving Madrid just before the outbreak of the Movement to my arrest, a few days later. Several times I am interrupted by their questions, and all of it is recorded by the secretary on long sheets of legal paper. The hearing lasts all morning. Finally, when it's close to two o'clock, they pick up their papers, bid me farewell, and say they will return tomorrow.

When Dr. Mendieta comes to see me later, he asks if I had read his medical certificate. I hadn't, I tell him.

"They're not bad, neither of them. Both are oldtimers in Busturia. They won't do anything in your favor, but I don't think they'll do anything to harm you, either. In my certificate I state clearly that any effort to move you prematurely could cause you serious circulatory troubles, total paralysis, or even death. Let me know how things develop."

The Busturia officials return and resume the questioning. The first charges they discuss are those of my having manufactured bombs and the fact that I am a Mason. This last one is serious enough to bring about a death sentence in any zone held by the fascists. I know that. I and other brothers of the Zurbano lodge of Logroño owe our lives to a young mechanic who, at the risk of his life, destroyed the records of our lodge. Thus, that accusation is short, confused, and anonymous. The next one concerns having participated in the burning of convents in Logroño in the early spring of 1936. The difference between this charge and the previous ones is its length and the names involved. I have to make a mental effort to remember pertinent details. . . .

. . . After the brutally repressed uprising of miners in Asturias, in October of 1934, when the rightist government had prevailed, I was dismissed as a municipal engineer from Logroño's City Hall without explanation or proceedings. The victory of the Popular Front in the elections of 1936 rectified that, as it did many abuses committed by the rightists during the "black biennial" in which they held power. I was anticipating my reinstatement and had to go to Madrid to wind up some personal business. I decided to take the morning train for the capital. That very afternoon the burning of convents started in Logroño. I went to the mayor's office and offered my services as a volunteer fireman. After talking with Mayor Gurrea and coordinating operations with Erce, chief of the Urban Guard, I took over the Guard's fire brigade and dispatched the men to the areas most affected. In fifteen minutes we had the firefighting machines and equipment out in the streets. I deployed them to the convent of the Carmelites and the convent of the Adoration nuns. The men fought both disasters swiftly and courageously, doing as little damage as possible as they put out the flames. But it was impossible to do the same in all other places affected simultaneously. The convents of Enseñanza and Mother of God, the building of the newspaper Diario de la Rioja, and the monarchists' headquarters were favorite targets of the arsonist hordes.

By the time we got to the newspaper office the building had been already gutted. We proceeded to the convent of Enseñanza and began spreading out the equipment, but the hundreds who were watching the fire brandished knives and threatened to cut the hoses if we used them. (Among them were a few I later recognized serving in the first execution patrols that performed the "sacas" at the Avenida prison.) I telephoned lawyer Rupérez, an advisor to the governor. Upon his promise to send reinforcements, I left the equipment protected by some urban guards and proceeded with the firemen to the convent of Mother of God. The ancient wooden structure was crumbling already. I returned to the convent of Enseñanza. With several teams of Assault Guards sent by Rupérez as promised, we were able to turn on the hoses at last. My assistant, Amaranto, chief of the municipal plumbing division, worked incessantly all through the night. A smoking beam falling from the roof miraculously missed us by two yards. We were able to save a good part of the building. At dawn, wet, tired, my suit torn to shreds, I went home to rest for a couple of hours before my departure for Madrid.

The irony in the secretary's expression now compels me to tell him and the judge another story concerning the burning of convents. This took place in Madrid around the middle of May, 1931, shortly after the change from the monarchy to the Republic.

I was at the old café Millares when alarming news came: The convents of the district of Chamartín had been set afire. Half an hour later I was parking my car in front of the Sacred Heart convent in

the company of three friends. The whole structure was enveloped
in flames. The nuns had escaped, except for three who ran back and
forth in terror at the main gate, not daring to make a dash through
the hostile crowd watching the fire. With the help of a taxi driver
my friends and I were able to get to the three nuns, showing our
political identification cards. The taxi driver and one of my friends
took one of the nuns and sped toward the highway to France while
I and my other companion took the road from Madrid through the
Chamartín township with the other two nuns in my car.

A couple of hours before, the mobs had tried to set fire to the
Jesuit school next to the Sacred Heart, and the Civil Guard had
had to shoot over their heads. News spread around the workers'
quarter of Tetuán de las Victorias that the people were being shot
at, that already several were dead and wounded. Huge crowds then
marched toward Chamartín de la Rosa to burn the Jesuit school. I
saw the throng coming and hardly had time to turn around before
all exits were blocked. They threw rocks at us, breaking both head-
lights and denting the body of the car. I drove away as fast as I
could.

It took us more than two hours to get to town through the suburb
of Cuatro Caminos with stops and detours. The nuns' white wimples
attracted attention. We asked them to remove them; they refused
and we had to force them to do so and lent them our jackets for
headcover. Finally we delivered them to the addresses they had
given us: the first one to the house of an architect, Fernando Escon-
drillas, on Zorrilla Street, across a side entrance from the Congress
building; the second at the house of a Sr. Betancourt, on Príncipe
de Vergara Street, close to the avenue of Alcalá. The latter, an aging
whitehaired gentleman, embraced us and thanked us profusely for
saving his niece. Upon saying farewell, he was quite surprised to
learn we were not monarchist youths, but Republicans who supported Spain's new regime with wholehearted enthusiasm.

The judge, who has been listening to this last story with marked
interest, switches back to his impersonal attitude. "That has nothing
to do with this inquest. Besides, Madrid has not been liberated yet
and it would be difficult to verify that story." He turns to the secretary. "We must be brief. We can't give so much time to this case."

The rest of the questions are brief, and so are the answers. They pertain to my friendship with notable leftists, to my having expressed revolutionary feelings, having read newspapers such as the *Heraldo* of Madrid and *The Socialist,* harboring antireligious ideas, contributing to subversive funds, and finally, hiding explosives for revolutionary purposes.

At the end they wish me an early recovery and depart. Obviously, they don't relish this interruption of their routine work.

A few days later Dr. Mendieta tells me he has met the judge in Busturia and asked him about my case. "He is an honest man," the judge told him. "But I haven't the faintest idea what they're going to do about his case in Burgos. It's up to them."

The Catalonia front collapsed and on January 26th the rebels entered Barcelona. According to news reaching our little town, there was a big military parade with General Gambara's Italians at the head. Dr. Mendieta said that all the big noise about the Italian victory was necessary to boost Mussolini's prestige before European opinion and soothe him for the beating his troops suffered at Guadalajara. The fall of Barcelona was celebrated in some houses in Busturia and also among the soldiers convalescing at La Colonia.

A group of legionnaires—they called themselves "those betrothed to Death"—stop to sing their anthem below my window while celebrating the victory at Barcelona. It is late at night and all the lights are out. I hear one of them say:

"If you didn't have a broken back we'd go in and make you dance!" The remark can be excused because of the wine they've obviously consumed in their celebration.

A few days later the pope died and Cardinal Pacelli was elevated to the pontifical chair as Pius XII. Along with the extensive news about the new pope, there was a speech from General Franco directed to the Republican zone:

"When you had all the gold, all the metallurgical plants, almost all the arms depots, the munitions and powder works, the most important coal and iron mines, large stocks of food and raw materials, three-fourths of our coasts, nine-tenths of our navy, hundreds of airplanes and tanks, and an army that, counting only its shock troops, numbered 100,000 internationals and in the north another army integrated by the best of the Marxist labor organizations, well equipped and well supplied. . . . When you had all that you lost every battle and you were defeated constantly. Consider therefore your situation now that you have lost all that we ourselves have gained. Deprived of factories, without iron or coal, without planes, subjected to a sea blockade, your navy powerless at port, your starving families. . . . You cannot possibly entertain further hopes. You are lost!"

One afternoon I hear Dr. Mendieta's comments on that famous speech.

"Those statements practically admit to the foreign intervention that helped him! What he said is partly true, as far as the situation that prevails now. But he failed to explain how he was able to compensate for those tremendous differences, unless he implies he circumvented them with his military genius. And that genius was nowhere in sight when he had to face a well-armed Republican army in Guadalajara, Madrid, Teruel, and on the Ebro. Not until he got reinforcements from his pals Hitler and Mussolini! He sure stretches the number of international brigades. From fifteen thousand to one hundred thousand, no less! And as for his blockading a coastline three times as large as his, with a navy nine times smaller than his opponent's, according to his words . . . why, that's a feat that makes a midget of Nelson!"

"Don't you think the Republic still has important factors on hand to negotiate an honorable capitulation? We have the fleet, the gold of the Bank of Spain, we have Madrid, Valencia, Cartagena, other important centers. . . ."

"Franco knows very well that nobody wants to sell arms to the government and that everything will soon fall into his hands. And easily, too. Only if he is made aware that the Republicans will destroy everything before surrendering, would he accede to that honorable capitulation. That is, a surrender with guarantees of safety for life and property and the right, for those who wish, to leave the country."

"You're right, Doctor. The fascist victory is a reality by now. The difficulty would be to find the formula and the persons capable of conducting those negotiations."

"My dear Escobal, only the foreign powers could give validity to Franco's guarantees. Remember the Santoña surrender!"

When I tell the physician that I am unaware of that surrender, he explains it.

"A detachment of 2,000 Basque troops at Torrelavega found their retreat to Asturias cut off. Colonel Facina, of the Italian contingent, made a pact with Leizola and Minzón, as representatives of the Basque Government. The Basques were to:

1. Surrender their arms and equipment to the Italian legion who would occupy the Santoña area without opposition.
2. Maintain law and order in the territory still under their control.
3. Guarantee the life and freedom of the political prisoners and hostages in the Laredo and Santoña prisons.

"The Italians, on their part were to:

1. Guarantee the life of the Basque officials in the Santoña and Laredo jurisdictions and authorize their leaving the country.
2. Guarantee the life of all surrendering Basques.
3. Declare the Basque troops free from the obligation to take part in the Civil War.
4. Guarantee the Basque population loyal to the Basque Government that they would not be persecuted.

"After the Basques had fulfilled their part and their troops were making ready to leave the country by boat, Franco officials appeared, prevented their departure and made prisoners of all of them. A good number were shot later. And to think that the leaders of the Movement, starting with Franco, go to confession and communion and make much ado about their religious beliefs! How can anyone expect that such hypocritical and infamous conduct will guarantee the fulfillment of any pact?"

The incision in my back has healed without apparent trace of infection. I dream of leaving the wheel bed, but the doctor cautions me. One or two months will ensure complete recovery, and . . . what can a couple of months more mean now? He will soon order an orthopedic corset that I'll have to wear for nearly a year after I get up.

On the high rise of town there is a little chalet whose garden borders on the sea cliffs. It is occupied by a young girl called Garmiñe, her mother, and an old servant. Garmiñe suffers from the same illness I have, and our wheels beds are twins, made by the same smith in town. Garmiñe's mother is a close friend of Amelia, and together they go twice a week to the market at Guernica. On her way to the station she stops and chats with me, if I am out on the terrace. When she finds out about my "promenades on wheels" in the orchard and on the pier, she comes in with Amelia and begs me to extend the ride as far as her house and visit her daughter. It would be such a pleasure for the invalid girl. . . . I promise to engage a few strong boys in town to wheel me up the hill. I do, and in a few days, with unexpected ease, I am rolled up by four boys right to Garmiñe's house. There are her mother, the old servant, and two visitors expecting me. One of them is the son of Busturia's pharmacist. He speaks of his days as a Basque miliciano. He fought until he was made prisoner in the fall of Bilbao. His wealthy mother engaged the influence of priests and church officials and succeeded in liberating him from jail after a few months.

We talk about a torpedo recently found on our beach, a popular topic of that day. A team of experts from Bilbao has been assigned to examine it and transport it to the nearby fort on the Cape of Machichaco. The other visitor at Garmiñe's house is from the town of Durango, which was subjected to an attack almost identical to the one suffered by Guernica. "The first bomb fell on the chapel of Saint Susana," he tells us. "It was a direct hit that completely destroyed the building. I'll never forget the scenes after the raid, when I went to do rescue work with other volunteers. The nuns' bodies lay amidst a rubble of broken images of saints, bricks, and masonry. A woman went out of her mind as she held the dismembered body of her child. Another bomb hit the Santa María church, just as the priest Carlos Morilla was raising the host during consecration. He was found dead, surrounded by the bodies of the faithful who were awaiting communion when they were hit by the explosion. But the greatest number of dead were found at the Jesuit church, which was hit when the priest Rafael Billabeitia was starting mass. That March day will not be forgotten in Durango. . . ."

By nightfall, the boys roll me down hill and back home. The return proves to be more tricky than the climb because the road is dark and slippery.

Next morning, Pedro Plasta, the old seawolf, who like everybody in town has heard of my visit to Garmiñe's house, comes to see me with the latest news. The experts showed up at midnight, and after examining the torpedo concluded it was a harmless World War I piece. They loaded it into a truck and took it away. The town let out a sigh of relief when the contraption was well on its way on the road to Bermeo. He then shows me a newspaper clipping with pencil markings underlining certain paragraphs. It is a speech by falangist leader Sánchez Mazas which ends paraphrasing the Apostle Paul:

"We shall win over the pharisees with prodigious deeds and the pagans with wisdom; to win over the first we shall make a just and a great Spain; the latter will be won with the wisdom of our lofty ideals of justice and culture. Yet there is a third thing that neither one would know how to ask from us, but which we shall also give them: love."

Those words, to Pedro, mean the possible release of his nieces jailed in Saturdarán. When Dr. Mendieta comes over later that morning, I show him the clipping Pedro left in my room. After reading the last paragraph he comments:

"In Barcelona they keep on with the executions by the thousands. Perhaps what this illustrious falangist writer had in mind when he said 'love' was the love of death."

Meanwhile, the head of the Republican Government, Dr. Juan Negrín, after remaining with the remnants of the Republican Catalonian Army on its march to France, flew back to the central Republican zone which was still holding on, in a desperate attempt to repeat the epic of the defense of Madrid in 1936. It was a futile attempt under the circumstances, the troops were demoralized, without food and with very little armament.

Segismundo Casado, the military chief of the shrinking Republican zone, together with Julian Besteiro, a leader of prestige in the Socialist Party, held some murky negotiations with Franco, which entailed their battling the Communist Party inside Madrid, and surrendering the capital of Spain to the Rebels. They thought that in exchange for surrender they had closed a deal with Franco whereby the lives of the defenders of Madrid would be guaranteed together with permission for those who wished, to embark from the Mediterranean ports still held by the Republicans and go into exile.

Once the Republican and Socialist troops had fought and defeated the Communists inside Madrid, Franco demanded the unconditional surrender of the city. The Casado-Besteiro Junta and its forces, exhausted after battling the Communists, were in no position to argue and had to surrender unconditionally.

All resistance collapsed. Tens of thousands of troops that had withdrawn toward Alicante, for instance, surrendered *en masse* to General Gambara, under promise that their lives would be respected. His authority was later countermanded by Franco and he could not keep his promise. The Basque surrender at Santoña was repeated over and over again on a much larger scale.

Years later I heard accounts from soldiers which would fill a thick book with horror stories. While the Italians were in charge of the vast concentration camps, there were no executions; food, although not abundant, was enough to ease the pangs of hunger. As soon as the Franco Army took command, murders and famine started.

Franco's entry in Madrid on April 1st, 1939, marked the end of the Civil War and the beginning of one of the longest and most cruel periods of persecution in the history of Spain.

Among the many iniquities perpetrated by the fascists upon their occupation of the city was to cast Don Julian Besteiro into prison. This eminent Socialist, ex-speaker of parliament and Professor of Logic at the Central University of Madrid, had not participated in any political activity during the course of the Civil War. Only at the end did Besteiro intervene in politics when he lent his prestige to General Segismundo Casado's Junta seeking to eliminate further Communist armed resistance in the city and ease the way for the surrender of the capital. It is possible that without his collaboration, the Communists would have put up a last-ditch fight to the bitter end, thus increasing destruction and famine among the population, since Madrid could expect no help from the rest of the Republican zone or what remained of it. Besteiro, unlike Casado, chose to stay. With a clear conscience, he thought he had nothing to fear. He refused to be evacuated.

He was rewarded with ignominious treatment at the hands of his falangist captors. Then, later he was to die of ill health, an aged, broken man in prison, where his tormentors had interned him. Shortly after my arrival in New York, I saw a photograph distributed by the Basque Government-in-exile, in which Besteiro appeared in the company of some thirty Basque priests jailed with him, in the courtyard of the Ocaña prison.

With communications somewhat restored, my mother came to Pedernales in the middle of April, accompanied by a nephew of mine. The trip from the south had been long and full of inconveniences because of the ravages of three years of war on the rolling stock and the rail lines.

She told me about the destruction of our Madrid house in the Argüelles quarter. First it had been hit by the fascist artillery firing from El Pardo in November, 1936, and she had to move in with some relatives in the Salamanca section of the city. A few days later, during a fascist air raid, the house was hit again, and anything that had not been destroyed by the bomb was looted—everything was lost: furniture, clothing, books, jewels.

At the end of 1936 she left Madrid to live with some nephews in Andalusia who had a house near Puebla de Don Fadrique, in Almería Province, where she spent the rest of the war in relative peace.

People coming from Madrid bring news of the butchery going on in the capital. Teachers, professors, and those who belong to the liberal professions are the choice victims of the fascist manhunts. Dr. Mendieta commented to me:

"Human political evolution turns 'round in circles. You struggle for freedom. Then, once you have it, it degenerates into demagogy, and then into anarchy. Anarchy brings back despotism, and, in turn, it is replaced by freedom once more. Millions of men have died in the tug-of-war without giving permanence to any one system. We are now to live in the stage-before-the-last of the cycle. But more than anything, it is arrogance that has reached satanic proportion here. Look, for instance, how they react with insults, mockery, and haughty rejection when those even faintly tainted by liberalism accept the new regime."

"What do you think," I asked him, "about the return of the monarchy? Maybe it'll help curb the executions, free the majority of the prisoners, and give some confidence to the people."

"Germany and Italy would not allow it," he answers. "Franco would reject the idea because he does not want a king over him. All dictators are the same in their greed for absolute power. The monarchy could perhaps alleviate the harshness of the situation, but the monarchists are as overbearing and as filled with hatred as any of the other forces that make up this dictatorship."

Then he adds, "Anyway, the important thing is that soon you'll resume your normal life. Do you remember our first chat? Now you are cured. Yet you must take care of yourself and avoid risks."

Teresa's aunt and uncle come to make the house ready for the summer and look over their property. The long-avoided clash occurs one day when I answer Don Ricardo's impertinences with harsh words. His reaction to the violent scene is contained in a letter we receive a week later in which he advises us he needs the premises for summer tenants. The problem, under the circumstances, has no easy solution. My mother-in-law placates Don Ricardo, telling him we'll quadruple the monthly rent. He accepts and we stay through the summer season, until we find another house, close to the railway station.

One afternoon, Amelia comes crying to me on the terrace with the news that Dr. Mendieta died half an hour ago. His well-known little car in which he used to move around to take care of his patients in the community and nearby villages, was confiscated by the falangist authorities upon his arrest and imprisonment in Vitoria. After his release, he used a horse to reach patients living up the mountains, and a bicycle for those in the valley. Sometimes, his eldest son, a strong and handsome boy of twelve, would accompany him on his rounds. Many of the roads had been damaged during the Civil War, including the beautiful and well-kept shore drives along the Bay of Biscay. These are now full of potholes. It was one of those potholes that caused Mendieta, while pedaling back to his house, to lose control of his bike and strike his head against a large rock, fracturing his skull. He died almost instantly.

The death of my friend hurts me deeply and he is mourned among the inhabitants of Busturia and Pedernales. It was just the previous afternoon that he gave me the address of the man who would make the orthopedic corset I'll have to wear. We had also discussed the problem of the thousands of prisoners in the Bilbao jails. According to the press, thirty three prisoners were set free one day, and forty a week later, seventy three during the entire month. That is but a drop in comparison to the total. The last words I heard from him were about the prisoners:

"As we all know, those are only provisional releases, and they can be thrown back in jail any time. It's hopeless, unless there is an outcry abroad. . . ."

Vacationers begin coming to our village and soon Pedernales takes on the brisk rhythm of its summer life. Among the tourists I recognize some whom I met last year. Meanwhile the dark clouds of war are gathering on the European horizon. It is obvious to anyone that the major conflict is approaching, but those in any way identified with the Franco regime repeat their new slogan, "Nothing will happen."

At last the man in charge of fashioning my orthopedic corset comes from Bilbao, a short deformed creature who strings me up with thongs and ropes and calmly proceeds to take my measurements, jotting them down in a notebook. He unstraps me, bids me good-by, and informs me that the corset will be ready for delivery in two weeks.

In mid-July, a week later than he promised, "Quasimodo" returns with his masterpiece. The corset is almost perfect; he has to make only one slight alteration, by hand. Next morning I get up from the wheel chair. Bursting with joy I try my first steps. They are difficult and painful. I have to lean most of my weight on the crutches because my muscles, inactive for so long, refuse to hold me up. My legs feel like brittle glass. Like a child learning to walk, I do better each day until in a week I can walk a short distance. Three weeks later I discard the crutches for a strong walking stick with a broad non-skid tip.

One of my best friends from Madrid comes with his wife to spend a few days with me. His eldest son was killed in the first skirmishes of the Civil War. I remember him, a strong, intelligent idealistic nineteen-year-old who enlisted as volunteer with other young Republicans, only to have their throats slit by Franco's Moors in their advance from Talavera. My friend is an impassioned liberal, a man with a tremendous heart to whom a life of youthful adventures and the love for the sport of soccer has always linked us. We spend a short week reminiscing and he proceeds to San Sebastián with his wife.

Postwar Madrid provides some humor besides the daily diet of terror. For days the press displays news of a sensational story: An Austrian national, an adventurer who entered Madrid with Franco's troops, claims to have discovered a method of making gasoline with plain water and a few special herbs mixed in some contraption of his own invention. According to a neighbor I see at Ramona's tavern when I get around, the official state bulletin has announced that a concession was granted for planting the herb somewhere on the banks of the Jarama River. The Basques give the "gasoline" the name of "Purrusalda" a famous regional soup because some of its condiments are among those prescribed by the Austrian for his concoction. I get the biggest laughs reading about the new great falangist empire ready to declare its independence of foreign oil suppliers and reach self-sufficiency in gasoline production.

The Spanish press was a good mirror of the image of the nation, transformed by the new regime: It was the adoration of the God-figure incarnate in the dictator.

The pall of fear kept Spain silent as a cemetery. Press, radio, books, and personal conversations were subject to violent suppression if they strayed from the strict guideposts of the Falange. Remarks or commentaries about speculation in high offices and of the *estraperlo* (black market) operations carried out by officials, were made at one's own risk, even in whispers. Bread, the main staple of the working class, was of the lowest quality. With the same violence, any talk about scarcities of food, medicines and clothing was suppressed as a form of sabotage against the new Imperial Spain personified in the *Caudillo*. You had to look happy in order to give the impression that in Spain, under Franco, things were not only normal, but flourishing and prosperous.

That was the state of Spain when Hitler, on that September dawn of 1939, invaded Poland. Two days later Britain declared war and the world was plunged into the second man-made cataclysm of the first half of the Twentieth Century, whose dress rehearsal had been the so-called Spanish Civil War.

Among Republicans, Socialists, and trade unionists, great hopes were kindled by the expected triumph of the democracies whose victory they never doubted. But to the fascists, in their blind faith and admiration for German military power, the war was but the curtain call that would open the golden age of a New Order in which Nazi Germany and Fascist Italy would split between themselves the map of Europe. The leftovers would be picked up by the little Spanish fascists . . . such morsels as French Morocco, Gibraltar, and other African colonies.

My walks in town are short. My legs are not yet strong enough for long promenades. As soon as I can I begin to return Pedro, the sailor, his many visits. One morning I find him hard at work breaking the ground in his back garden with a spade, beret tilted forward to shade his brow, pipe firmly stuck between his teeth. The work has parched his throat, he tells me. Of course, the best way to take care of that is to leave immediately for Ramona's tavern. After several glasses of wine he finishes a long story about a girl his nieces know from the Saturdarán jail. It seems their friend has a cousin who is having a love affair with an army colonel. The good cousin begs and cajoles and intrigues until her lover has no recourse but to help get the girl out of jail.

What Pedro Plasta says is:

"One hair from a woman's cunt is more powerful than Franco and all the generals in the world."

One day I go to Guernica by bus. The town is a pile of rubble stacked along the debris-littered streets. The only buildings that have escaped the disaster are a few chalets on the outskirts of town and the small arms factory. The legendary famous oak of the Basque Fueros—symbol of their centuries-old liberties—is still standing. They've made some makeshift stands with the stones of the destroyed buildings in the square and are holding market day as they have done since ancestral times. I remember Dr. Mendieta's descriptions, but they pale before the Dantesque spectacle spread before my eyes. I inquire discreetly about the German bombings. I get only evasive or false answers. Later I find out that many have landed in jail for speaking about the destruction of the town. The official version is that Guernica was razed and pillaged by the "Reds" on their retreat to Bilbao, and nobody dares say otherwise in public.

Returning to Pedernales, seated on the hard seat of the bus, uncomfortable in my orthopedic corset, I remember the words of Rabindranath Tagore: "The powerful ones believe that the convulsions of their victims are mere signs of ingratitude."

London is already suffering from the Nazi air raids perpetrated by the same men who already have left their devastating mark on Spain. The allies, architects of the International Committee of Non-Intervention who prescribed hands off Spain—while no committee checked Italy and Germany—are now getting their own medicine, I reflect. In a moment I am ashamed of my acid rejoicing. The cowardice, indecision, and blundering of the world's statesmen who devised the Committee should not be blamed on the men, women, and children of London.

At any rate, the picture of devastation I saw in Guernica surpassed all I had heard and imagined. The genius of Picasso epitomized the horrors, the death, and the destruction of defenseless Guernica for a mural that was to warn future generations of more appalling things to come.

PACO'S BAR

After we move I begin to patronize Paco's Bar. This property is made of two buildings separated by a patio, with a garden in back, a combination bar, hotel, and café. Its balconies rising above the road offer a full view of the bay and the island of Chacharramendi. Since this is the only hotel on the river mouth, it is always full in the summer. In the winter, its customers are priests, wealthy landlords from the area, transients, and the new doctor who has replaced the late Dr. Mendieta. Almost every afternoon after supper I go over to Paco's, where men gather to discuss the latest developments of the world war, still in its early stages. Although most of them are sympathetic to the Allies, few of them actually express it.

Paco, the owner, is a clever and likeable fellow. His wife and older cousin, Vicente, live with him. Vicente is a vegetarian.

One morning I go to the bar to borrow a hammer. Paco directs me to his cousin, who seems to be in charge of the tools. He is working in the garden, and I call out to him, expecting his customary plain good morning. I am surprised when instead he gives me a warm handshake, saying:

"I shut up to avoid any trouble. Two of my cousins were killed in an ambush in Ponferrada, in the mountains of León. They had gone there with a group of Asturian miners to pick up weapons promised them by the authorities in Oviedo. This took place at the beginning of what those bastards call the 'Glorious Movement.' Most of the people who come to my cousin's bar are cowards, butchers, and hypocrites, and that goes for the priests too."

I am puzzled by his strong words and frenzied look. I mention the possibility that things might change in the not-too-distant future.

"That won't bring back the dead, but that's all we can hope for. At heart, Paco is one of us, but he's soft by nature, and his business forces him to pretend," he replies.

He gives me the hammer I'm looking for. Paco has been watching us from the window, and as I leave he asks, "What was that mad cousin of mine saying? This is the first time I've seen him mumble more than a couple of words to anyone."

From then on, whenever I sit in the café and listen to the stupid praise which some customers heap upon the Caudillo, Vicente looks at me, trying to remind me of what he said in the garden.

Paco needs a blueprint of the hotel for a tax assessment pending in Guernica. It's hard to find anyone in the vicinity to do the job, and it would be too expensive to get a draftsman from Bilbao. I offer my services and he accepts gladly. A few days later I give him a plan of the property. Since I don't accept payment he gives me a case of wine. This incident strengthens my friendship with the two cousins.

Some afternoons the café is half empty, and Paco leaves his wife and the waiters in charge while we go up to Vicente's room, where we drink cognac and speak freely. Only Paco and I enjoy the liquor, for Vicente faithfully follows his vegetarian diet and neither drinks nor smokes. The first time I notice a collection of books neatly arranged on top of a large piece of furniture. Among the authors are Zola, Victor Hugo, Galdós, Unamuno, and Dostoyevski. And on a separate shelf were his vegetarian cookbooks. In his room we discuss freely the news about the European war, without running any risk. We agree that the Germans will be turned back at the Maginot line, that the British naval blockade will soon have Germany poverty-stricken, and that with the inevitable fall of Hitler the end of the Franco regime in Spain will come.

Vicente likes to discuss books with me. One afternoon he takes down one of his volumes and a bundle of notes fall from its pages. One of these is the text of the preface to a law of appropriations to support the clergy as part of the government budget. It was taken from a recent edition of *La Gaceta del Norte*. "The law pays tribute to the Spanish clergy, which has cooperated with our cause most selflessly and efficiently."

According to Paco, Vicente is keeping this strange sheaf of notes for a relative who has fled to France, a man of letters. I am particularly interested in two of the notes I copy down. The first is a declaration of the Spanish bishops on the proclamation of the Republic in 1931.

"True political sovereignty derives from God, who is the source and basis of all authority; and the Church, as its guardian, has never failed to teach the respect and obedience owed to the constituted power, even when its sanctifiers or representatives abuse it and direct it against the Church itself."

The second note was written by Cardinal Gomá a few months after the outbreak of the Civil War:

"As I write these lines, thousands of soldiers from the Russian steppes equipped with vast amounts of war matériel are landing in Barcelona. That city is being converted into a branch of the Russian Komintern and the seat of the Soviet Republic in the Mediterranean, a center for the communization of Western Europe. Everyone knows that communism was plotting a subversive uprising in Spain at the time the National Movement started."

Time has elapsed quickly and it is pitch black outside. I gulp down the rest of my cognac and leave my two friends.

With the end of the Civil War, La Colonia is reconverted from a military to a children's hospital, and its rooms once again are filled with young patients from Bilbao. Unlike previous years, these winter Sundays are very cheerful, and a good number of people visit their small loved ones in the hospital.

One day we see some nuns accompanying a group of children down the road, and Vicente comments:

"While those children are being cured, they are also being taught how to think."

"Everyone who can, teaches children how to think," Paco replies. "Fathers teach their sons, and teachers teach their pupils. It's no different in Russia."

"What's Russia got to do with it? What's bad in Guernica is equally bad in Sevastopol and I don't try to defend it in either place. Freedom of thought is the cornerstone of human progress, and when a man reaches a certain age he should be free to listen to or read whomever he wants, whether it's Lenin, Saint Augustine, Mohammed, or anyone else."

"This cousin of mine sometimes loses his head and makes a big fuss about little things."

"Never mind. You're only thinking of your business, always your business. I've known you since childhood and I know very well that you often hide your ideas."

I've never seen the two cousins so excited. I intervene with some conciliatory words which calm down Vicente.

"Pedro, you're a very sober man and for that reason I'm very fond of you, but you won't deny that all those officers covered with medals are shitting in their pants in fear that people could think for themselves. Because, in the final analysis history teaches us that once the masses begin to think for themselves, tyrants are doomed."

Much later when I read one of Bertrand Russell's works I came across a passage which expressed with more precision and beauty the meaning of Vicente's words.

"Men fear thought as they fear nothing else on earth, more than ruin, more even than death. Thought is subversive and revolutionary, destructive and terrible; thought is merciless to privilege, to established institutions, and comfortable habits; thought is anarchic and lawless, indifferent to authority, careless of the well-tried wisdom of the ages. Thought looks into the pit and is not afraid. It sees man, a feeble speck surrounded by unfathomable depths of silence; yet it bears itself as if it were lord of the universe. Thought is great and swift and free, the light of the world, and the chief glory of man."

I continue to have frequent contact with the two cousins until my departure from Pedernales. Paco was very moved when I took leave of him two months later, and he shook my hand, wishing me luck and a good trip. Vicente threw his arms around me and said:

"If I were as young as you, I too would try to escape from these stagnant waters and seek to breathe freedom in other lands."

One morning toward the end of March, a car from the Italian Embassy stops in front of my house. Two officers from the staff of General Gambara—who has already been named Ambassador of Italy in Spain—come in and, after greeting me, hand me a copy of an unexpected document: a stay of proceedings on my case, of which I've heard nothing since my interviews with the Judge of Busturia. On the basis of various articles in the military code now in force, the charges against me are proven false and I am free! Although this whole business is the result of General Gambara's intervention on my behalf, I can't help but smile at the contradictions of this code, one article of which could condemn me to thirty years in prison and another set me free.

To celebrate the news, we go to Paco's Bar for lunch, while the Italian driver goes to Ramona's tavern. Teresa and I enjoy an excellent meal in the company of the Italian officers, who are very polite and pleasant. These men have absolute faith in a German victory, and believe that Italy will enter the war in due time. Of course, the final decision is up to Il Duce, who as always will do what is best for Italy. They criticize the revenge which characterizes the fascist regime in Spain; they consider it erroneous and unnecessary. Afterwards they reminisce about the Northern Campaign, when both were in the main body of the Italian army pressing from the coast of the Bay of Biscay. One of them was almost taken prisoner when transmitting a message to Bermeo, at the time when the Mundaca bridge was recaptured by the Basque Republicans.

The younger officer remarks, "It was a rough campaign. It took us a few months to cover the thirty kilometers between us and Bilbao. The courage of the Basques and the detachments of Asturian reinforcements was overwhelming, in spite of their inferior weapons and their lack of planes. Our aircraft would bomb their positions in order to open the way for our infantry to take the high ground. At night, they counterattacked and recaptured the positions at bayonet point. The following morning the front lines were back in the same place and we'd have to start all over again. What men! How we would like to have them fighting on our side!"

These words sound sincere, and I conclude that, in spite of their admiration for mechanized warfare, these officers attach great importance to the human element. As far as the European struggle is concerned, they foresee a German victory, but not a quick or easy one. Their knowledge of their profession doesn't make them invulnerable to the popular myth about the indestructability of the Maginot line. They also believe in the great capacity of the French army, especially of its lower ranks. As for England, they take into account its powerful navy and the help she could get from her dominions, particularly Australia, Canada, and India. When analyzing the industrial potential of these dominions, the older officer alludes to the discovery and naming of Australia: Fernández de Quirós, toward the end of the reign of Felipe III had baptized the island-continent with the name of the Austrian dynasty then reigning in Spain. He has considerable knowledge of history, and boasts about it a little. I recall some words which the late Dr. Mendieta spoke in one of our conversations:

"Vanity exists in all men to one extent or another, and those who hide it best are said to be modest."

When we finish eating, the Italian officers leave on a special mission to Bilbao. They offer us the hospitality of the Italian Embassy if we ever decide to return to Madrid. My wife and I see them disappear, driving at the high speed customary for the Italian military cars.

For the remainder of spring we work steadily at preparing to leave Spain as soon as possible. Now free, I can help expedite our departure, although I am aware that our exodus will be impossible without the influence of those who have helped obtain my freedom.

I begin visiting nearby towns, wearing the orthopedic corset to which at last I have become accustomed, and carrying my sturdy cane. At times, those journeys take me over twenty kilometers from home. I have visited the other side of the estuary: that is, Laida and the Laga Beach. But it is on the Pedernales side that I move around more frequently, particularly to the towns of Busturia, Guernica, Bermeo, and Mundaca. I witness the picturesque transactions of the Bermeo fishermen upon the arrival of their fishing boats. I have heard their songs and laughter from my wheel bed. Traditionally, the fishermen end their sardine and tuna season with a dinner at Ramona's tavern, after sharing their earnings and settling all accounts. A great joy characterizes those banquet celebrations, where the men share long hours of rare human warmth. But Mundaca is the place I've found most interesting. Its streets are clean and quiet, flanked by large, ancient houses and chalets whose façades, some bearing great coats of arms, recall the simple dignity of seafaring people. There is an imposing air of sober, marine elegance to that town inhabited by sea captains. Its streets are redolent of salty breeze and tar.

Well into spring, a curious episode breaks my daily routine for a few hours.

THE PRIEST FROM LAIDA

Among the occasional patrons of Paco's Bar there is the priest from Laida, a tall, emaciated, grey-haired man with protruding eyes. His long and bony hands look like pincers. We have exchanged greetings at the bar, where they tell me that he is one of the most fanatical Carlists in the district. One day I receive a strange letter signed simply: "The priest from Laida." In mysterious terms he asks me to meet him across the estuary to discuss a matter of great importance. I wonder why he has omitted signing his own name. Perhaps after so many years of serving the community he has come to be known only by that title.

In the days preceeding the meeting I also wonder if it could be a trap. I am undecided and fearful. The situation is far from normal, particularly for persons known to have no sympathy for the Franco dictatorship. On the other hand, if the letter was truly sent by the priest, there is little reason to believe it could be a trap. That man can't possibly have any resentment toward me. Still, I thought I'd better not tell my wife of the forthcoming meeting. It would cause her anxiety. Between my contradictory reflexions and my vanity, I arrive at this somewhat absurd conclusion: The meeting is a test of my integrity. If fear prevents me from going, it will mean that suffering and illness have rendered me a coward. But if I do go, whatever the consequences and motives of the meeting, it will be an indication that I haven't been crushed by misfortune and I am the same man I was before. Forgetting all risks, I decide to attend.

The appointed day begins grey, cold, and windy. Several times in the early morning I am seized by suspicion and doubts. Suppose I am lured into a trap? What have I got in common with the Laida priest? I control my nervousness, and at three in the afternoon I await at the embarcadero with a half dozen other passengers for the launch that will take us across the estuary. The crossing takes about fifteen minutes and we arrive at a little pier at the edge of the canal. There is a dynamite factory not far from the beach, and the freighters carrying the product cross this very narrow and choppy canal.

Before I step on land I see a windblown figure extending his arms toward me in a gesture of welcome. The cassock and the large umbrella he carries give the Laida priest the look of a giant eagle. The moment I set foot on terra firma he shakes my hand warmly.

"I knew you'd come," he says smiling. "There may be a storm coming later, but there'll be no rain until the wind changes. What do you say if we take a walk toward the Laga Beach so we can talk freely?"

In a few minutes I am trying to keep up with the priest's long strides, walking on the solitary road. I ask him the reason for his urgent request to meet with me. The man stops in his tracks and grips me with his eyes.

"There is plenty of time, my friend. High tide won't be ready for your return till eight o'clock, so we have four hours to talk." He resumes walking. "I am a village priest, and although I have a kind of warring spirit, I've never harmed anyone.

"I am Basque," he continues, "but my family is of Navarrese ancestry, they come from near the Pyrenees. We lost seven men during the Carlist wars of the nineteenth century. But those were other times. Now they come and kill priests. Why? Perhaps wars are to humanity what illnesses are to Man. If that's the case, maybe they'll invent a moral vaccine to immunize people against wars. Do you see the great rock?"

From the road bend we can see the deserted rock of Izaro. The little rocky island seems lonely and sad. I try to take advantage of the pause to answer some of his barrage of questions, but he gives me no chance. He seems to be hungry for expression. Nothing will deter him from his talk.

"Centuries ago there was a monastery on the rock," he continues. "Every night, a young priest swam across the bay to meet with a great lady of Mundaca. After a night of love he would return to the monastery at dawn. There are two versions to the end of the story. One of them tells that the Father Prior of the Order one day surprised the young priest returning from his tryst and sent him away to another monastery, where the young man died of sorrow. The other one concerns the lady's husband. Apparently he discovered her infidelity through the servants' gossip, and one night he waited for the priest and killed him with his sword. No one will ever know the truth. All that happened so many years ago. . . . The most difficult phase of a priest's life is his youth, when he has to fight with all his strength against the temptations of the flesh. I've left all that behind, long ago. But only a few chosen ones can live cleanly through that trying period in order to reach the greatest heights of spiritual life, ecstasy, and nirvana. In the first greatness is positive, and in the second negative. Nirvana is a state which seems foreign to our temperament; perfect quietude, that well-being without agitation, that infinite vacuum, none of that has ever been achieved by anyone in Spain. Whereas in the other direction, in ecstasy . . . how truly rich we are in Spain! Think of it! Saint Teresa, Saint John of the Cross, Friar Luís de León, and other mystics. . . ."

At the next bend, to the right of the road, there is a "caserio," the last one before the Laga Beach. The wind has stopped wailing and now great drops of rain begin to fall. With a tremendous effort I stop the priest from talking and remind him that the storm is upon us. It's silly to continue our walk. If we turn around now we'll be able to take cover before the storm rains down on us in full force. Perhaps we can continue our talk in some inn near the embarcadero, I add.

He turns about face and opens his great umbrella, inviting me to share it with him. On the way back the wind is against us and rain strikes us in the face.

Under the scallops of the umbrella I see some random "caserios," houses isolated in the mountains and spread out through all the Basque country. The priest notices my look of longing toward these possible places of refuge, and says, "The distance to the pier is greater, but the road is in better shape, and water is always preferable to mud. Do you see those "caserios" drenched in rain? There is where innocence has taken cover. There is great wisdom in the cities, but there is also evil and corruption in them. Innocence is God's preferred virtue. When I was a student priest a book of Balzac fell into my hands. I read it avidly, as did some of my fellow-students. Not because we were literary fans but moved by a youthful curiosity for a forbidden book. Something has remained forever in my mind about that book: two children looking at a painting depicting Adam and Eve. One of the children asked the other who was Adam. And, you know what the child answered? 'It's impossible to tell because they're not wearing clothes.' "

At this point, I ask the priest what he reads mostly.

"I read little in summer, but in the long winter nights I have more time. Winter is a slow season for a priest. Not so many weddings, baptisms, and masses."

We continue our talk until we reach an inn, a sprawling, decayed house which like most others in the district has no electricity during the winter months, reserving the expense of the luxury for the summer. The innkeeper apparently is a friend of the Laida priest. She escorts us into a dining room. There is a great table in the center, but the chairs are piled up against a wall. The priest is apparently familiar with the inn's customs, he takes down two chairs and places

them close to the table. We sit across from each other. The innkeeper, a hefty Basque woman, leaves the candle on the table and
departs.

She returns with a wine bottle, a decanter of sparkling water, and
two glasses. After asking the priest if he needs anything else, she
leaves quietly.

The storm is at its zenith. Great gusts of wind whip the windows. Lightning and thunder flash and rumble intermittently. There
is no head or tail to this adventure, no sense whatsoever. I am still
awaiting some special confidence that will reveal the motive of this
meeting.

Extending his arms slowly, the priest invites me to drink with
him. From the first glass the conversation becomes almost incoherent. By now my doubts as to his sanity have been confirmed.
He tackles new subjects of conversation. The millennium, about
which there are ill-interpreted prophesies—not because they are
untrue, but because they apply to the second millennium. The real
terror, the total cataclysm, will not reach us until the year two
thousand. The victory of the Germans will mean nothing in all this,
although Hitler is to be congratulated.

A tremendous thunder clap shakes the building to the basement,
followed by a brilliant ray of lightning which flashes on the priest's
face and stops his speech for a while.

"See," he tells me, "how my right eye trembles? Maybe you
haven't noticed before, but every time that happens I think my
heart is going to stop. I've had this handicap since childhood."

One of his hook-like fingers points to his eye, which I don't see
moving and trembling as he says he feels. I am impatient to end the
visit. I look at my watch. I still have a long hour ahead before the
last launch. When he notices my impatience he continues. "Don't
look at your watch. I know a little about celestial things and thus can
tell the right time, day or night. But just to make sure. . . ."

He takes out a tremendous pocket watch and places it on the
table with great care. He continues as before:

"It's a long time since I have had such an interesting conversation."

I think that monologue would be a more fitting word than conversation. From then on his talk is so incoherent that I can't make
any sense out of it.

The influence of the Scandinavian arch and the development of Protestantism, without which Luther would have failed after burning the papal edicts. The balance between East and West. The difference between respectful and disrespectful persons. . . . These are some of the topics he tackles at length. Finally he expounds upon a special and very original economic theory. According to him, gold should again be put in circulation. The international monetary system would then become a lot simpler, to the great advantage of commerce, because now paper money is often subject to forgery. To support this theory he says he has had the experience of losing money in the First World War, when he bought marks because of his blind admiration for Germany.

The pier is not far from this house and although I still have fifteen minutes before the launch takes off, I at last succeed in taking him away, after toasting his health. Wind and rain buffet us on the way to the little embarcadero. At last I take my place in the boat with four other passengers, after an affectionate handshake with my priest friend.

From the departing launch I see the figure of the madman becoming smaller and smaller. Now his flapping cassock gives him more the look of a raven than an eagle. Sitting at the bow of the launch, breathing the salty sea air, I regain my peace of mind. The short and silent crossing is disturbed only by a few Basque words exchanged among the passengers. Upon our arrival at the isle of Chacharramendi my fellow passengers jump down with their bundles and disappear.

The pilot is a man of thirty, a splendid specimen of virile beauty and strength. I've made this crossing with him several times without exchanging a word with him. Now, as I pay my fare, he says:

"I know who you are. You are Don Pedro, the dangerous sick man."

It is dark, so I'm sure he doesn't see me smile. As he puts the money away, he extends the other hand. "You are one of us," he says, adding, "good night."

I walk the slippery path across the isle until I reach the bridge. I see the lights in the houses facing the road. Can it be that I have a special attraction for mad people, or is it that mad people have a special attraction for me?

I get home close to nine o'clock. I've never been away this

long, and Teresa, worried, has already been to Paco's Bar to inquire about me.

PROFILES

On his way to Bermeo during a business trip I meet Alberto, an old friend I haven't seen in almost five years. He has a little time and it's a sunny afternoon, so we take a long walk together and talk.

Alberto was in Barcelona on July 18th of 1936, at the outbreak of the military rebellion. Two months later he escaped to France, from where he got to the zone held by Franco, looking for his family.

"As you know," he tells me, "although I've never liked politics, I am a liberal at heart. Actually, I place my family above all else and that's the reason I escaped from Barcelona. I agree with much of what you say, and now I want to tell you a couple of incidents which are like a double mirror, reflecting the characteristics of the Civil War. In a way, they'll confirm our conversation:

"During the first days of the military rebellion in Barcelona, the quarter of San Andrés was severely punished. When the anarchists took over San Andrés they installed a committee who established their own dictatorship with their own militia, cemetery, and secret prisons. It became a fortress within the city. Among those who were detained first by the committee were three priests. The committee decided to have some fun before executing them. The president of the tribunal proposed the following to the first priest: Say: 'I shit on God' and your life will be spared.

"The poor man, dying of terror, breathed the blasphemy, to the general laughter of the members of the tribunal.

"They called the second priest and proposed the same thing. Again, the priest complied. Then came the third priest, who said: 'Forgive me, compañeros. Go ahead and shoot me, but don't ask me to repeat that. No threats or torture will make me go back on my faith. I will never utter such blasphemy.'

" 'That's wonderful!' said the committee's president, extending his hand. 'This is a man of principle, like us.' And, turning to his companions, he ordered them: 'Shoot the other two right now, but leave this one. I want to talk to him. I think he may be the man we need to fill the post of committee secretary.'

"But every coin has its other side," Alberto tells me. "A few months later, in Burgos, three Masons were brought in front of the fascist tribunal. The 'gentlemen' members of the tribunal had the three Masons brought before them, and as an example of justice and generosity, proposed the following to the first one:

'If you retract your Masonic oath we will spare your life.' The terrified Mason mumbled his retraction, while all members of the tribunal beamed a smile.

"The second Mason was called and offered the same way out. This one answered firmly that it was unnecessary to confess his retraction because he had already done so to himself before the trial. Still, he added, to make a public confession was a great source of pleasure for him. And so he did.

"Now came the turn of the third Mason. 'My life is in your hands,' he said. 'Kill me or torture me. I'll never go back on the ideals I consider true and just.'

" 'Take this man to the execution wall,' said the president of the fascist tribunal. 'The other two are to go to jail. Let's see if we can extract some information from them before we execute them too.' And with the approving nod of the rest of the tribunal, the trial was closed."

By the time Alberto finishes the story, we've reached the bus stop in front of Ramona's tavern. In a moment the bus arrives, Alberto wishes me luck in my forthcoming departure from Spain, and we embrace each other in farewell.

We are getting ready for our trip to the United States, something Teresa and I decided to attempt some time ago. This creates much commotion in our lives and the need to make several trips to Bilbao. When I try to get our visas I find that the American consul in Bilbao refuses to extend them. We don't know each other, we don't speak each other's language. . . . The interview becomes difficult and even embarrassing. Despite my insistence and explanations, the most he offers is to put me on the quota list of Spaniards awaiting their turn to emigrate to the United States. I refuse the generous offer which would delay my leaving Spain almost indefinitely, in view of the ridiculously low number allotted to the Spanish quota. But I must leave Spain for whatever country will have me. I decide to try the Cuban consul. This time I am more fortunate.

The next day we say farewell to our friends and acquaintances in Pedernales.

The 15th of June, 1940, on the S/S *Magallanes,* Teresa, Pedrito, my little son, and I cross the Portugalete bridge and leave behind the Basque coast. I watch it disappear from deck, leaning on the railing, last week's incidents and faces cross my mind as if on film. . . . The man in charge of the Cuban Consulate in Bilbao from whom —after a long talk and five hundred pesetas—I was able to get transit visas for Havana. . . . My mother, crying as we left on the train from Bilbao to Portugalete. . . . The many friends we leave behind, some of them forever. . . .

My fellow passengers are mostly Jews, liberals, leftists from various European countries. Some of them I first saw at the steamship company's offices, begging to be sold a passage to America at any price. They have just crossed the French frontier ahead of the German divisions. The breath of Hitler still seems to be at their backs, *'Ils son très forts'* (they are all-powerful) they repeat, every time they talk.

I think of myself, my life: What could I do in Spain? Wherever one looks one sees only hypocrisy, vanity, and humiliation. Mendacious justice applying the death penalty and dispensing thirty-year sentences left and right. . . . Some priests kneeling in front of the new idol, their cassocks stained with blood. . . . Assassinations by silence. . . . The military intoxicated by a victory which is not rightly theirs. . . . The middle class split in two. . . . Those who collaborated with the Republic, suffering misery and persecution after having endured terror and jail. . . . The fascists exploiting their own sufferings and casualties to receive advantages and jobs. . . . The workers, powerless, their rights lost, are allowed to join only the falangist syndicates; they are now without the support of the press, without civil liberties, reduced to the status of slaves, and try to survive the chaos with their children, by accepting any meager salary under any conditions. . . . The newspapers reduced from 250 to less than 100 in all of Spain, 39 notable Republican editors already executed. . . . No true religion, no respect for science. . . . More than fifty per cent of the teachers, from grade school to university assassinated or in exile. . . . Poverty and fanaticism reigning supreme. . . . Dignity and ideals vanished from the land.

The ship continues to touch the principal ports of northern Spain: Santander, Gijón, Vigo, and finally, Lisbon. I know those towns, but I have scant time to visit them in our short port calls. Only in Lisbon do we go ashore and exchange our currency, shop, and . . . taste white bread again! How marvelous! We return to the ship at midnight, one hour before departure. There is a great bustle of visitors on deck.

My orthopedic corset has forced me to have a fitted, oversize suit made by a tailor in Bermeo. I am overweight because of my long immobility, and still have to use the sturdy unsightly cane when I walk. Altogether, I look like a banged-up tank.

Among the passengers there is a busybody of a lady: the kind we call in Spain "handy parsley for all sauces." She talks incessantly with all alike: children, old people, the sailors, visitors, priests, with everyone she meets. During our days on board, my wife and I have not been able to escape her attention. She has even made inquiries about my corset, my cane, my difficulty in getting around. Perhaps because she has only gathered unclear information, she has arrived at some confused deductions of her own.

In one of the groups standing on deck just before departure, was the inquisitive woman, next to Nicolás Franco, the Caudillo's brother, Spain's ambassador to Portugal. As we cross in front of them on our way to our cabin, the woman stops us and addresses the ambassador.

"This lady," she tells him, pointing at my wife Teresa, "is the sister of Dr. Castroviejo, and this is her husband. Look at him, Don Nicolás. See what the Reds have done to the poor young man."

As soon as Don Quixote found himself in the open country, free to roam at will and without being annoyed by Altisidora's advances, his spirits rose and he felt at peace, ready to take up once more the pursuit of his ideals of chivalry. "Freedom," he said, turning to Sancho, "is one of the most precious gifts that the heavens have bestowed on men; with it the treasures locked in the earth or hidden in the depths of the sea are not to be compared; for the sake of freedom, as for the sake of honor, one may and should risk one's life, and captivity, on the other hand, is the greatest evil that can befall a human being.
Miguel de Cervantes